SCHOLARS' GUIDE
TO WASHINGTON, D.C.
FILM AND
VIDEO COLLECTIONS

THE WILSON CENTER

W

SCHOLARS' GUIDE
TO WASHINGTON, D.C.

FILM AND
VIDEO COLLECTIONS

BONNIE G. ROWAN

With Contributions by

DAVID CULBERT

Consultants
THOMAS CRIPPS
LAWRENCE LICHTY

Series Editor
ZDENĚK V. DAVID

WOODROW WILSON INTERNATIONAL CENTER FOR SCHOLARS

SMITHSONIAN INSTITUTION PRESS
WASHINGTON, D.C.
1980

A grant from the Ford Foundation provided part of the financial support for the preparation of this *Guide*.

The preparation of this volume was also made possible in part through a grant to the author from the Program for Research Tools and Reference Works of the National Endowment for the Humanities, an independent federal agency.

Library of Congress Cataloging in Publication Data

Rowan, Bonnie.
    Scholars' guide to Washington, D.C. film and video collections.

    (Scholars' guide to Washington, D.C.; no. 6)
    Bibliography: p. . .
    Includes indexes.
    Supt. of Docs. no.: SI 1.20:Sch6
    1. Moving-pictures—Information services—Washington, D.C.—Directories. 2. Television broadcasting—Information services—Washington, D.C.—Directories.
    I. Culbert, David Holbrook.
    II. Woodrow Wilson International Center for Scholars.
    III. Title.   IV. Series.
    PN1998.A1R68   001.4'025'753   80-607014
    ISBN O-87474-818-6
    ISBN O-87474-819-4 pbk.

CONTENTS

FOREWORD

This is the sixth in a series of *Guides* to the scholarly riches of the Washington area published by the Woodrow Wilson International Center for Scholars. This particular volume reflects the Wilson Center's interest in the development of film and television studies. The Center has accommodated a number of distinguished scholars with major projects in these areas during the last six years.

Taken as a whole, the series of *Guides* exemplifies the Wilson Center's "switchboard function" of facilitating connections between the vast resources of the nation's capital and those with scholarly or practical needs—or simply curiosity. These *Guides*—like the Center's annual fellowship program—are designed largely to serve the national and international scholarly communities. At least 20,000 visiting scholars come each year to Washington with serious research proposals from elsewhere in America and abroad. It is hoped that the *Guides* will inform scholars, many of them outside the major university research in the United States, about the possibilities for engaging in research on particular topics in Washington.

The series of *Guides* is under the general editorship of Zdeněk V. David, the Wilson Center librarian. Elizabeth Dixon is largely responsible for the design and publication arrangements. Two former Wilson Center fellows, Thomas Cripps of Morgan State College, and Lawrence Lichty of the University of Wisconsin, served as consultants in the preparation of the *Guide,* and the project also benefitted in both the initial and concluding stages from the advice of another former Center fellow, Erik Barnouw, now at the Library of Congress, and David Thaxton, a film historian and former staff member of the Center. The author of this volume, Bonnie Rowan, has taught film history and production at Towson State College, Maryland, and has used many of the Washington collections for scholarly research. The Center separately commissioned the introductory essay, "The Scholar and the Visual Image," and Appendix VII, both by David Culbert, also a former Wilson Center Fellow and Associate Professor of History at Louisiana State University.

The Center wishes to thank the Ford Foundation for its indispensible financial support of the *Guide's* preparation, as well as the Morris and Gwendolyn Cafritz Foundation of Washington, D.C., for additional support. The author also secured support from the National Endowment for the Humanities.

So far the Center has prepared *Guides* for scholars in the fields of Russian/ Soviet (1977), Latin American and Caribbean (1979), East Asian (1979), African (1980), and Central and East European studies (1980). All were published by the Smithsonian Institution Press. Forthcoming volumes will include surveys of resources in the Washington area for scholars interested in the study of the Middle East and South Asia.

James H. Billington, *Director*
Woodrow Wilson International Center for Scholars

WOODROW WILSON
INTERNATIONAL CENTER FOR SCHOLARS

The Wilson Center was created by the United States Congress as the nation's official living memorial to its twenty-eighth President. As a national institution with international interests, the Center seeks to encourage the creative use of the unique human, archival, and institutional resources in the nation's capital for studies illuminating man's understanding of his past and present.

The Center's programs attempt to commemorate the Wilsonian connection between ideas and affairs, between intellect and moral purpose. At the heart of the Center stands its Fellowship Program, which enables the institution to appoint annually fellows from the U.S. and abroad to conduct research on major projects at the Center for periods ranging from four months to one year or more. The Center has no permanent or tenured fellows. The Center's fellowship program consists of two broad divisions (Social and Political Studies and Historical and Cultural Studies) and four special programs (Russia and the Soviet Union, Latin America and the Caribbean, international security issues, and environmental problems). There is a Guest Scholar Program which brings visiting scholars and specialists to the Center for shorter periods of time. The Center's continuing interest in film and television studies, especially through the Social and Political Studies and Historical and Cultural Studies divisions, has resulted in both the sponsorship of this *Guide* and the appointment of a number of fellows and guest scholars whose work has focused on film and television. Since 1975, Center fellowships have been awarded to Peter Braestrup, Marc Ferro, Erik Barnouw, Thomas Cripps, Lawrence Lichty, David Culbert, Frank McConnell, Gladys Lang and Kurt Lang.

The Center's activities include frequent colloquia, evening seminars, and other discussions designed to foster intellectual community among the participants. The scheduled events are announced in a monthly calendar of events which is available to scholars.

Other volumes in the Wilson Center series of *Scholars' Guides to Washington, D.C.* survey collections, institutions, and organizations pertinent to the study of particular geographic areas. In addition to the *Scholars' Guides,* the Center publishes a journal, *The Wilson Quarterly,* a national review of ideas and information.

The Center's librarian, Zdeněk V. David, who is also editor of the series of *Guides,* should receive any comments, additions, or corrections which would assist in an up-date of this *Guide.* The Wilson Center is located in the Smithsonian Institution Building, 1000 Jefferson Drive, SW, Washington, D.C. 20560. (202) 381-5613.

THE SCHOLAR AND THE VISUAL IMAGE

By David Culbert

We hear a great deal these days about the role of mass media in a technological society. John Harrington tells us in his *Rhetoric of Film* (1973) that "by the time a person is fourteen, he will witness 18,000 murders on the screen. He will also see 350,000 commercials. By the time he is eighteen, he will stockpile nearly 17,000 hours of viewing experience and will watch at least 20 movies for every book he reads. Eventually, the viewing will absorb ten years of his life" (p. v). But statistics is only one way of comprehending the prevasiveness of mass media in our current lives.

Everyone believes that media affect us; most fear for the worst. Do adolescents turn to violence because of what they see on television? Does our society suffer from an "information overload" that dulls our ability to distinguish between the important and the trivial? Do network moguls in New York City manipulate what society thinks about public issues? In short, what effect do visual images have on the way we live, or how we make decisions? The questions abound; so do "authoritative," albeit uninformed, answers.

Right from the start the necessity for scholarly analysis of visual media has been recognized by the few—usually those professionally involved in filmmaking or film criticism. This *Guide* is intended to help locate primary visual sources for a wide scholarly audience.

Only in the past decade have historians begun to look carefully at mass media as a field for scholarly research. Indeed, the two leading historical journals in this country, the *Journal of American History* and the *American Historical Review*, have yet to publish a single review of any film or television program. Only one article relating to the history of visual media has appeared in either journal. Nor until 1977 did the Organization of American Historians create a national Committee on Radio-Television-Film Media.

Media study remains needlessly compartmentalized in Schools of Education or Departments of Radio-TV-Film. Traditional departments sometimes add a film or two to current courses but our society is uncertain of what role visual images play in the way we learn. We all watch television, to be sure, but we have not really thought about the implications of visual literacy. We watch but we do not see. A challenge to scholars for the remainder of this century will be to understand a technological society in which mass media define our visual impressions of the world around us. Thus the records of our visual past are crucial to such understanding, and Washington, D.C., is their principal location.

I first became interested in the scholarly analysis of media in graduate school, though an undergraduate degree in organ performance had helped prepare me for the interpretation of aural material. In playing the pipe organ the distance between sounds is often critical to interpretation and this is generally true of broadcast speech. My dissertation traced the development of radio news in the 1930s and argued that radio as a medium created, for the first time in America, a general interest in foreign affairs because the sounds of overseas events could be heard at home. The resulting book, *News for Everyman: Radio and Foreign Affairs in Thirties America* (1976) was based on extensive materials from the Washington, D.C., area. The Library of Congress provided me with hundreds of recorded news broadcasts and correspondence relating to the impact of individual commentators. State Department records in the National Archives showed how commentators tried to influence those who made foreign policy.

I had particular difficulty in locating copies of broadcasts for Boake Carter, banned from CBS in 1938 for his vituperative remarks. He left no papers and everyone assured me that his broadcasts had disappeared. The networks in New York certainly had nothing, but National Archives did. A chance remark solved my dilemma. An archivist told me I might want to check a long-ignored collection of broadcast transcriptions assembled by the Federal Trade Commission in the 1930s for an investigation of food commercials. In the stacks I saw thousands of transcripts, arranged chaotically. But some were filed by station call letter so I looked to see whether there might be something under WCAU, the Philadelphia station from which Carter broadcast nationally over CBS. I found over 100 stenographic transcriptions, which enabled me to analyze Carter's broadcasts during his period of greatest notoriety. This experience taught me a couple of important lessons: always discuss fully one's research interests with archivists, and always look for paper records when studying topics relating to aural and visual media. Government print records can seem intimidating for someone attempting to use them the first time but my article (Appendix VII) at the back of this *Guide* can help reduce the element of chance, which obviously played an important role in my search for Boake Carter's broadcasts.

In the summer of 1974 I returned to Washington to begin work on another book. I decided to visit the top floor of National Archives to see what was available for research in film and newsreel. William Murphy showed me some films which the Army had used for morale and instruction in World War II, among them Private Snafu, a cartoon character who always deviated from Army policy and learned the hard way why there were rules and regulations. One episode involved some marvelous imagery with a mosquito whose harpoon (laden with malaria) sends Snafu to the next world for ignoring preventive medicine and proper netting. I looked at every Snafu cartoon, went several floors below to see what might be found in Modern Military Records relating to production and distribution of this series, and soon found myself on the way to Tobyhanna, Pennsylvania, where the Army stores some Snafu films and production records. Tobyhanna is an equipment depot and it is a strange experience to study amid rows of warehouses storing thousands of trucks and jeeps. My summer research convinced me that I had a wonderful topic, if greatly broadened, for it seemed to me that I was looking at the origin of the audiovisual revolution in American education. I settled on *The American Military's Use of Film in World War II* as a working title.

I was soon attracted to the Frank Capra *Why We Fight* series, especially vast paper records showing step-by-step official supervision of the series from start to finish. It was astonishing to discover that no film scholar had ever located any of this documentation for such a noted group of films. What surprised me the most, I suppose, was to find that thousands of World War II training films were stored at National Archives, along with supporting production files, distribution records, detailed shot lists, supplementary instructional material, and records relating to censorship, much of the latter material at the Washington National Records Center in Suitland, Maryland. (Appendix VII explains how to locate some of these materials.)

In 1975, at a meeting of the Popular Culture Association in St. Louis, I met Patrick Sheehan, of the Library of Congress's Motion Picture Section. Sheehan told me about the interest of the Woodrow Wilson International Center for Scholars in projects dealing with mass media which used Washington area resources. I gave a great deal of thought to a proposal during the summer, applied in October 1975, was accepted, and in June 1976 arrived in Washington to begin work.

As soon as I got to the Wilson Center I talked with another Fellow, Erik Barnouw, who was full of suggestions. He had worked in educational broadcasting for the Army's radio service during World War II and had known some of those in charge of military film utilization. I soon met another Fellow finishing his year at the Center, Thomas Cripps, and served as a critic for his colloquium paper describing an Army orientation film, *The Negro Soldier* (1944). I gently suggested that Cripps had made insufficient use of government paper records.

A couple of months later Cripps called me one Saturday morning at 8:30 a.m. and asked if I wanted to meet him at a Washington theater in one hour to attend a press preview of *Network*. He told me to call Erik Barnouw but I did not feel I should call a senior scholar so early in the morning and without notice. I rushed across town to meet Cripps and there were Barnouw and his wife standing out front (they had been invited by the *Washington Post's* television critic). Afterwards Cripps suggested that he and I join forces to write an article about *The Negro Soldier*. I was flattered by his offer and redoubled my efforts to find paper records relating to this pioneering film in race relations. The result, after numerous revisions, appeared in the Spring, 1980, issue of *The American Quarterly*.

Cripps introduced me to the possibility of long distance telephone interviews, something I had not thought about. He shared unlisted numbers, and suggested persons that I might think about seeing. Thanks to his suggestion, I went to Macungie, Pennsylvania, for a long interview with Donald Young, the War Department's official expert on race relations in World War II. Cripps's ideas confirmed my growing conviction that communications media needed serious study by use of both paper and audiovisual records.

Months passed. I worked week after week viewing films, and going through hundreds of thousands of pieces of paper in endless Federal Record Groups. One day I got into a conversation with Robert Williams, a student of Russian history who was a Fellow of the Wilson Center's Kennan Institute for Advanced Russian Studies. He had heard that I was interested in film and, in a chance remark, told me he had found State Department files relating to police surveillance of Sergei Eisenstein during the latter's trip to Hollywood. I was not working on the 1920s, and did not have a special interest in Eisenstein, but I hastened to National Archives to see what the State Department files had relating to film, for it seemed possible that if there were something on Eisenstein there might be something about World War II film.

An excellent archivist, Gerald Haines, found my subject fascinating and suggested some likely decimal numbers. I soon found documents relating to wartime distribution of American feature films within the Soviet Union, in particular material about a 1943 film, *Mission to Moscow.* I told Williams what I had found. He was writing a book about the entry of Russian art into the United States and since Ambassador Joseph E. Davies, whose career had inspired *Mission to Moscow,* had collected a great deal of Russian art, Williams's interest was not merely academic. Williams told me to interview one of Davies's daughters who lives in Washington. She proved most helpful in giving me access to the closed section of her father's papers in the Library of Congress.

Soon Williams and I began to think that a symposium focusing on Davies as art collector and filmmaker might be a good idea. Wilson Center Director James Billington agreed, and invited a group of senior retired diplomats who had served with Davies in Moscow during the 1930s. I contacted Howard Koch, *Mission to Moscow*'s screenwriter, and invited him to come to Washington. National Archives allowed us to screen their beautiful 35mm print and on June 23, 1977, we saw the film in the morning and discussed Davies in an afternoon symposium. The experience was memorable, for Williams and I gained important substantive material from responses made by those present. As a result of the symposium I developed ideas about the feature film's documentary flavor, and some of those present later sent data I would never have thought to seek on my own.

I soon had assembled a vast amount of paper records relating to *Mission to Moscow,* particularly from my use of the Office of War Information records at Suitland, Maryland, and the Davies Papers in the Library of Congress. How, I wondered, could film scholars have overlooked such valuable material when all along everyone had suspected that the federal government was involved in the making of this notorious effort to promote Soviet-American friendship? Thanks to a suggestion by Thomas Cripps, I was able to put this material to good use. I am editing the script of *Mission to Moscow,* to be published by the University of Wisconsin Press in 1980. Meanwhile my essay about this film has appeared in John O'Connor and Martin Jackson, eds., *American History/American Film* (1979).

My stay in Washington led to one other activity based upon media resources. I decided to make a documentary film. Peter Rollins had made an award-winning film, *Will Rogers' 1920s* (1976), and wanted to do something relating to Vietnam. He invited me to join Townsend Ludington and him in a project focusing on television coverage of the war in Vietnam during the Tet offensive of 1968. We were fascinated by the way that visual images affect public perceptions of overseas events and sought to discover what television had contributed, if anything, to altering the way Americans decide about foreign policy. Once again the Wilson Center turned out to be an excellent source of additional ideas. Peter Braestrup, editor of the *Wilson Quarterly,* was finishing up his *Big Story* (1977), a massive two-volume story of media coverage of Tet 1968, and Lawrence Lichty arrived in August, 1977, to continue to work on his major study of television coverage of the Vietnam war. Lichty planned to make use of the recently-opened George Washington University television news archive.

In February, 1978, the Wilson Center and the University of North Carolina sponsored a symposium on the tenth anniversary of Tet. At Chapel Hill, Rollins, Ludington, and I filmed interviews with participants, including Lawrence Lichty, Peter Braestrup, William Westmoreland, and Robert Northshield, producer of NBC's "Huntley-Brinkley Report" in 1968. Rollins, Ludington, and I came to the Wilson Center as Guest Scholars in June 1978 to work on our film. We spent our time at National Archives studying Department of Defense kinescopes of network television coverage of Vietnam, 1967-68. We then went to the Marine Corps Film Archive in Quantico, Virginia, to look at several hundred thousand feet of color footage shot by Marine cameramen during 1967-68; at the Marine Historical Division in Washington's Navy Yard, we went through nearly 8,000 still photographs and hundreds of examples of combat art, and listened to oral history interviews conducted by the Marines in 1968. Thanks to a grant from the Rockefeller Foundation we spent July, 1979, back in Washington conducting additional film interviews and selecting footage for further study. I feel that as an historian of mass media I have an obligation to make a documentary film as a means of exploring contemporary problems. We believe our film will make an important contribution to a subject on which passions continue to run high.

Yet another Fellow at the Wilson Center made excellent use of Washington-area visual materials. James Gibbs is an anthropologist with a fine film to his credit, *The Cows of Dolo Ken Paye: Resolving Conflict Among the Kpelle* (1970). He talked with me at length about anthropological film and we made frequent trips to the Smithsonian's Anthropological Film Center, where Gibbs was doing research and where we previewed films for a special course he planned dealing with anthropological films of trance.

These experiences offer one sort of guide to ways in which Washington area resources may be used; my intent has been to show how often the combination of print records and visual materials is essential for proper research. I also hope that I have properly emphasized the element of chance—but also how often "chance" has been aided by discussing my interests with others in the Washington area. It is so much fun picking up good ideas from colleagues who share my enthusiasm for conducting serious research in visual materials.

Now let me suggest some other kinds of research which might be done in the Washington area. My background as historian no doubt explains some of my preferences.

A. Film and Television Documentaries. Traditionally the visual holdings in Washington have been used only by television and film crews making films about such familiar topics as World War II, Adolf Hitler, or ghetto life. There is a tendency to use images selected by the last person to make a film about the same topic. The editor or producer rarely selects the footage himself and his assistants rarely have much background in the topic being undertaken. Such documentaries would be much stronger if film researchers brought something besides an eye for visual material to their assignments. As things stand, most documentaries rely on excellent subject card files created by major newsreel companies and now in National Archives. Use of the kinds of textual records described in Appendix VII to this *Guide* would help keep those using visual records from making assessments solely in terms of the visual image itself.

B. *The "Interior" of a Film.* Film scholars have long been fascinated by aesthetics, which includes such topics as the visual meaning of a released film, the analysis of film language, differences between television and film as media, the artistic implications of editing, and a current enthusiasm, semiology. So far this latter outgrowth of linguistic theory has yet to prove its worth. Marc Ferro's elaborate analysis of *Tchapaev* (1934) in Paul Smith, ed., *The Historian and Film* (1976) is a representative example of the difficulty in moving from fascinating ideas to substantive conclusions, though semiology is the most promising area for further work in a field which has attracted a great deal of attention.

C. *The "Exterior" of a Film.* This is an area of study of particular interest these days. Under this rubric can be found such topics as societal context, the sociology of film and television, and attempts to determine who deserves credit for what. Since television and film are collaborative media it is often hard to decide who made a particular artistic contribution and who did not. Film history can mean an analysis of all of the films by a particular director, the evolution of film and television programming (a type of history which has tended to ignore context), and the quest for accurate data about distribution or audience grosses.

In all exterior analysis of film or television programming there is no substitute for a "paper chain" of primary documentation. The field of film history has suffered from too much reliance on oral history interviews in which the credulous have imagined that anything said in a tape-recorded interview was somehow ennobled with a special kind of veracity. Textual records in the Washington area offer innumerable leads for the scholar who wants, for example, to find out—without having to rely on the director's uncertain memory—what changes the Pentagon demanded before releasing John Huston's *San Pietro* (1945). National Archives has the unedited outtakes for this film in case someone wants to see what was cut in the final version. Both the Library of Congress and the American Film Institute have important collections of periodicals to help in the writing of film history but the media scholar should particularly look for unpublished primary documents. To bring media history up to the evidential standards of more traditional history will be a major task in the next decade.

In a field with no fixed rules a good place to begin is by looking at John O'Connor, ed., *Film and the Humanities* (1977), which reprints some excellent articles describing the use of film by teachers of philosophy, history, English, and anthropology and which includes a fine bibliography. The book may be had free of charge by writing the Rockefeller Foundation, Publications Office, 1133 Avenue of the Americas, New York, N.Y. 10036.

Media is a research subject I feel very strongly about; it has become a magnificent obsession, which helps explain why I was asked to write this introduction. Not Hollywood, not New York, but Washington, D.C., is the place to come for media research, for nowhere else are you able to gain access to visual materials and supporting paper records in such close physical proximity. I hope this *Guide* will stimulate serious use of some marvelous research material.

INTRODUCTION

In 1894, William K. L. Dickson, co-inventor with Thomas Edison of the motion picture camera, predicted a significant future for the motion picture as historical record:

> *The advantages to students and historians will be immeasurable. Instead of dry and misleading accounts, tinged with exaggeration of the chronicler's mind, our achives will be enriched by the vitalized pictures of great national scenes, instinct with all the glowing personalities which characterize them.*

While Dickson clearly foresaw the importance of such a record for scholars, he would have been disappointed with the reality that since 1894 few scholars have actually used film and television footage as documents.

Considering the enormous global influence and appeal of film and television, it seems surprising that scholars have often ignored this resource. But film and video present significant new problems for the scholar familiar only with print and manuscript resources. Motion pictures are more expensive and time-consuming to study; they are difficult to annotate. The analysis of film and video resources demands not only some awareness of the culture that produced them, but also an understanding of the visual language, the grammar and syntax of the moving image.

Methods for handling these problems are evolving as today's historians, anthropologists, sociologists, and scholars in other fields use archival film and video materials. The bias which once existed against the use of non-print resources in scholarly study is gradually disappearing. The product of scholarly research in film and television history, visual anthropology, film aesthetics, and semiology can be found in dozens of books published in the last decade, as well as in new journals and scholarly periodicals devoted to the subject.

This research is being done without the aid of a tool taken for granted by those who use books, serials, manuscript collections, and oral histories. There is no union catalogue of film and video collections. Guides such as *NICEM Media Indexes* and the *Library of Congress Catalogs, Films and Other Materials for Projection* may list a title's distributor, but provide no information on the holdings of film and video libraries and archives.

The realities of the growing scholarly interest in the use of film and video materials and the lack of a union catalogue, combined with the estimate that

Washington, D.C., has the largest and most important film and video achives in the Western Hemisphere prompted the Woodrow Wilson International Center for Scholars to sponsor this *Guide*. It is one of a series of *Scholars' Guides to Washington, D.C.*, designed to serve resident scholars and the estimated 20,000 visiting scholars, American and foreign, who come to Washington each year to do research.

The information in the *Guide* may in fact save a researcher a trip to Washington. As many entries indicate, materials from a large number of Washington area collections are available through the mail or at regional libraries and centers.

Scope and Content: The *Guide* describes Washington, D.C., area collections of film and video available for scholarly research as well as organizations which can provide information about such collections. The collections included serve several different groups. American and international scholars will be most interested in the large, often unique collections located only in the Washington area. Many of these will be found within the U.S. Government section, which has its own introduction (p. 142). Many entries, especially those for local libraries, colleges, and universities, and the TV stations and school systems described in the Appendixes I and II, are included to serve the needs of those already in the Washington area. These listings may also indicate to scholars elsewhere possible sources of materials in their own city. It is hoped that filmmakers, researchers, and those wishing to borrow films to show to groups will also find this *Guide* useful.

No attempt has been made to list the roughly 192,000 titles and 80 million feet of unedited footage available in Washington but each entry includes descriptions of the location, holdings, and conditions for use of individual collections. Significant manuscript and non-print materials of interest to scholars working with visual materials are identified. The appendixes add several more categories of resources and services. Six indexes assist users in locating materials.

The geographical scope of the *Guide* is the Washington, D.C., area: the District of Columbia; Montgomery and Prince Georges counties in Maryland; and Alexandria, Arlington, and Fairfax counties in Virginia. A few exceptional collections within a 100-mile radius are included as well as a list (Appendix III) of major government collections, embassy libraries, and large film and video archives throughout the U.S.

The collections listed in the *Guide* are limited to those of interest to scholars in the humanities and social sciences. Scientific and evidential footage collections and strictly medical, technical, or instructional collections of film and video are not covered. Large collections, included because of their materials in the humanities and social sciences, often contain technical materials and these are noted. Television stations, public school systems, and commercial rental libraries which offer limited services to scholars are listed in Appendixes I, II, and VIII, respectively.

Methodology: Research began with a list of organizations and institutions which might hold collections of film or video, compiled using reference works listed in the Bibliography. All Washington area embassies, associations, and academic departments were contacted. Departments within the federal government were queried at several levels. Each collection was then investigated in person or by telephone. The information in this volume came from interviews with staff members, inspection of libraries and card files, and analysis of printed materials. The description of the holdings of the National Archives Audiovisual Division is based upon its own published description of holdings. The description of the special collections within the Library of Congress Motion Picture, Broadcasting, and Recorded Sound Division was done with the assistance of Annette Melville, compiler of *A Guide to Special Collections of the Library of Congress* (in press).

Bonnie Gail Rowan

ACKNOWLEDGMENTS

The author owes much to the experience and good judgment of both David Thaxton, a Washington film historian who first developed the concept for the *Guide,* and Fay Schreibman, of the George Washington University Television News Study Service; to the editorial guidance of Zdeněk V. David, editor of the Wilson Center's series of *Scholars' Guides;* to conceptual guidance and careful review of the manuscript by Lawrence Lichty of the University of Wisconsin and Thomas Cripps of Morgan State University; to assistance from Barbara Humphrys of the Library of Congress and William Murphy of the National Archives and to special help from Erik Barnouw. The National Endowment for the Humanities and the Ford Foundation provided financial support. Joyce Savage and Mary Pat Rowan brought initiative and skill to the initial research and final preparation stages. Many women and men who work with the collections contributed their time and knowledge to this project. Only some of them are listed in the entries. Finally a special thanks you to my whole California Street family.

HOW TO USE THE GUIDE

Format: The main body of the *Guide* contains 186 entries arranged alphabetically by the name of the institution or organization. Entries for the federal government are found together under "U.S. Government." The introduction to government entries which precedes entry #183 provides information on the Freedom of Information Act and recent regulations on the handling of audiovisual materials. All embassies are listed as "Embassy of . . ."and so are found together. For those interested in finding all of the entries in other institutional categories, there is an Organization Index at the end of this volume.

Standard Entries: Among the entries are three distinct types of resources for scholars interested in locating collections of film and video. The great majority of entries are actual collections and are labeled Collection. Referral Service entries are organizations such as the American Film Institute which hold no film or video but which have staff members and written resources to assist a scholar in locating collections. Academic Program entries list the faculty, degrees, and courses at area colleges and universities of interest to scholars using film and video materials for research.

Other sections of the standard entry formats which may need explanation are:

Names, addresses, telephone numbers, hours of operation—This information is correct as of summer, 1979. Hours of operation for academic institutions often change during the summer months.

Eligibility—Specific information on who is eligible to use the facilities and collections is located at the beginning of each entry. Scholars and others with varied backgrounds and projects are directed to those organizations and institutions which are most willing and able to serve them. Information on many collections was provided only on the condition that eligibility restrictions be made clear.

Collection—The numerical descriptions of the collections are approximate in most cases. Titles refer to single, completed productions. Feet, hours, and reels are different measures used to quantitatively describe unedited footage and uncatalogued collections.

The prose descriptions of the collections seek to highlight groups of titles and the general focus of the holdings. Individual items are mentioned to further describe the collection or to represent the range of the holdings. Since the focus of the *Guide* and its indexes is necessarily limited to directing scholars to groups of titles rather than individual items, this is the only part of the entry where information on an individual title may be found.

Referral Aids—Referral Service entries and many of the Collection entries list staff, publications, and in-house finding aids which assist researchers in locating film and video collections in Washington and throughout the world.

Access—This section includes information concerning the borrowing of materials, reservation requirements, and viewing facilities as well as the copyright status of a collection and its availability for use by filmmakers and others interested in reproducing the materials.

Many collections may only be viewed on the premises, those that may be borrowed are generally lent for one day and are expected back or in the mail on the day following the play date. The borrower of a film by mail generally must pay return postage and insurance. Many collections are subject to detailed reservations policies. In all cases it is crucial to call or write before visiting a collection to view a film or tape. Walk-in service, the standard in most libraries of print materials, is almost unknown in film and video libraries.

The descriptions of viewing facilities distinguish between those equipped for viewing and those equipped for analysis. Viewing equipment refers to film projectors and television monitors which allow little or no stopping and rewinding. Analysis equipment in the case of film is usually an editing console (Moviola and Steenbeck are the brand names) which allows a researcher to view a film forward, backward, in slow motion, and in fast motion. These capacities permit frame by frame analysis and a quick review. Video analysis equipment is usually a cassette unit (Betamax or VHS) which allows the viewer to stop, rewind the tape, or view a single image; videotape cannot be viewed in slow motion, in fast motion, or in reverse. In all cases the equipment described is for use on the premises. Information on equipment rental is included in Appendix VIII.

Filmmakers and others interested in copies of films and video should note that these collections are not commercial stock film libraries with the exception of National Geographic Society. The government stock film libraries, listed in the Organizations Index, are useful to filmmakers who have time to wait for copies of the requested footage. Most of the other organizations and institutions included in the *Guide* hold only completed productions. They are not averse to assisting filmmakers but do not have ready access to information on the status of copyright or the location of the preprint materials.

Other Materials—Resources highlighted in this section include primarily nonprint materials such as audio recordings and slides. Manuscript collections and documentation related to the collections of film and video are listed.

The standard format of the Academic Programs entries includes three sections: *Faculty* lists faculty members who specialize in the study of film and video rather than production; *Degrees* presents the degrees offered to indicate the level and size of the program; and *Courses* provides a sampling of academic offerings to give the reader an idea of the activities and screenings which may be available on each campus.

Appendixes: Most appendixes supplement the information included in the entries. Others provide special information for visiting scholars. Consult the Table of Contents for a list of the appendixes; the titles are self-explanatory.

Indexes: Six indexes guide the reader to information in the text.

Organization Index—This breakdown of the entries by the type of organization or institution guides the readers to both the entries and the information in the appendixes. This index provides lists of all government entries, all academic institutions, and so on, allowing generic access to the strictly alphabetically arranged entries in the *Guide*. It includes variant titles, especially helpful in the case of government entries.

Named Collections Index—This mechanism directs the user to each entry which holds special collections not readily identified by the title of the entry. Collections within the federal government are not prefaced by U.S., and common names and abbreviations are used.

All other indexes direct readers to groups of films or tapes rather than to individual titles. A title by title indexing of the collections was beyond the scope of this *Guide*.

Foreign Productions Index—Groups of films and videotapes produced outside of the U.S. are divided by both country and geographical area. Not included in the index are the foreign films in the Library of Congress Copyright Collection (entry No. 165A) which were released in this country and registered for copyright with the Library. Also not included are many American and other films about foreign locations; these are cited in the Content Index.

Production Date Index—Collections which contain groups of films produced before 1960 are included in this index. The categories are broad but should serve scholars interested in historical material.

Type Index—Groups of films and videotapes within collections are indexed according to their format, purpose, length, and technique.

Content Index—Directs users to groups of films and videotape according to their content. Exceptions are the broader headings of "Film Art and History," which includes older films and experimental films as well as productions about the art and history of the motion picture; "Video Art," which lists collections of the work of video artists; and "Films for Children," films created or recommended for children. The headings reflect the content of the large public library and academic collections. See the National Archives (entry No. 155) for a separate detailed subject index of that collection.

COLLECTIONS
REFERRAL SERVICES
ACADEMIC PROGRAMS

Entries

1. Alexander Graham Bell Association
2. American Association of Community and Junior Colleges
3. American Federation of Labor
4. American Federation of State, County and Municipal Employees
5. American Federation of Teachers
6. American Film Institute
7. American Institute of Architects
8. American Mining Congress
9. American Petroleum Institute
10. American Red Cross
11. American Trucking Association
12. American University—Academic Programs
13. American University—Performing Arts
14. American University—Visual Media Film
15. American University—Visual Media Video
16. Anti-Defamation League of B'nai B'rith
17. Association Films
18. Association for Childhood Education International
19. Association of American Railroads
20. BNA Communications
21. Bowie State College
22. Broadcast Pioneers' Library
23. Catholic Archdiocese of Washington
24. Catholic Diocese of Arlington
25. Catholic University
26. Coordination Council for North American Affairs
27. District of Columbia—Martin Luther King Memorial Library
28. District of Columbia, University of—Academic Programs
29. District of Columbia, University of—Black Film Institute
30. District of Columbia, University of—Media Services—Van Ness Campus
31. District of Columbia, University of—Harvard Street Library
32. District of Columbia, University of—Media Services Department
33. Embassy of Australia
34. Embassy of Austria
35. Embassy of Barbados
36. Embassy of Belgium
37. Embassy of Brazil
38. Embassy of Canada
39. Embassy of China, Peoples Republic of
40. Embassy of Cyprus
41. Embassy of Czechoslovakia
42. Embassy of Egypt
43. Embassy of the German Democratic Republic
44. Embassy of Germany, Federal Republic of
45. Embassy of Ghana
46. Embassy of Guyana
47. Embassy of Hungary
48. Embassy of Iceland
49. Embassy of India
50. Embassy of Indonesia

51. Embassy of Iran
52. Embassy of Ireland
53. Embassy of Israel
54. Embassy of Jamaica
55. Embassy of Japan
56. Embassy of Korea
57. Embassy of Kuwait
58. Embassy of Liberia
59. Embassy of Libya
60. Embassy of Malaysia
61. Embassy of the Netherlands
62. Embassy of New Zealand
63. Embassy of Nigeria
64. Embassy of Norway
65. Embassy of Pakistan
66. Embassy of Peru
67. Embassy of Poland
68. Embassy of Saudi Arabia
69. Embassy of Singapore
70. Embassy of South Africa
71. Embassy of Spain—Audiovisual Department
72. Embassy of Spain—Information Department
73. Embassy of Thailand
74. Embassy of Trinidad and Tobago
75. Embassy of Tunisia
76. Embassy of Turkey
77. Embassy of Uganda
78. Embassy of USSR
79. Embassy of Venezuela
80. Embassy of Zambia
81. Enoch Pratt Free Library
82. Farm Film Foundation
83. Folger Shakespeare Library
84. Fondo Del Sol
85. Gallaudet College—Academic Programs
86. Gallaudet College—Media Distribution
87. George Mason University—Academic Programs
88. George Mason University—English Department
89. George Mason University—Research Center for the Federal Theatre Project
90. George Washington University—Academic Programs
91. George Washington University—Anthropology Department
92. George Washington University—Asian Languages and Literature
93. George Washington University—Media Resources Department
94. George Washington University—Television News Study Service
95. Georgetown University—Academic Programs
96. Georgetown University—Audiovisual Department
97. Georgetown University—Lauinger Library
98. Howard University—Academic Programs
99. Howard University—Afro-American Studies Resource Center
100. Howard University—Center for Learning Systems
101. Howard University—Institute for the Arts and Humanities
102. Independent Curators, Inc.

103. International Visual Literacy Association
104. Japan Foundation
105. Jewish Teacher Center
106. Maryland, University of—Academic Programs
107. Maryland, University of—Anthropology Department
108. Maryland, University of—Audiovisual Services
109. Maryland, University of—Educational Technology Center
110. Maryland, University of—Non-Print Media Services
111. Middle East Institute
112. Modern Talking Picture Service, Inc.
113. Montgomery College—Rockville—Academic Programs
114. Montgomery College—Rockville—Learning Resources Department
115. Montgomery College—Takoma Park—Academic Programs
116. Montgomery College—Takoma Park—Learning Resources Department
117. Mount Vernon College—Academic Programs
118. Narcotics Education, Inc.
119. National Association for Foreign Student Affairs
120. National Geographic Society—Stock Film Library
121. National Trust for Historic Preservation
122. Northern Virginia Community College—Alexandria—Academic Program
123. Northern Virginia Community College—Extended Learning Institute
124. Northern Virginia Community College—Film Collection
125. Organization of American States
126. Prince Georges Community College—Academic Programs
127. Prince Georges Community College—Learning Resources Center
128. Prince Georges County Memorial Library System
129. Project HOPE
130. Public Broadcast Service—Public Television Library
131. Public Broadcast Service—Public Television Archive and Study Center
132. Public Citizen Visitor's Center
133. Resources for the Future
134. Special Olympics
135. Suburban Washington Library Film Service
136. Trinity College—Academic Program
137. UNICEF Information Centre
138. United Nations Information Center
139. United States Catholic Conference
140. United Way of America
141. U.S.-China Peoples Friendship Association of Washington, D.C.
142. USER (Urban Scientific and Educational Research, Inc.)
U.S. Government—Introduction
143. U.S. ACTION
144. U.S. Agriculture Department
145. U.S. (Agriculture) Food and Nutrition Information Center
146. U.S. Central Intelligence Agency
147. U.S. Defense Department
148. U.S. (Defense) Air Force Department
149. U.S. (Defense) Army Department
150. U.S. (Defense) Marine Corps
151. U.S. (Defense) Marine Corps Film Depository
152. U.S. (Defense) Navy Department
153. U.S. (Defense) Naval Photographic Center

154. U.S. Energy Department
155. U.S. (GSA) National Archives and Records Service—Audiovisual Archives Division
156. U.S. (GSA) National Archives and Records Service—National Audiovisual Center
157. U.S. (GSA) National Archives and Records Service—Stock Film Library
158. U.S. Health, Education, and Welfare Department
159. U.S. (HEW) National Library of Medicine
160. U.S. Housing and Urban Development Department
161. U.S. (Interior) National Park Service
162. U.S. International Communication Agency
163. U.S. Justice Department
164. U.S. (Justice) Law Enforcement Assistance Administration
165. U.S. Library of Congress—Motion Picture, Broadcasting and Recorded Sound Division
166. U.S. National Endowment for the Arts
167. U.S. (Smithsonian) Anacostia Neighborhood Museum—Center for Anacostia Studies
168. U.S. (Smithsonian) Anacostia Neighborhood Museum—Education Department
169. U.S. (Smithsonian) Anacostia Neighborhood Museum—Outreach Program
170. U.S. (Smithsonian) Archives of American Art
171. U.S. (Smithsonian) Hirshhorn Museum
172. U.S. (Smithsonian) Museum of History and Technology
173. U.S. (Smithsonian) National Air and Space Museum
174. U.S. (Smithsonian) National Anthropological Film Center
175. U.S. (Smithsonian) National Collection of Fine Arts
176. U.S. (Smithsonian) National Gallery of Art
177. U.S. (Smithsonian) National Zoological Park
178. U.S. (Smithsonian) Office of Museum Programs
179. U.S. (Smithsonian) Office of Telecommunications
180. U.S. (Smithsonian) Renwick Gallery
181. U.S. State Department
182. U.S. (Transportation) Coast Guard
183. U.S. (Transportation) Federal Aviation Administration
184. U.S. (Transportation) Federal Highway Administration
185. U.S. (Transportation) Federal Highway Administration National Highway Institute
186. U.S. Veterans Administration Central Office Film Library

Collection

1 Alexander Graham Bell Association for the Deaf

3417 Volta Place, NW
Washington, D.C. 20007
(202) 337-5220

9:00 A.M.-4:30 P.M.   Monday-Friday

Virginia Gilmer, Staff Coordinator

Eligibility

Open to the public. Call ahead to make an appointment.

Collection

10 titles. The collection includes materials on deafness, educating the deaf, and diagnosis of deafness. Copies of the films and videotapes are for sale through the association.

Catalogue

A descriptive list is available by mail.

Access

The collection does not circulate but can be viewed at the association's offices.
Reservations should be made in advance.
Video analysis equipment is available.

Collection

2 American Association of Community and Junior Colleges

One Dupont Circle NW, Suite 410
Washington, D.C. 20036
(202) 293-7050

8:30 A.M.-4:30 P.M.   Monday-Friday

James Zigerell, Mass Media Programs Director

Eligibility

Scholars and researchers may use the collection.

Collection

80 titles: samples of college course lessons. The American Association of Community and Junior Colleges publishes a catalogue of lower division college courses produced for video, audio, or print media. The 80 videocassettes in the collection are samples of the courses listed in the catalogue, which includes social science, humanities, arts, science, health, consumer and occupational courses.

Catalogue

The sample lessons which make up the collection are from courses described in *The Mass Media College Catalogue,* a directory of lower division college course material in national distribution for use via the mass media.

Access

The collection does not circulate.

Those wishing to view the collection should call ahead to check on the availability of viewing equipment.

Video analysis equipment is available.

Information on rights is included in the *Catalogue.*

Other Materials

In addition to the sample lessons on videocassettes, the Association's library contains print materials and evaluation studies related to the courses listed in the *Catalogue.*

Collection

3 American Federation of Labor and Congress of Industrial Organizations

815 16th Street, NW
Washington, D.C. 20006
(202) 637-5153

9:00 A.M.-4:30 P.M. Monday-Friday

Louise McLaurin, Film Librarian

Eligibility

Open to the public. There is a rental charge.

Collection

157 titles. Included are groups of films on labor history, building a union, political education, human rights, social and economic issues, and techniques for training organizers. About one-third of the collection was produced by unions but there are also television documentaries from the networks, public television, and local stations. There are numerous titles from the Canadian Film Board and three films produced in Europe. Many date from the 1950s. Individual titles and topics include *The Inheritance,* health care, women's rights, and biographies of Susan B. Anthony, Eleanor Roosevelt, and A Philip Randolph.

Catalogue

A descriptive catalogue is available by mail.

Access

> Borrowing is by mail and in person. There is a rental charge for most films.
> > Reservations should be made two weeks in advance.
> > There are no viewing facilities.
> > For TV rights and purchase of copies of AFL-CIO films, contact the committee which produced them.

Collection

4 American Federation of State, County and Municipal Employees

1625 L Street, NW
Washington, D.C. 20036
(202) 452-4800

8:30 A.M.-6:00 P.M.   Monday-Friday

Joyce Casey, Department of Education and Leadership Training

Eligibility

> Open to the public.

Collection

> 20 titles. These films, produced by labor unions and labor-related organizations, cover labor history, union activities, and organizing.

Catalogue

> A descriptive catalogue is available by mail.

Access

> Borrowing is by mail and in person.
> > Reservations should be made two weeks in advance
> > There are no viewing facilities.

Collection

5 American Federation of Teachers

11 Dupont Circle, NW
Washington, D.C. 20036
(202) 797-4400

8:00 A.M.-5:30 P.M.   Monday-Friday

Barbara Lee, Order Department

Eligibility

> Open to the public, but a deposit is required.

Collection

> 7 titles. The collection contains short documentaries, some produced by the American Federation of Teachers but most purchased. The majority deal with labor unions, especially teachers' unions. Individual topics include arbitration, Black Americans, Joe Glazer telling labor history through song, and a documentary on conditions of the black worker in Dimbaza, South Africa.

Catalogue

> A descriptive catalogue is available by mail.

Access

> Borrowing is in person and by mail. The $10.00 deposit required to reserve a film is returned if the film is returned within 24 hours after use.
> Reservations should be made in advance.
> There are no viewing facilities.
> Information is available on TV rights and purchase of copies for films produced by A.F.T.

Referral Service

6 American Film Institute

> *National Information Services*
> *John F. Kennedy Center for the Performing Arts*
> (take the elevator next to the AFI Theater entrance)
> *Washington, D.C. 20566*
> *(202) 828-4088*
>
> 9:00 A.M.-5:30 P.M.   Monday-Friday
>
> Abby Nelson, Senior Information Associate
> Chris Spillsbury, Information Assistant
> Debbie Davidson, Information Assistant

The National Information Services of the American Film Institute (AFI) provides limited reference service by phone, letter, and in person, and offers scholars the use of a library designed to serve researchers in film and television. The emphasis is on American entertainment films. This is the best source of information in Washington on recent American films and foreign films in general. It is not a film or television archive. The large AFI Film Collection is at the Library of Congress (entry #165C).

The AFI is a private, non-profit organization established in 1967 and funded by the National Endowment for the Arts and others. Its purpose is to preserve the film and television heritage of the United States and to advance the art of film and television. AFI supports preservation and documentation activities, the National Education Services, the AFI Theater in the Kennedy Center, *American Film* magazine, and the Center for Advanced Film Studies in Beverly Hills, California, which includes the Charles K. Feldman Library.

Eligibility

Open to the public. The benefits of membership in the AFI, currently $15.00 per year, include information on AFI services and activities, reduced prices at the AFI Theater and on publications, and a subscription to *American Film.*

Referral Aids

National Education Services

National Information Service. This phone, letter, and in-person reference service responds to questions about film and television. It is a fine source of information on distributors of 16mm films, archival sources of feature films and television programs, and recent and foreign entertainment films.

AFI Library. The library has a large collection of film books and periodicals; some television books and periodicals; a clippings file arranged by title, personalities, and country of origin, with strength in recent films; transcripts of the AFI Film History Project's taped interviews; and the basic film reference works.

The AFI Library is a pleasant place to do research since the entire collection is accessible and the staff is available to assist researchers. Getting into the Kennedy Center before 10:00 A.M. may be a problem, and in any case a call should be made before visiting the library.

Stills Collection. From a variety of sources, AFI has acquired a collection of 30,000 motion picture stills. They are in the process of being catalogued and are available for in-house and archival use.

Factfiles. This series of periodically updated documents contains annotated reference information on various topics. Individual titles are available by mail for $3.00 each or $2.00 to AFI members. In the Library, and available to researchers, are files with much more information than is printed in the *Factfiles. Factfiles* titles include: "Film/Television: A Research Guide," "Film/Television: Grants, Scholarships, Special Programs," and "Film and Television Periodicals in English." Other subjects include careers, festivals, independent film and video, classroom use of film, women, nostalgia, film music, animation, and Third World Cinema.

Curriculum Advisory Service. This service provides teachers of high school and college level film and television courses with advice on textbooks and a syllabus exchange.

The AFI Guide to College Courses in Film and Television. The 1978/79 edition contains notes on the courses, faculty, and facilities of nearly 1,100 schools. It is available for $9.75 or $7.50 to AFI members. The *Guide* is published biennially. The most recent information is available from the *Guide's* editorial staff.

The AFI Theater

Located in the Kennedy Center, the AFI Theater shows two or three films each day, with several series running each month. In the past it has presented series on foreign films, genre, and individual filmmakers or stars, as well as children's films and the Washington premieres of several films. (See Appendix IV.)

American Film

A subscription to the AFI journal of film and television arts, published ten times a year, is one of the benefits of AFI membership. The magazine features popular entertainment articles as well as short scholarly pieces on film and television.

Preservation and the AFI Collection

The preservation program has resulted in the AFI Collection of films at the Library of Congress as well as preservation activities at other archives in the U.S. The AFI Collection is described in the entry for the Library of Congress (entry #165C), and 14,124 films are listed in the recently published *Catalogue of Holdings of the American Film Institute Collection and the United Artists Collection at the Library of Congress* (Washington, D.C.: American Film Institute, 1978). The *Catalogue* lists title, production date, producer, director, actors, and availability of a reference print. It is a valuable guide to the vast holdings of the Library of Congress and an impressive tribute to AFI's efforts.

Documentation and *The AFI Catalogue*

The goal of *The American Film Institute Catalogue of Motion Pictures* is to catalogue every feature, short, and news film produced or exhibited in the United States since 1893. The projected series will have 22 volumes, two of which have been completed, *Feature Films 1921–1930* (New York: R. R. Bowker, 1971) and *Feature Films 1961–1970* (New York: R. R. Bowker, 1976). The planned third volume will document feature films 1911–1920. Each catalogue includes an alphabetical listing of titles with credits, release date, country of origin, a detailed plot synopsis and other information. There also are detailed credit and subject indexes and lists of the output of film companies, countries of origin and literary sources of films.

This essential reference work should be available in most large libraries or can be ordered from AFI. The 1921–30 volume is $57.00 or $47.00 to AFI members; the 1961–70 volume is $90.00 or $72.00 to AFI members.

Programs for Filmmakers

AFI supports the work of filmmakers through the Center for Advanced Film Studies in Beverly Hills, California, and grant programs for independent filmmakers. A small collection of films which came out of these programs may be made available to scholars in the Washington office. There is no catalogue and viewing facilities are very limited. A complete collection of these productions is available at the Center for Advanced Film Studies.

Collection

7 American Institute of Architects

Audio-Visual Library
1735 New York Avenue, NW
Washington, D.C. 20006
(202) 785-7295

8:30 A.M.-5:00 P.M.   Monday-Friday

Barbara Heiberger, Audio-Visual Librarian

Eligibility

Open to the public. Some films are not available on loan to non-members.

Collection

30 titles: architecture and city planning. The loan collection includes ten films about buildings, design, and people, along with short documentaries sponsored by the American Institute of Architects. A small archival collection contains out-of-date AIA films and donated films. Individual topics include urban schools. Louis I. Kahn, and renovation.

Catalogue

A descriptive catalogue is available by mail.

Access

Borrowing is by mail and in person. Archival films do not circulate.
Reservations should be made three weeks in advance.
A projector is available for viewing the films. Arrangements should be made in advance.
AIA-sponsored films are cleared for TV

Referral Aids

The Audio-Visual Librarian maintains a file of films and slides on architecture and planning that are available from sources other than AIA. Bibliographies on more than 60 subjects are available by request.

Other Materials

The loan collection contains 10 slide presentations. A collection of over 10,000 additional slides may be viewed at the Library only.

Collection

8 American Mining Congress

1100 Ring Building, NW
Washington, D.C. 20036
(202) 331-8900

9:00 A.M.-5:00 P.M.   Monday-Friday

Carmen Grenier, Films

Eligibility

Open to the public.

Collection

6 titles: mining. These are general films about mining, the economy and the environment.

Catalogue

A list of over 170 films about mining provides the names and addresses of the distributors as well as descriptions of the films. This list is available by mail.

Access

Borrowing is by mail and in person.
Reservations should be made.
There are no viewing facilities.

Collection

9 American Petroleum Institute

Public Relations Department
2101 L Street, NW
Washington, D.C. 20037
(202) 457-7046

9:00 A.M.-5:00 P.M.   Monday-Friday

Dick Drew, Photographic and Film Services Coordinator

Eligibility

The collection is available to researchers upon application. The "Movies About Oil" catalogue is available to the public.

Collection

9 current titles; 88 archival titles. Films in the collection deal with oil technology, the oil industry, and the environment. Current films are for sale, and some preview prints are available to scholars. The archival materials are films made by the Petroleum Institute over the past 25 years.

Catalogue

Films available from the American Petroleum Institute are listed in their publication "Movies About Oil." This list describes over 150 films about oil and films sponsored by the oil companies on other technologies and history. The archival collection is in a card index.

Access

Scholars must apply to the Institute for permission to use its archival and preview collections.

There are no viewing facilities.

For information on TV rights and purchase of copies, contact the Institute.

Collection

10 American Red Cross

Audio-Visual Productions Center
5816 Seminary Road
Falls Church, Virginia 22041
(703) 379-8160

8:30 A.M.-4:45 P.M. Monday-Friday

George Manno, Manager

Eligibility

Scholars and researchers may request to view the collection. Free loan films, available to the public, are described below.

Collection

500 film titles; 300 videotapes. The Production Center holds a wide variety of films and videotapes about the Red Cross and events with which the Red Cross is often asked to assist. Refugees, food parcels, celebrity fund appeals, and natural disasters are among the subjects in the collection. One Japanese Red Cross film dates back to the 1930s; many are from the 1940s and 1950s; and there is a beautiful film about Vietnam produced in Saigon in 1966. A number of films were produced by Red Cross organizations in Europe and the East Asia. Also included are public service announcements and other short Red Cross productions from 1950 to the present.

Catalogue

Completed productions are included in a card file which provides descriptive information—the only card catalogue with a sense of humor that was discovered in researching this *Guide*.

Access

The free loan collection is available by mail and in person. The Production Center collection does not circulate.

For additional information on both the free loan library and the Center's collection, write or call Mr. Manno.

Special Collections

The American Red Cross Audiovisual Loan Library is a free loan service located in the same facility as the Production Center. The collection is available to the public and contains films, videotapes, and other audio-visual materials on the blood program, disasters, health, and water safety. A descriptive catalogue is available by mail.

Activities

George Manno is the president of the Washington chapter of the International Television Association (ITVA), an organization of non-broadcast television producers and users. One ITVA program provides for an exchange of video productions among members. For more information, call or write Mr. Manno.

Collection

11 American Trucking Association

Public Relations Department
1616 P Street, NW
Washington, D.C. 20036
(202) 797-5243

8:30 A.M.-4:30 P.M.   Monday-Friday

Jerry Buckman, Public Relations

Eligibility

Open to the public.

Collection

14 current titles; 12 archival titles. These films deal with the trucking industry, safety, and industries which depend on trucks. One film chronicles 200 years of freight transportation in the U.S. The archival collection goes back to the 1940s.

Catalogue

A descriptive list of the current films is available by mail. The archival collection is not catalogued.

Access

Borrowing is by mail and in person. The archival collection does not circulate.

Reservations should be made two weeks in advance.

A projector is available. Arrangements should be made in advance to view films at the Association.

Information on TV rights and purchase of copies is available from the Association.

Academic Programs

12 American University

Massachusetts and Nebraska Avenues, NW
Washington, D.C. 20016
(202) 686-2000

Note: Programs in film and video at American University are cooperative and cross departmental lines. This results in a lively program and an
economical sharing of resources but creates some difficulty in listing
them in this *Guide.*

COMMUNICATION, SCHOOL OF
309 Mary Graydon Center
(202) 686-2559

Faculty

Lincoln Furber—Broadcast journalism
Glenn Harden—Documentary film
Janet Keefer—Broadcast journalism and management
Larry Kirkman—Non-broadcast video
Jack Orwant—Mass media research
Ron Sutton—Film and society, Media education

Degrees

The B.A. in Visual Media and the M.A. in Film are interdepartmental
majors composed of courses in the Literature Department, the Performing Arts Department, and the School of Communication. There are also
B.A. programs in Broadcast Journalism and Public Communication.

Program

The Visual Media program, under Professors Sutton and Harden, combines film and video production with courses in fiction film taught by
Literature faculty, courses in non-fiction film and video taught by Communication faculty, and courses in media performance taught by faculty
in Performing Arts. Professor Kirkman, an editor of *Televisions* magazine and a producer for Public Interest Video Network, teaches non-
broadcast video and works with artists, dancers, sociologists and others.
Professor Harden offers a summer workshop which introduces print-
oriented communicators to film, video and photography.

Professor Sutton, former chairman of the National Association of
Media Educators, specializes in media education. He also teaches the
history of the documentary.

HISTORY DEPARTMENT
Clark Hall
(202) 686-2401

Faculty

Alan Kraut—Social and political history

Courses

Professor Kraut teaches U.S. media history in the School of Communication.

LITERATURE DEPARTMENT
Cinema Studies Program
Gray Hall
(202) 686-2450/2103

Faculty

Jack Jorgens—Shakespeare and film
Arnost Lustig—Screenwriting

Degrees

The B.A. and M.A. in Cinema Studies are interdepartmental majors composed of courses in the Department of Literature and the School of Communication.

Courses

Professor Jorgens is the author of *Shakespeare on Film* (Bloomington, Ind.: Indiana University Press, 1977). Professor Lustig is a Czechoslovakian author of several novels and a collection of stories which he has adapted for the screen. Janus Films distributes his *Diamonds in the Night*. Jorgens and Lustig teach courses in the fiction film, national cinemas, directors, and film and literature of the Holocaust.

PERFORMING ARTS DEPARTMENT
Kreeger Music Building
(202) 686-2315

Faculty

Elizabeth Monk Daley—Media performance
James T. Hindman—Media performance
Naima Prevots—Dance

Courses

As part of the integrated media effort, Professors Daley and Hindman teach a sequence of courses in performance and directing for film and television. *TV Acting: A Manual for Performance,* published by Hastings House, is the work of Daley, Hindman, and Professor Larry Kirkman of the School of Communication.

Professor Prevots's students have done theses in video dance and regularly work with Kirkman and the Visual Arts Program.

SOCIOLOGY DEPARTMENT
232 McCabe Hall
(202) 686-2414

Faculty

Muriel Cantor—Social aspects of television
Professor Cantor, the author of *The Hollywood Television Producer:*

His Work and His Audience (New York: Basic Books, 1972), is a specialist in the content analysis of television drama and the effects of television on children.

Collection

13 American University—Performing Arts Department

Kreeger Music Building
Massachusetts and Nebraska Avenues, NW
Washington, D.C. 20016
(202) 686-2315

Naima Prevots, Dance faculty

Eligibility

The film collection is rented to the general public. The video collection is in the Performing Arts Library (686-2165).

Collection

20 titles: dance. The film collection of the Modern Dance Council of Washington is housed in the Department. Its five titles are available for rent. The Department also has videotaped performances by students, faculty, and visiting artists. These tapes are designed for use by the faculty and students but might be made available to the public.

Catalogue

No list is available.

Access

Films must be picked up and returned to the Department.
Advanced reservations should be made by phone.
A projector and video analysis equpiment are available.

Collection

14 American University—Visual Media Film Collection

Media Center
1 Ward Circle Building
Washington, D.C. 20016
(202) 686-2103

Ron Sutton or Jack Jorgens, Faculty

Eligibility

Available to scholars by appointment.

Collection

75 titles. This collection, which serves the needs of courses in film history and film study, consists of 25 classic features and 50 shorts. Included are

three films by Arnost Lustig, a faculty member and screenwriter from Czechoslovakia; films directed by Alfred Hitchcock and Jean Renoir; and several examples of independent cinema and classic documentary.

Catalogue

A title list is available by mail. Send a self-addressed, stamped envelope.

Access

The collection does not circulate.
Reservations should be made to view the films at the Media Center.
A projector is available.

Collection

15 American University—Visual Media Video Collection

School of Communication
227 Mary Graydon Center
Massachusetts and Nebraska Avenues, NW
Washington, D.C. 20016
(202) 686-2055

Larry Kirkman, Faculty

Eligibility

Scholars may view the videotapes at the Media Center or in the Library.

Collection

The collection serves the academic program in non-broadcast video with a substantial array of video art, video dance, independent video, and experimental video generated by anthropologists, sociologists, communication researchers, and others. Also included are selections for use in the documentary history course and several examples of the best work of industrial television units.

Access

The collection does not circulate.
Reservations are required to view tapes at the Media Center. No reservations are needed to view tapes in the Library.
Video analysis equipment is available.
TV rights and copies of tapes are not available.

Collection

16 Anti-Defamation League of B'nai B'rith

1640 Rhode Island Avenue, NW
Washington, D.C. 20036
(202) 857-6660

9:00 A.M.-5:00 P.M.   Monday-Friday

Amy Goott, Community Services

Eligibility

Open to the public. There is a rental fee.

Collection

160 titles. The primary focus of the collection is Judaism, Jews, and Israel, but there are also numerous films on Black Studies, other ethnic and religious minorities, prejudice, and civil rights.' The films were produced by American TV networks, the Anti-Defamation League, and others. The small archival collection includes films from the 1950s and early 1960s.

Catalogue

A descriptive catalogue is available by mail.

Access

Borrowing is by mail or in person.

Reservations should be made up to one month in advance.

Scholars may request to view the collection in the League auditorium. The collection is intended to serve teachers in the Washington area. Most films rent for $10.00.

Information on TV rights is in the catalogue. For purchase of copies, contact the League.

Referral Service

17 Association Films

600 Grand Avenue
Ridgefield, New Jersey 07657
(201) 943-8200

Washington office (for information and telephone request for catalogue):
1111 North 19th Street
Arlington, Virginia 22209
(703) 525-4475

Association Films (formerly Association-Sterling) has a free loan collection of films available by mail to groups in the Washington area through the New Jersey film exchange. There are other exchanges throughout the U.S. The borrower pays only the return postage.

Referral Service

18 Association for Childhood Education International

3615 Wisconsin Avenue, NW
Washington, D.C. 20016
(202) 363-6963

8:30 A.M.-4:30 P.M.   Monday-Friday

This non-profit association provides information to its members on the education and well-being of children and concerns itself with legislation which affects children.

Eligibility

The public may use the collection of copies of the Association's journal and may purchase copies of pamphlets. Members have access to extensive files.

Referral Aids

"Films for Childhood Educators" ($1.25) discusses and provides rental and purchase information on films about education, childbirth, the pre-school years, and international education.

"Four Million Neighbors" describes and evaluates films for children about children in other cultures.

Each issue of *Childhood Education*, the Association's journal, has a column devoted to films for parents and teachers.

Collection

19 Association of American Railroads

Office of Information and Public Affairs
1920 L Street, NW
Washington, D.C. 20036
(202) 293-5016

8:30 A.M.-5:15 P.M. Monday-Friday

Ann Bennof, Educational and Informational Services

Eligibility

Open to the public.

Collection

2 films plus archival collection. The two films that are available deal with safety and the modern railroad. The archival collection contains about 20 films which are uncatalogued and unavailable.

Referral Aid

Railroad Film Directory lists the two films available from the Association of American Railroads and 165 other films about railroads, with descriptions and information on the distributors.

Access

Borrowing is by mail and in person.

Reservations should be made several weeks in advance.

Limited screening facilities are available to individual scholars.

Information on TV rights and purchase of copies is printed in the *Directory*.

Collection

20 BNA Communications, Inc.

9401 Decoverly Hall Road
Rockville, Maryland 20850
(301) 948-0540

8:15 A.M.-5:15 P.M.   Monday-Friday

Preview Center

Eligibility

The preview center is available to those interested in renting or licensing the films distributed by BNA. Scholars are welcome to use the collection also.

Collection

200 titles. Most of the films are from a series on management training and have such titles as *Management by Objectives, Effective Communication,* and an intriguing *How to Advance Your Husband's Career.* Individual films include advice for salespeople, jurors, and labor negotiators.

Catalogue

Descriptive catalogues are available by mail.

Access

Films may be screened at the preview center free of charge. There is a charge for previews by mail.
Reservations should be made to preview films.
Projectors are available.
Information on TV rights and purchase of copies is available from BNA Communications.

Academic Program

21 Bowie State College

Department of Communication
Jericho Park Road
Bowie, Maryland 20715
(301) 464-3283

Faculty

James Hinson—Visual literacy
Neal Alperstein—Video

Courses

Courses are offered in visual arts, broadcasting, and film history and documentary. Professor Alperstein teaches the uses of videotape in data collection and has written about his work with video as an approach to consumer education for the mentally handicapped.

Referral Service

22 Broadcast Pioneers Library

1771 N Street, NW
Washington, D.C. 20036
(202) 223-0088

9:00 A.M.-5:00 P.M.   Monday-Friday

Catharine Heinz, Director
Michael Kissko, Librarian

The Broadcast Pioneers Library was created to preserve and make readily accessible information about the history of broadcasting. It maintains a core collection of archival material relating to radio and television and serves as a referral center, directing scholars to broadcasting history materials in other libraries.

Eligibility

The Library is open to researchers, writers, students, official organizations, and the public, as well as the broadcasting industry.

Referral Aids

Director Heinz has extensive experience in broadcasting research.
Two unpublished reference works of special interest are "Sources of Television Programs Available to Educators and Librarians" and "Television Programs in the Collection of the Library of Congress, 1973."
The Library has a good collection of catalogues, reference books, and a referral file.

Other Materials

The Library's traditional print holdings include 1,450 books, 4,600 pamphlets, 200 early and current broadcast periodical titles.
Also available in the Library are the unpublished Broadcast Pioneers' papers; 3,000 photographs; a microfilm system with 1,600 documents; a small archival collection of motion pictures with no viewing prints; 22 titles of TV programs from the 1940s and 1950s; and 535 oral history tapes of Broadcast Pioneers, primarily those who worked in early radio management and technology.

Access

The collection does not circulate.
Appointments should be made to use the collection.

Collection

23 Catholic Archdiocese of Washington—Bishop Spence Center

Marist Building, Room 15
Catholic University
4th Street and Michigan Avenue, NE
Washington, D.C. 20064
(202) 832-0567

8:30 A.M.-4:30 P.M.   Monday-Friday

Sr. Ursula Butler, Director

Eligibility

The collection is for use by teachers in the Catholic schools of the Archdiocese. Others may request access to the collection.

Collection

300 titles. This collection of classroom films dates from the 1940s to the early 1970s. Strengths are in science and social studies. Of particular interest are 80 issues of the Hearst Metronome News Screen Digest dating from the mid-1960s to the present. These short films cover both current events, such as presidential inaugurations, and broader topics, such as American farmers or the history of the motion picture industry. These films are donated to each local school system's media center by PEPCO, the electrical utility.

Catalogue

A descriptive catalogue is available by mail for $4.50.

Access

Borrowing is in person only.
Reservations should be made in advance to borrow films.
There are no viewing facilities.

Collection

24 Catholic Diocese of Arlington—Multi-media Center for Religious Education

200 Glebe Road
Arlington, Virginia 22203
(703) 841-2530

9:00 A.M.-3:00 P.M.   Monday-Friday

Sr. Marie Paul

Eligibility

The public may rent the films for a small fee. Scholars may view the films at the Center.

Collection

> 65 titles. The short films that constitute this collection either explore values or teach religious principles. The intended audience ranges from primary school children to adults.

Catalogue

> A descriptive catalogue is available by mail for $2.50.

Access

> Borrowing is in person only.
> Advance reservations should be made to borrow the films. Scholars who wish to view the films at the Center should call a few days in advance.
> Projectors are available.

Academic Program

25 Catholic University of America

Politics, Department of
4th Street and Michigan Avenue, NE
Washington, D.C. 20064
(202) 635-5129

Faculty

> Michael Robinson

Courses

> Two courses in media analysis are offered by Professor Robinson: an undergraduate "TV and Political Systems" and a graduate "Seminar in Mass Media and Politics."

Collection

26 Coordination Council for North American Affairs

National Press Building, Room 552
14th and F Streets, NW
Washington, D.C. 20045
(202) 657-2130

9:30 A.M.-5:30 P.M.   Monday-Friday

Austin Chiang

The Coordination Council handles the films and other services formerly provided by the Embassy of the Republic of China.

Eligibility

> Open to the public.

Collection

> 81 titles: China. Recent short documentaries on Chinese culture and life in the Republic of China make up half of the collection. Individual topics include ceramics, dance, education, fishing, opera, shadow plays, and Tai Chi. There are also 38 feature length entertainment films in Chinese with English subtitles.

Catalogue

> A title list is available by mail.

Access

> Borrowing is by mail and in person.
> Reservations should be made two to three weeks in advance.
> Screening facilities are not available.
> For information on TV rights and purchase of copies, contact the Council.

Collection

27 District of Columbia Martin Luther King Memorial Library

Audio-Visual Division
901 G Street, NW
Washington, D.C. 20001
(202) 727-1265

9:00 A.M.-9:00 P.M.   Monday-Thursday (September-May)
9:00 A.M.-5:30 P.M.   Friday, Saturday

Diane Henry, Chief, Audio-Visual
Lynne Bradley, Video Librarian

Eligibility

> All persons who are 21 years of age or older and who live, work, or own property in the District of Columbia are eligible to borrow films. Anyone may view videotapes.

Collection

> 3,600 titles. Over half of the 3,000 films are aimed at young viewers, with special emphasis on pre-school materials. Subject strength is in animation, animals, biography, city life, art films and film history, race relations, and sports. There are also smaller collections of government-produced films, U.N. films, Canadian travel films, and feature films.
> The video collection includes 400 purchased titles and 200 in-house productions; the latter are primarily video documents of performances and events at the Library.

Catalogue

> Printed catalogues are available for use at each branch in the library system.

Access

Films circulate for one day or one weekend. They must be picked up in person. The video collection does not circulate.

Reservations in writing must be made five days before the scheduled show date.

There are no film viewing facilities.

Video viewing facilities can be arranged for individual or group use.

Note on University of the District of Columbia Entries

The University of the District of Columbia was formed by a recent consolidation of what were previously Federal City College, D.C. Teachers College, and Washington Technical Institute. Because the University is still in organizational transition, titles and locations of its components may change. Consult the District of Columbia telephone directory for a campus locator number.

Academic Program

28 District of Columbia, University of

Library Science and Instructional Systems Technology
724 9th Street, NW
Washington, D.C. 20001
(202) 727-2756

Faculty

Robert Jordon—Information science, African library resources

Courses

Professor Jordon teaches courses in history of film and contemporary film.

Referral Service

29 District of Columbia, University of—Black Film Institute

Library and Media Services
425 Second Street, NW
Washington, D.C. 20001
(202) 727-2396

Anthony Gittens, Director

The Black Film Institute is a Black and Third World repertory film theater offering film series and lectures. (See Appendix IV.)

Eligibility

Open to the public.

Referral Aids

> Mr. Gittens has catalogues, lists and books on Black and Third World films and is in contact with Black directors and independent filmmakers.

Collection

30 District of Columbia, University of—Media Services—Van Ness Campus

4200 Connecticut Avenue, NW
Washington, D.C. 20008
(202) 282-7128 (Media Services)
(202) 282-7536 (Library and Media Services Division)

8:00 A.M.-9:00 P.M. Monday-Thursday
8:00 A.M.-6:00 P.M. Friday
9:00 A.M.-1:00 P.M. Saturday

Albert Casciero, Director, Library and Media Services Division
Edward S. Jones, Associate Director, Media Services

Eligibility

> Open to the public for use within the Center. UDC faculty and staff may borrow the materials.

Collection

> 1,100 titles. The collection consists primarily of purchased instructional films and videotapes. Many of the films were purchased from the National Audiovisual Center. Strengths are in medical and technical subjects. There are a few documentaries produced by local television stations.

Catalogue

> A listing by subject is available in the Center. A consolidated catalogue by subject for all UDC campuses is in production.

Access

> Materials circulate only to UDC faculty and staff.
> There are no reservations.
> Video analysis and film projection facilities are available.

Referral Service

31 District of Columbia, University of—Harvard Street Library

1100 Harvard Street, NW
Washington, D.C.
(202) 673-7018

Raoul Kulberg, Librarian

Mr. Kulberg maintains up-to-date lists of film series and media activities in the Washington area and is willing to provide this information to those who telephone or visit the Library.

Collection

32 District of Columbia, University of—Media Services Department at Mt. Vernon Campus

Room 2161
425 2nd Street, NW
Washington, D.C. 20001
(202) 727-2465

8:00 A.M.-5:00 P.M.   Monday-Friday

Gregory Stewart, Circulation and Distribution Supervisor

Eligibility

Open to the public for use within the Department. UDC faculty may borrow the films and videotapes.

Collection

574 film titles; 332 video titles. The collection, designed primarily for classroom use, includes some interesting films on dance and political protest, an instructional series on film and TV production, classic short films such as *Night and Fog* and *Spanish Earth*, biographies of Martin Luther King, Jr. and Harriet Tubman, and several silent film shorts. Subject strength is in biology, physics, fine arts, and the social sciences. The 25 films for children include many fables and folk tales.

The video collection includes several BBC series, a series on African life, programs produced by local television stations, and network news specials. There are video documents of local government events and speakers such as Angela Davis.

Catalogue

A descriptive list and subject index of the films is available. A title list of the videotapes is available.

Access

The public may view the film and video collections in the Department.
Reservations are not necessary to view the films and tapes.
A projector and video analysis equipment are available.

Collection

33 Embassy of Australia

1601 Massachusetts Avenue, NW
Washington, D.C. 20036
(202) 797-3175

9:00 A.M.-5:30 P.M.   Monday-Friday

First Secretary for Information

Eligibility

The embassy film collection is located in New York. A descriptive catalogue with fee schedule is available by mail. (See Appendix III.)

Scholars should contact the embassy to inquire about the possibility of having films sent on free loan to the embassy from the New York library.

Collection

200 titles: Australia and Southeast Asia. Composed primarily of recent short documentaries, this collection features Australian aborigines, armed forces, arts, architecture, music, development, education, environment, geography, the handicapped and health, history, marine life, sports, recreation, and wildlife. Of special interest are fiction and documentary compilation films with footage dating back to 1896. One series of films was produced by the Australians in cooperation with the government of Thailand, Malaysia, Indonesia, and India. There are individual films on World War I, film history from 1896 to 1929, jazz, the Namatjira, urban life, and the architecture of the Victoria Gallery and the Sydney Opera House.

Catalogue

A descriptive catalogue is available by mail.

Access

Borrowing is by mail through the New York library and in person for scholars working with the embassy.

For reservation policies, contact the New York library.

The embassy cannot make screening facilities available.

For purchase of copies, contact the New York library.

TV rights must be negotiated with the Australian Film Commission, Suite 720, City National Bank, 9229 Sunset Boulevard, Los Angeles, California 90069. (213) 275-7074.

Collection

34 Embassy of Austria

2343 Massachusetts Avenue, NW
Washington, D.C. 20008
(202) 483-4474 ext 64

9:00 A.M.-5:00 P.M.   Monday-Friday

Press Department

Eligibility

Open to the public. (See Appendix III for larger collection.)

Collection

> 12 titles: Austria. Short documentaries feature the geography, music and recreational activities of Austria. Individual subjects include Spanish Riding School, Tirol, gourmet dining, Schoenau Castle, UNO city.

Catalogue

> A descriptive list is available by mail.

Access

> Borrowing is by mail and in person.
>> Reservations must be made at least one month in advance of showing.
>> Films must be borrowed to be viewed. The Embassy has no screening facilities.
>> For TV rights and purchase of copies, contact the Embassy.

Collection

35 Embassy of Barbados

2144 Wyoming Avenue, NW
Washington, D.C. 20008
(202) 387-7373

9:00 A.M.-5:00 P.M.   Monday-Friday

Film Collection

Eligibility

> Open to the public

Collection

> 5 titles: Barbados. Recent short documentaries cover the geography and recreation facilities of Barbados. Individual subjects include housing, school meal program, sports, industry.

Catalogue

> There is no printed list.

Access

> Borrowing is by mail and in person.
>> Reservations should be made either in writing or by telephone.
>> A projector is available.
>> For information on TV rights, contact the Embassy.

Collection

36 Embassy of Belgium

3330 Garfield Street, NW
Washington, D.C. 20008
(202) 333-6900 ext 219

9:30 A.M.-1:00 P.M.   2:30 P.M.-5:30 P.M.   Monday-Friday

Cultural Service

Eligibility

A small collection is available on the premises. Under certain circumstances, scholars can arrange to have films sent to the Embassy from Brussels.

Collection

500 titles: Belgium. The material available at the Embassy includes about 40 short documentaries. The collection in Brussels contains over 200 documentaries, 70 animated films, 20 experimental films, and about 125 fiction films, including 35 features.

Documentaries focus on the fine arts, history, architecture, technology, folklore, sports and science. Other topics and titles include Toone puppets, prehistory of the cinema, cybernetics, Bejart, Rubens, Magritte, Bruegel, Meunier, van de Velde, Belgica, *Chromophobia.* A number of documentaries by Henri Storck are included in the collection.

Some films are in French without subtitles.

Catalogue

A descriptive catalogue is available by mail.

Access

Borrowing is by mail and in person.

Reservations should be made in writing several weeks in advance. The collection is heavily booked.

Films must be borrowed to be viewed. There are no screening facilities at the Embassy.

For TV rights and purchase of copies, contact the Embassy.

Collection

37 Embassy of Brazil

Document Section
3006 Massachusetts Avenue, NW
Washington, D.C. 20008
(202) 797-0210

9:00 A.M.-1.00 P.M.   2:00 P.M.-5:00 P.M.   Monday-Friday

Eligibility

Open to the public.

Collection

31 titles: Brazil. Short documentaries cover the geography and culture of Brazil, with special emphasis on city architecture and the work of Brazilian poets and writers. Topics include carnival, Brasilia, Pele, Amazonia, baroque sculpture, architecture.

Catalogue

A descriptive list is available by mail.

Access

Borrowing is by mail and in person.
Reservations should be made in advance.
A projector is available for very limited use.
For TV rights and purchase of copies, contact the Embassy.
Note: Seven of the titles are also available from the Brazilian-American Cultural Institute, (202) 362-8334.

Collection

38 Embassy of Canada

Public Affairs Division
1771 N Street, NW
Washington, D.C. 20036
(202) 785-1400 ext 341

9:00 A.M.-4:00 P.M. Monday-Friday

Audio-Visual Librarian

Eligibility

Open to the public.

Collection

300+ titles: Canada. Most of these films are documentaries on the arts, history, industry, science, sports and people of Canada. Of special interest is a group of experimental films by Norman McLaren and others. Both English language and French language films are included. There are short biographical films of celebrated Canadians including Norman Bethune, Leonard Cohen, John Grieson, Norman Jewison and others. A nine-part series explores Canadian-U.S. relations using extensive archival material. Other compilations use much archival motion picture footage. The life of the Netsilik Eskimos is explored in a two-part documentary and a thirteen-part series for children. Other topics include Jane Jacobs, Castleguard Cave, Cree Indians, Blissymbols, early film history, aviation history, the Yukon gold rush, restoration, explorers, salmon fisheries, the Northwest Passage, arctic oil, space telecommunication, wheat, wildlife, mental retardation, skiing, gliding, snowmobiles, skating, hockey.

Catalogue

A descriptive catalogue is available by mail from the Embassy. Supplements and updates on films not in the main catalogue are available by special arrangement.

Access

Borrowing is by mail and in person.

Reservations should be made several weeks in advance of showing. Four films may be borrowed at one time.

A projector is available at the Embassy but only for very special and limited use.

Information on TV rights and copies can be found in the printed catalogue.

Bibliography

Canada Today. Vol. 3, No. 7, September, 1972, is entirely devoted to the National Film Board of Canada.

Other Materials

The large Embassy library contains materials on film and broadcasting in Canada.

Collection

39 Embassy of China, Peoples Republic of

2300 Connecticut Avenue, NW
Washington, D.C. 20008
(202) 797-9000 (Switchboard)
(202) 797-8878 (Cultural Section)

9:00 A.M.-Noon   2:00 P.M.-5:00 P.M.   Monday-Friday

Lon Gon Shih, Cultural Section

A collection of films is housed at the Embassy but the policies for their distribution have not yet been established.

Collection

40 Embassy of Cyprus

2211 R Street, NW
Washington, D.C. 20008
(202) 462-5772

9:00 A.M.-4:30 P.M.   Monday-Friday

Film Section

Eligibility

Open to the public.

Collection

6 titles: Cyprus. Four of the six films deal with the 1974–75 Turkish invasion and the plight of the Greek-Cypriots. Several were produced in Great Britain.

Catalogue

A descriptive list is available by mail.

Access

Borrowing is by mail and in person.
Reservations should be made in writing or by telephone.
Films must be borrowed to be viewed. The Embassy has no screening facilities.
For TV rights and purchase of copies, contact the Embassy.

Collection

41 Embassy of Czechoslovakia

3900 Linnean Avenue, NW
Washington, D.C. 20008
(202) 363-6315

9:00 A.M.-12:30 P.M.   Monday-Friday

Film Section

Eligibility

The films are available to institutions.

Collection

60 titles: Czechoslovakia. The collection consists primarily of recent films, 10 to 60 minutes in length on the culture, history, music, sports, and contemporary life of Czechoslovakia. There are a number of films on artists past and present.

Catalogue

There is no printed catalogue but information on available films may be obtained by phone or letter.

Access

Borrowing is by mail and in person.
Reservations must be made by letter.
Films must be borrowed to be viewed. The Embassy has no screening facilities.
For TV rights and purchase of copies, contact the Embassy.

Collection

42 Embassy of Egypt

2300 Decatur Place, NW
Washington, D.C. 20008
(202) 234-0980

9:00 A.M.-1:00 P.M.   3:00 P.M.-4:30 P.M.   Monday-Friday

Dina Andrawis, Press Section

Eligibility

Open to the public.

Collection

12 titles. Short documentaries depict both ancient and modern Egypt.

Catalogue

A descriptive list is available by mail.

Access

Borrowing is by mail and in person.
Reservations must be made in writing, one to two weeks in advance.
There are no viewing facilities.
For information on TV rights and purchase of copies, contact the Embassy.

Collection

43 Embassy of the German Democratic Republic

1717 Massachusetts Avenue, NW
Washington, D.C. 20036
(202) 232-3134

8:00 A.M.-4:30 P.M.   Monday-Friday

Cultural Attaché

Eligibility

Universities, German clubs, and large groups may use the collection. Additional films from the German Democratic Republic are available from:

U.S. Committee for Friendship with the G.D.R.
130 East 16th Street, Third Floor
New York, New York 10003

MacMillan—Audio-Brandon Films
34 MacQueston Parkway South
Mount Vernon, New York 10550

Collection

9 titles. Five short documentaries describe German cities and the life of Bach. Five recent features include two by Konrad Wolf, *Mom, I'm Alive* and *I was Nineteen*, plus *Beethoven, Lotte in Weimar,* and *Naked Among Wolves.* All features are in German. *I Was Nineteen* has English subtitles.

Catalogue

A descriptive list is available my mail.

Access

> Borrowing is by mail and in person.
> Reservations must be made in advance.
> There are no screening facilities. Films must be borrowed to be viewed.
> The Embassy will contact Berlin for information on TV rights and purchase of copies.

Collection

44 Embassy of Germany, Federal Republic of

4645 Reservoir Road, NW
Washington, D.C. 20007
(202) 331-3000 ext 323

9:00 A.M.-5:00 P.M.   Monday-Friday

Traude B. Blanks, Film Librarian

Eligibility

> Feature films are available from the Embassy to universities, colleges, and similar institutions for strictly non-commercial purposes.
> Short films, mostly documentaries, are available to educational and cultural institutions through Modern Talking Picture Service, Inc. (entry #112).

Collection

> 160 titles: German feature films. The collection of 25 silent films includes theatrical features dating from 1913 to 1929 by Fritz Lang, F. W. Murnau, Ernst Lubitsch, and others. One 1932 silent documentary feature shows life at the end of the Weimar Republic.
> The sound film collection includes theatrical and television feature-length films, both fiction and documentary. There are biographies of Schiller, Mozart, Luther, Rasputin, Alexander von Humboldt, as well as portraits of children, young lovers, the working class. Documentaries explore the Hunza of Karakorum in 1955, the Serengeti in 1959, and German railroads before 1935.
> There are 18 films from the 1930s and early 1940s, 17 from the 1950s, 38 from the 1960s and a large number from the 1970s. The most recent items are usually TV features or series. Some surprises, available only in German, are *Der Verlorene* (1951), directed by and starring Peter Lorre; *Liebelei* (1932), directed by Max Ophuls; and *Mazurka* (1935), starring Pola Negri and based on the same murder trial as *Confession,* a 1937 Warner Brothers' film. There is a special collection of opera films.
> The catalogue notes the language of each film: German, English, or German with English subtitles.

Catalogue

> A descriptive catalogue of features is available by mail. The catalogue of German documentary and cultural films distributed through Modern

Talking Pictures is also available by mail from the Embassy. A catalogue of German films for theatrical use is available from the Foreign Ministry.

Access

Borrowing is by mail and in person.
Reservations should be made well in advance of showing date. Most films are booked 10 months in advance. It is possible to reserve films on shorter notice if the loan period is just one day.
Films must be borrowed to be viewed. The Embassy has no screening facilities.
For TV rights and purchase of copies, contact the Embassy.

Collection

45 Embassy of Ghana

2460 16th Street, NW
Washington, D.C. 20009
(202) 462-0761

9:00 A.M.-12:30 P.M.   2:00 P.M.-5:30 P.M.   Monday-Friday

Ernest Tetteh, Information Section

Eligibility

Open to the public. Initial contact must be by letter.

Collection

14 titles: Ghana. Documentary films, most at least 30 minutes long, cover the industries, culture, and history of Ghana. Specific subjects include dance, education, cocoa, Nkrumah, agriculture, crafts.

Catalogue

A title list is available by mail.

Access

Borrowing is by mail and in person.
Reservations must be made at least two weeks in advance of showing. No more than two films may be borrowed at a time. Students must have their film requests countersigned by their department head.
Screenings at the Embassy can be arranged.
For TV rights and purchase of copies, contact the Embassy.

Collection

46 Embassy of Guyana

2490 Tracy Place, NW
Washington, D.C. 20008
(202) 265-6900

9:00 A.M.-5:00 P.M.   Monday-Friday

Information Officer and Press Attaché

Eligibility

Films may be borrowed by individuals and groups. The request must be made in writing on official letterhead.

Collection

20 titles. Guyana. The collection includes short news films of public events in Guyana, and longer films on the history and culture of the country. Individual topics include Defense Force, sculpture, Youth Corps, Phagwah Festival, Amerindians.

Catalogue

A descriptive list is available by mail.

Access

Borrowing is by mail and in person.

Reservations should be made one month in advance but one day loans are possible on shorter notice.

The Embassy has no screening facilities. Films must be borrowed to be viewed.

For TV rights and purchase of copies, contact the Embassy.

Collection

47 Embassy of Hungary

3910 Shoemaker Street, NW
Washington, D.C. 20008
(202) 362-6730

9:00 A.M.-4:00 P.M.   Monday-Friday

Istvan Fazekas, Cultural Attaché

Eligibility

Open to the public.

Collection

36 titles. The collection includes recent short documentaries on agriculture, folk arts and geography of Hungary. A small collection of entertainment features remains at the embassy for about one year and then is replaced by another group. Individual titles and topics include a film on the excavation of medieval Budapest and *Duel,* an award-winning animation.

Catalogue

A list is in preparation and will be available by mail.

Access

> Borrowing is by mail and in person.
> Reservations should be made on month in advance. Films may be borrowed for one day on short notice.
> There is very limited access to a projector.
> For information on TV rights and purchase of copies, contact the embassy.

Collection

48 Embassy of Iceland

> *2022 Connecticut Avenue, NW*
> *Washington, D.C. 20008*
> *(202) 265-6652*

> 9:00 A.M.-5:00 P.M.   Monday-Friday

> Dora Asgeirsdottir

Eligibility

> Open to the public.

Collection

> 16 titles: Iceland. Recurrent topics are geography, volcanos, and salmon fisheries of Iceland. *Iceland, Land of the Vikings,* made in 1939, is the oldest film in the collection. Specific subjects include Reykjavik, Westmann Islands volcano, ponies.

Catalogue

> A descriptive list is available by mail.

Access

> Borrowing is by mail and in person.
> Reservations should be made in advance.
> Films must be borrowed to be viewed. The Embassy has no screening facilities.
> For TV rights and purchase of copies, contact the Embassy.

Collection

49 Embassy of India

> *Information Service*
> *2107 Massachusetts Avenue, NW*
> *Washington, D.C. 20008*
> *(202) 265-5050*

> 9:30 A.M.-5:30 P.M.   Monday-Friday

> L. Sailo, Film Assistant

Eligibility

> Open to the public.

Collection

> 157 titles: India. This widely varied collection of short documentaries includes many films on dance, geography, science, industry and history of India. There are biographies of Ghandi, Nehru, Tagore, artist Nandlal Bose and others. A large number of films are about animals. A few use archival footage, including one on the history of the Indian film industry, 1913-1963. Folk tales are told in animation, live action, and dance.

Catalogue

> A descriptive catalogue is available by mail.

Access

> Borrowing is by mail and in person.
>
> Reservations four to five weeks in advance are recommended for borrowing by mail. Reservations are not required for one-day borrowing. Written requests on letterhead should be made for the films but area residents may telephone to check on the availability of a film.
>
> It is sometimes possible to view films on a projector at the Embassy.
>
> All films are cleared for TV. For purchase of copies, see notes in the catalogue.

Collection

50 Embassy of Indonesia

2020 Massachusetts Avenue, NW
Washington, D.C. 20036
(202) 293-1745

9:00 A.M.-5:00 P.M.   Monday-Friday

Pangi Soria

Eligibility

> Open to the public.

Collection

> 6 titles: Indonesia. The collection includes documentaries on the geography and culture of Indonesia produced by oil companies, National Geographic, and a Japanese TV station. Specific subjects include the Ramayan, batik, Bali.

Catalogue

> There is no printed list.

Access

Borrowing is by mail and in person.

Reservations should be made one week in advance.

A projector is available at the Embassy but only for restricted and very special use.

For TV rights and purchase of copies, th eindividual producers must be contacted.

Collection

51 Embassy of Iran (Embassy closed effective April 8, 1980)

Press and Information Department
3005 Massachusetts Avenue, NW
Washington, D.C. 20008
(202) 797-6571/6589

9:30 A.M.-5:30 P.M.   Monday-Friday

Mrs. Ferivari, Audio-visual Officer

Eligibility

Open to the public.

Collection

20 titles. The collection includes short documentaries on the geography, arts, crafts, and industries of Iran. Individual subjects include wool, woodcarving, folk dance.

Catalogue

A title list is available by mail.

Access

Borrowing is by mail and in person.

Reservations should be made one month in advance although one-day loans are available on shorter notice.

Films must be borrowed to be viewed. The Embassy has no screening facilities.

For TV rights and purchase of copies, contact the Embassy.

Collection

52 Embassy of Ireland

2234 Massachusetts Avenue, NW
Washington, D.C. 20008
(202) 462-3939

9:30 A.M.-5:30 P.M.   Monday-Friday

Barbara Edmundson, Third Secretary

Eligibility

Open to the public.

Collection

23 titles: Ireland. Short documentaries feature the geography, agriculture, industry, culture, and history of Ireland. *Cradle of Genius,* a 40-minute film from the 1950s, tells the history of the Abbey Theatre through interviews with actors and the playwright Sean O'Casey. There are biographical films on William Butler Yeats, Roger Casement, and others. Specific subjects include stone carving, dance, Easter Rising.

Catalogue

A descriptive list is available by mail.

Access

Borrowing is by mail and in person.

Reservations are not always necessary but one should call ahead to check on a film's availability.

Films must be borrowed to be viewed. The Embassy has no screening facilities.

For TV rights and purchase of copies, contact the Embassy.

Collection

53 Embassy of Israel

Films are handled by the Jewish Teacher Center (entry #105).

Collection

54 Embassy of Jamaica

1666 Connecticut Avenue, NW
Washington, D.C. 20009
(202) 387-1010

9:00 A.M.-5:00 P.M.   Monday-Friday

Director of Information

Eligibility

Open to the public.

Collection

15 titles: Jamaica. Recent 20- to 30-minute films about the geography, culture and history of Jamaica make up the collection. Specific subjects include Parboosingh, Marriott, Manley, farm life, Independence Day 1962.

Catalogue

A descriptive list is available by mail.

Access

> Borrowing is by mail and in person.
> Advanced reservations are recommended.
> A projector is available for small groups.
> For TV rights and purchase of copies, contact the Embassy.

Collection

55 Embassy of Japan

Information Section
2514 Massachusetts Avenue, NW
Washington, D.C. 20008
(202) 234-2266 ext 263/264

9:30 A.M.-12:30 P.M.   2:00 P.M.-5:30 P.M.   Monday-Friday

Eligibility

> Open to the public.

Collection

> 100 titles: Japan. Short documentaries cover the agriculture, architecture, history, geography, sports, theater, industry, cities, and women of Japan. Many are simply views of Japan in different seasons, different moods. Classic arts and contemporary problems are repeated themes. Specific subjects include bamboo, Bunraku, Noh, Kabuki, Chanoyu, Ikebana, paper, gardens, silk, plutonium, Tokaido line, aquaculture, mass communications.

Catalogue

> A title list is available by mail.

Access

> Borrowing is in person only. Films are available throughout the country at the ten diplomatic missions. The largest collection is in New York.
> Reservations should be made as far in advance as possible.
> Films and videotapes (¾ inch cassettes) must be borrowed to be viewed. There are no screening facilities.
> For TV rights and purchase of copies, contact the Embassy.

Collection

56 Embassy of Korea

Information Office
1414 22nd Street, NW, Suite 101
Washington, D.C. 20037
(202) 296-4256

9:00 A.M.-11:00 A.M.   2:00 P.M.-4:00 P.M.   Monday-Friday

Young Ho Cho, Assistant Cultural and Information Attaché

Eligibility

Open to the public.

Collection

20 titles: Korea. Short documentaries cover the geography and culture of Korea and a 60-minute film documents the Korean War. Specific subjects include the folklore museum, celadon, taekwondo, music, migratory birds, nirvana, ginseng, classical arts.

Catalogue

A title list is available by mail.

Access

Borrowing is by mail and in person.
Reservations should be made one to two weeks in advance.
Films must be borrowed to be viewed. The Embassy has no screening facilities.
For TV rights and purchase of copies, contact the Embassy.

Collection

57 Embassy of Kuwait

2940 Tilden Avenue, NW
Washington, D.C. 20008
(202) 966-0702

9:30 A.M.-5:00 P.M.   Monday-Friday

Press Officer

Eligibility

Open to the public.

Collection

20 titles: Kuwait. Recent 15- to 30-minute films explore the geography, education, and oil industry of Kuwait. Specific subjects include city planning, falconry, the handicapped.

Catalogue

A title list is available by mail.

Access

Borrowing is by mail and in person.
Reservations in writing two weeks in advance of showing are required. Reservations can be made no more than three months in advance.
Films must be borrowed to be viewed. The Embassy has no screening facilities.
For TV rights contact the Embassy.

Collection

58 Embassy of Liberia

Information Center
1050 17th Street, NW
Washington, D.C. 20036
(202) 331-0136

9:00 A.M.-5:00 P.M.   Monday-Friday

Mr. Tarty Teh, Film Circulation

Eligibility

Open to the public.

Collection

7 titles: Liberia. Short documentaries cover culture and industry of Liberia. There is a biography of President Tolbert. The oldest film is one on iron ore mining produced in the 1950s.

Catalogue

A printed catalogue is not available. Contact the Embassy for details.

Access

Borrowing by mail and in person. User must pay postage both ways.
Reservations in advance are recommended.
A projector is available for use at the Embassy.
For TV rights and purchase of copies, contact the Embassy.

Collection

59 Embassy of Libya

1118 22nd Street, NW
Washington, D.C. 20037
(202) 452-1290

9:00 A.M.-3:30 P.M.   Monday-Friday

Press Section

Eligibility

Open to the public.

Collection

20 titles: Libya. A small collection of short documentaries on folklore, medicine, development and tourism is available at the Embassy. A large collection is available on request from Tripoli.

Catalogue

There is no catalogue. Scholars should write for films on specific topics.

Access

Borrowing is by mail and in person.
Reservations are not necessary.
There is very limited access to a projector.
For information on TV rights and purchase of copies, contact the Embassy.

Collection

60 Embassy of Malaysia

2401 Massachusetts Avenue, NW
Washington, D.C. 20008
(202) 234-7600

9:30 A.M.-1:00 P.M.   2:00 P.M.-5:00 P.M.   Monday-Friday

First Secretary, Information

Eligibility

Open to the public.

Collection

26 titles: Malaysia and Southeast Asia. Short documentaries feature the geography, agriculture, history, arts and crafts of Malaysia. Several films present dance and dance drama from Malaysia and other Southeast Asian countries. Individual films focus on weaving, kites, silver, batik, development, the Jenka Project.

Catalogue

A descriptive list is available by mail.

Access

Borrowing is by mail and in person.
Reservations should be made at least two months in advance. The request must be in writing. Films may be kept for a maximum of two weeks, and two films may be borrowed at one time.
Reservation policies may be waived for those able to pick up films at the Embassy and return them the next day.
A 16mm projector is available for use at the Embassy but the staff prefers to lend the films.
For information on TV rights and purchase of copies, contact the Embassy.

Other Materials

The small library contains a collection of old black and white photographs.

Collection

61 Embassy of the Netherlands

Press and Cultural Section
4200 Linnean Avenue, NW
Washington, D.C. 20008
(202) 244-5300

9:00 A.M.-1:00 P.M.   2:30 P.M.-5:30 P.M.   Monday-Friday

Miss Bruyn, First Secretary

Eligibility

Open to the public.

Collection

63 titles: Netherlands. The geography, sociology and arts of the Netherlands are the subjects of these documentaries. There are biographical films on Queen Juliana, and artists Escher, Breitner, Mondriaan, Jongkind, Frans Hals, Van Gogh, and Rembrandt. Specific subjects include fishing; housing; mentally retarded, aged, and disabled persons; the sea; transportation; Westerbrook radio telescope. The collection includes the short film *Glass* and other films by Bert Haanstra.

Catalogue

A descriptive list is available by mail.

Access

Borrowing is by mail and in person.
Reservations should be made ten days in advance.
Films must be borrowed to be viewed. The Embassy has no screening facilities.
For TV rights and purchase of copies, contact the Embassy.

Collection

62 Embassy of New Zealand

37 Observatory Circle, NW
Washington, D.C. 20008
(202) 328-4800

9:15 A.M.-1:00 P.M.   2:00 P.M.-5:30 P.M.   Monday-Friday

Patricia Golden, Information Assistant

Eligibility

Open to the public.

Collection

51 titles: New Zealand. This collection of recent short documentaries includes groups of films on the geography of New Zealand and its sports activities, such as mountain climbing and racing. Films explore Maori arts and culture and include several animated Maori fables. There are special films on arts and the education and health of young children. Historical films present early railroads, a compilation of early photos and films, and a biography of James Cook.

Seven additional titles are available from Association Films, Inc. (entry #17).

Catalogue

A descriptive catalogue which includes both the Embassy and the Association films is available by mail.

Access

Borrowing from the Embassy is possible by mail and in person. Association films must be borrowed by mail. (See entry #17.)

Films should be requested as far in advance as possible. One-day loans can be arranged by calling the day before to check on the availability of the film.

There are no screening facilities at the Embassy. Films must be borrowed to be viewed.

For information on TV rights and purchase of copies, contact the Embassy.

Collection

63 Embassy of Nigeria

2201 M Street, NW
Washington, D.C. 20037
(202) 223-9300

9:00 A.M.-5:00 P.M.   Monday-Friday

Information Section

Eligibility

Institutions may borrow the films. Individuals may request to view the films at the Embassy.

Collection

39 titles: Nigeria. Short documentaries deal with the archeology, heritage, economic development, festivals, and history of Nigeria. There are individuals films on the Chief of Jos, the Alake of Abeokuta, dance, and economics.

Catalogue

A title list is available by mail.

Access

Borrowing is by mail and in person.

Reservations must be made in writing or by telephone at least two weeks in advance.

A screening room is available. Call the Embassy to request a reservation.

For TV rights and purchase of copies, contact the Embassy.

Collection

64 Embassy of Norway

Films are handled by Modern Talking Pictures (entry #112).

Collection

65 Embassy of Pakistan

Information Division
2315 Massachusetts Avenue, NW
Washington, D.C. 20008
(202) 332-8330

9:00 A.M.-5:00 P.M.   Monday-Friday

Naseer Tareen, Film Section

Eligibility

Open to the public.

Collection

20 titles: Pakistan. Recent documentaries, 20 to 30 minutes in length, show the geography, culture and history of Pakistan's diverse regions. Specific subjects include Gandhara, Kafiristan, painter Sadequain, weaving.

Catalogue

A descriptive list is available by mail.

Access

Borrowing is by mail and in person.

Reservations should be made as far ahead as possible. One-day loans are possible on short notice.

A projector and screening room are available for small groups.

For TV rights and purchase of copies, contact the Embassy.

Collection

66 Embassy of Peru

1700 Massachusetts Avenue, NW
Washington, D.C. 20036
(202) 833-9860

9:00 A.M.-5:00 P.M.   Monday-Friday

Miss N. Macedo, Attaché, Cultural Office

Eligibility

The collection is available only to institutions.

Collection

8 titles: Peru. Four films, available only in Spanish, explore the geography of Peru. Four films in English feature the ancient cultures of Peru. Specific subjects include Lake Titicaca, Chimu, Mochia, Inti Raymi.

Catalogue

A title list is available by mail.

Access

Borrowing is by mail and in person.
Reservations should be made in writing in advance.
Films must be borrowed to be viewed. The Embassy has no screening facilities.
For TV rights and purchase of copies, contact the Embassy.

Collection

67 Embassy of Poland

2460 16th Street, NW
Washington, D.C. 20009
(202) 234-3800

9:00 A.M.-4:30 P.M.   Monday-Friday

M. Wezyk, Information Officer

Eligibility

Open to the public. Priority is given to groups.

Collection

60 titles. This collection of recent documentaries focuses on the economy, traditions, and folk arts of Poland. There are groups of dance films and animated films for children.

Catalogue

> A catalogue is planned, but at the present time it is possible only to request films on a specific subject and have the librarian search the card file.

Access

> Borrowing is by mail and in person.
> Reservations must be made in writing.
> There is no screening facility at the Embassy but a projector might be set up for a group.
> For information on TV rights and purchase of copies, contact the Embassy. Polish feature films are commercially distributed in the U.S., and information on the distributor is available from the Embassy.

Collection

68 Embassy of Saudi Arabia

> Films are handled by the Farm Film Foundation (entry #82).

Collection

69 Embassy of Singapore

> *1824 R Street, NW*
> *Washington, D.C. 20009*
> *(202) 667-7555*
>
> 9:00 A.M.-5:00 P.M.   Monday-Friday
>
> Peter Chan, Counselor

Eligibility

> Open to the public.

Collection

> 9 titles: Singapore. Recent 20- to 30-minute documentaries feature the history, geography and festivals of Singapore. Specific subjects include housing, satellite communication.

Catalogue

> A title list is available by mail.

Access

> Borrowing is by mail and in person.
> Reservations can be made by phone.
> A projector is available for very limited use.
> For information on TV rights and purchase of copies, contact the Embassy.

Collection

70 Embassy of South Africa

3051 Massachusetts Avenue, NW
Washington, D.C. 20008
(202) 232-4400

9:00 A.M.-12:30 P.M.   2:00 P.M.-5:00 P.M.   Monday-Friday

Diana Huppert, Information Office

Eligibility

The collection is open to the general public in the Washington metropolitan area. Some films are available by mail from Association Films
(entry #17).

Collection

27 titles: South Africa. The geography, people, and industry of South
Africa are the subjects of these short documentaries. Half of the collection is at least 15 years old. Specific subjects include minerals, game
reserves, pollution, the Bantu, Namaqualand.

Catalogue

A title list with descriptions of some of the films is available by mail.

Access

Borrowing is in person only.
Reservations should be made two weeks in advance.
There are no screening facilities.
For TV rights and purchase of copies, contact the Embassy.

Collection

71 Embassy of Spain—Audiovisual Department

Cultural Office
4200 Wisconsin Avenue, NW, Suite 520
Washington, D.C. 20016
(202) 966-1077

9:30 A.M.-4:00 P.M.   Monday-Friday

Audiovisual Department

Eligibility

Universities, schools, and cultural institutions may borrow these films if
they send an official letter.

Collection

410 titles: Spain and Latin America. This collection of 15- to 30-minute
documentaries, all with Spanish language soundtracks, covers the geography, arts, architecture, fiestas, and cities of Spain. Many of the films

present sights in a single city of Spain or Latin America. Specific subjects include Cervantes, Juan Carlos, museums, monasteries, food, wine.

Catalogue

A descriptive list in Spanish is available by mail.

Borrowing is by mail and in person. Those requesting films by mail must send $2.00 per film ordered.

Reservations must be made two weeks in advance.

Films must be borrowed to be viewed. There are no screening facilities.

For TV rights and purchase of copies, contact the Embassy.

Collection

72 Embassy of Spain—Information Department

785 National Press Building
14th and F Streets, NW
Washington, D.C. 20045

(202) 347-6777

9:00 A.M.-3:00 P.M.   Monday-Friday

Eligibility

Schools and travel agencies may borrow these films.

Collection

62 titles: Spain. This collection of short documentaries about the geography and culture of Spain is similar to the one offered by the Embassy's Cultural Office, but Information Department films are available in both English and Spanish versions and all are in color. Specific subjects include castles, ceramics, bullfighting, Moslem art.

Catalogue

A descriptive list is available by mail.

Access

Borrowing is by mail and in person. Films are mailed C.O.D.

Reservations should be made far in advance. Only two films may be borrowed at one time and the films may be kept for three days.

Films must be borrowed to be viewed. There are no screening facilities.

For TV rights and purchase of copies, contact the Embassy.

Collection

73 Embassy of Thailand

Office of the Public Relations Attaché
2300 Kaloramo Road, NW
Washington, D.C. 20008
(202) 667-3108

10:00 A.M.-5:00 P.M.   Monday-Friday

Public Relations Office

Eligibility

Open to the public.

Collection

8 titles: Thailand. Thirty-minute documentaries show the geography and culture of Thailand. There is also a 90-minute film in Thai, *Investiture of the Crown Prince.* Other specific subjects include museums, life of a Buddhist monk, silk, sculpture.

Catalogue

A descriptive list is available by mail.

Access

Borrowing is by mail and in person.
Reservations should be made one month in advance.
A projector is available for very limited use.
For TV rights and purchase of copies, contact the Embassy.

Collection

74 Embassy of Trinidad and Tobago

1708 Massachusetts Avenue, NW
Washington, D.C. 20036
(202) 467-6490

9:00 A.M.-5:00 P.M.   Monday-Friday

Simone Deane, Information Officer

Eligibility

Open to the public.

Collection

15 titles: Trinidad and Tobago. Documentary films, most produced in the 1960s, cover the history, geography, and culture of Trinidad and Tobago. Specific subjects include the 1964 Carnival, wild birds, Independence, the first anniversary of Independence.

Catalogue

A descriptive list is available by mail.

Access

Borrowing is by mail and in person.
Reservations at least one month in advance are required. The loan period is two weeks.

Films must be returned by registered mail and insured.

Films must be borrowed to be viewed. There are no screening facilities.

For TV rights and purchase of copies, contact the Embassy.

Collection

75 Embassy of Tunisia

2408 Massachusetts Avenue, NW
Washington, D.C. 20008
(202) 234-6644
9:00 A.M.-5:00 P.M.   Monday-Friday
Mr. Kaak, Counselor

Eligibility

Open to the public.

Collection

6 titles: Tunisia. Three charming films set in Tunisia supplement the collection of general tourist documentaries. Some of the films are in French.

Catalogue

A descriptive list is available by mail.

Access

Borrowing is by mail and in person.

Reservations should be made six to eight weeks in advance of showing. One-day in-person loans are possible on short notice.

Films must be borrowed to be viewed. The Embassy has no screening facilities.

For TV rights and purchase of copies, contact the Embassy.

Collection

76 Embassy of Turkey

2523 Massachusetts Avenue, NW
Washington, D.C. 20008
(202) 462-3134

9:30 A.M.-4:30 P.M.   Monday-Friday

Chanan Big, Office of the Press Counselor

Eligibility

Open to the public.

Collection

>19 titles: Turkey. Short documentaries made in the last 20 years feature the geography, culture, and history of Turkey. The collection includes a 1961 CBS documentary on Ataturk and a short documentary, *La Turquie,* by Claude LeLouch. Specific subjects include Ataturk, Istanbul, the Hittites, old cars.

Catalogue

>A descriptive list is available by mail.

Access

>For borrowing by mail, contact the Embassy.
> For borrowing in person, make reservations through the Embassy but pick up and return the films to Modern Talking Pictures (entry #112).
> Reservations at least three weeks in advance are recommended.
> The Embassy has no screening facilities. The films must be borrowed to be viewed.
> For TV rights and purchase of copies, contact the Embassy.

Other Materials

>The small library contains recordings of Turkish music and a collection of still photographs.

Collection

77 Embassy of Uganda

5909 16th Street, NW
Washington, D.C. 20011
(202) 726-7100

9:00 A.M.-5:00 P.M.   Monday-Friday

Information Attaché

Eligibility

>Open to the public.

Collection

>10 titles: Uganda. Ugandan geography and culture are the subject of these 30-minute documentaries. Specific subjects include wire drawing, Makerere University, the East African Safari, tea, dairy farming.

Catalogue

>A descriptive list is available by mail.

Access

>Borrowing is by mail and in person.
> Advance reservations are recommended.

Films must be borrowed to be viewed. The Embassy has no screening facilities.

For TV rights and purchase of copies, contact the Embassy.

Collection

78 Embassy of the USSR

Film Library
1706 18th Street, NW
Washington, D.C. 20009
(202) 387-2084 (Cultural Office)

9:00 A.M.-Noon   Monday-Friday

Eligibility

Open to the public.

Collection

100 titles. Short documentaries in both English and Russian explore Soviet life, geography, nature, Republics of the USSR, industry, agriculture, culture, history, sports, and children. Historical films cover World War II and the life of Lenin. There are individual films on space, education, libraries, medicine, architecture, crystal, folk artists, the circus, Young Pioneers.

Catalogue

A descriptive catalogue is available by mail.

Access

Borrowing is by mail and in person.

Reservations should be made in a letter containing information on the organization assuming responsibility for the film. Those who can pick up films at the Film Library can get them on short notice.

Viewing facilities are available.

Prints may be purchased and rented from: Artkino Pictures, Inc., 165 West 46th Street, New York, New York 10036. The Artkino collection includes entertainment features.

Collection

79 Embassy of Venezuela

Information and Cultural Service
2437 California Street, NW
Washington, D.C. 20008
(202) 797-3880

9:00 A.M.-1:00 P.M.   2:00 P.M.-4:00 P.M.   Monday-Friday

Gonzalo Palacios G., Ph.D., First Secretary

Eligibility

Open to the public.

Collection

15 titles: Venezuela. Two of the three current films feature the work of artist Jesus Soto and the meeting of Spanish civilization with the cultures of Mexico, Peru, and Venezuela. The older films in the collection are uncatalogued but may be of interest to scholars.

Catalogue

There is no printed list.

Access

Films must be picked up at the Embassy.
Reservations can be made by telephone.
Screening facilities can be arranged with advance notice.
For TV rights and purchase of copies, contact the Embassy.

Collection

80 Embassy of Zambia

2419 Massachusetts Avenue, NW
Washington, D.C. 20008
(202) 265-9719

9:00 A.M.-1:00 P.M.   2:00 P.M.-5:00 P.M.   Monday-Friday

Moses M. Belemu, Press and Information

Eligibility

Open to the public.

Collection

45 titles: Zambia. The collection is primarily composed of recent 20- to 30-minute films on the geography, industry and history of Zambia. Specific subjects include dance, the life of a fish trader, Kaunda.

Catalogue

A title list is available by mail.

Access

Borrowing is by mail and in person.
Reservations should be made at least one month in advance. Shorter notice is permitted for in-person pick-up and return.
A projector is available for a single viewer.
For TV rights and purchase of copies, contact the Embassy.

Collection

81 Enoch Pratt Free Library

Audio-Visual Department
400 Cathedral Street
Baltimore, Maryland 21201
(301) 396-4616 (toll call from Washington)

This is one of three collections located outside the Washington area but included in the *Guide* because of their size, content, and proximity to Washington.

9:00 A.M.-5:00 P.M.   Monday-Saturday
5:00 P.M.-9:00 P.M.   Monday-Thursday (pick-up and return only)

Helen Cyr, Department Head

Eligibility

The collection is available to holders of adult library cards from any public library in Maryland. A non-resident card is available for a fee. Films may not be shown where any admission is charged or for fund-raising. Films may not be copied or shown on television. With few exceptions, films may not be borrowed by schools for classroom use.

Collection

3,340 titles. This large collection reflects both the varied needs of public library film-borrowers and the determination to build a few important specialized collections. Large groups of films are intended for children or cover the arts, biography, geography, history, social issues, and sports. Over 100 feature films and 350 eight millimeter (8mm) shorts are of general entertainment value.

Of interest to scholars is Pratt's excellent collection on the art and history of the motion picture. More than 100 experimental films provide a scholar with examples of film as the work of individual artists. There are also over 300 animated films. The almost 500 theatrical shorts and features include examples of the earliest productions; silent era films from the U.S., Germany, France, and the USSR; groups of American, British, and French sound features; and single titles from African, Latin American, Eastern European, and Asian filmmakers. Silent and genre classics in the collection of 8mm films are of limited interest, since most of them are edited versions.

The Black Studies collection includes over 100 documentaries by and about Blacks in the U.S. and a small group of American feature films with all-black casts. African films include both documentaries and feature films from Senegal and South Africa. Smaller special collections of note include groups of films on fairytales and folklore, films by Baltimore-area filmmakers, and several series on videotape produced by the Maryland Center for Public Broadcasting.

Catalogue

A descriptive catalogue with supplements can be purchased from the central library and its branches in Baltimore. Copies of the catalogue are available in public libraries throughout the state of Maryland. Both the film descriptions and the subject index seem to have been prepared with the scholar in mind, making this catalogue more valuable than most public library film catalogues.

Access

Reserved titles may be picked up and returned to the main library, branch libraries in Baltimore, and county libraries in Maryland. This in effect makes the Pratt collection available to scholars in Washington through the Prince Georges County Library (entry #128) and the Montgomery County Library (entry #135).

Reservations must be made two weeks in advance by telephone, mail, or in person. Reservations by mail must be made on the library's own reservation form and be accompanied by a stamped, self-addressed envelope for confirmation. Walk-in service is available at the main library.

Films may be borrowed for only one day except for films picked up on Friday which may be returned on Monday.

8mm films may not be reserved, are available only from the main library, and may be borrowed for seven days.

Video analysis equipment is available for viewing the small collection of videotapes. Both 16mm and 8mm films must be checked out to be viewed.

Other Materials

Slides, filmstrips, and audio recordings, as well as discussion and study guides for many of the titles in the collection, are available.

Collection

82 Farm Film Foundation

1425 H Street, NW
Washington, D.C. 20005
(202) 628-1321

9:00 A.M.-4:45 P.M.   Monday-Friday

Eligibility

Films are available to institutions and groups. The Farm Film Foundation is a non-profit educational film distribution service which provides free-loan films to specific audiences.

Collection

80 titles. The collection includes 11 films from the Embassy of Saudi Arabia. The rest are films about agriculture.

Catalogue

A descriptive list is available by mail.

Access

Borrowing is by mail and in person.
Reservations should be made in advance.
There are no viewing facilities.
Information on TV rights is in the catalogue.

Collection

83 Folger Library Shakespeare Film Study Collection

Folger Shakespeare Library
201 East Capitol Street, SE
Washington, D.C. 20003
(202) 546-4800

8:45 A.M.-4:30 P.M.   Monday-Friday (Film Study Collection)
8:45 A.M.-4:30 P.M.   Monday-Saturday (Library)

Note: The Library may be closed due to construction.

Barry Parker, Film Curator

Eligibility

The Folger Shakespeare Library is an independent research institution devoted to the study of the Renaissance with special emphasis on the humanities. The film study collection was established in 1975 to provide serious scholars with a facility for the study and preservation of Shakespeare on film. Services include a clearinghouse for information about Shakespeare films.

Use is restricted to recognized scholars, Ph.D.'s, and those actively engaged in dissertation research. Application should be made to the Registrar of the Library.

Collection

108 titles: Shakespeare. This well-managed and convenient facility has the following materials on 16mm film or videocassette: 32 feature-length sound versions of the plays, 15 feature-length sound adaptations, 26 silent film versions and adaptations, and 35 short and educational films.

Catalogue

A title list of the Study Collection is available by mail. There is also a list of the Shakespeare films in the collection of the Library of Congress.

Access

The Collection does not circulate.

Reservations should be made one to two months in advance since the facility is very busy. Reservations may not be necessary during the slower months of October, March, and April.

Film analysis and both color and black-and-white video analysis equipment are available.

The Collection may not be rented, loaned, copied in any form, or used for broadcast.

Other Materials

Books and periodicals on Shakespeare and film as well as a small collection of papers related to the films in the Collection are available.

Collection

84 Fondo Del Sol—Osiris Productions

2112 R Street, NW
Washington, D.C. 20008
(202) 483-2777
(202) 265-9235

Rebecca Crumlish, Media Director

Fondo Del Sol is a non-profit artists' collaborative of educators, filmmakers, and visual artists who share a common interest and involvement with the art and culture of the Americas. Osiris Productions is the media division of Fondo Del Sol. It produces and exhibits films and videotapes. The visual art and media center provides gallery and workshop space for Washington artists.

Eligibility

Community groups, museums, and colleges may rent the films and videotapes. Individual scholars should contact Fondo Del Sol to make arrangements to view the collection.

Collection

25 titles. The emphasis of this collection is art; the films and tapes are the work of media artists and many feature music, sculpture, painting, and poetry of Latin Americans and Spanish Americans in the U.S. Individual titles and topics include *Blood of the Condor,* flying pole dance, murals, Diego Rivera, Maya, Yanomami Indians, United Farm Workers.

Catalogue

A descriptive catalogue is in production. Copies will be available for a fee.

Access

Borrowing is by mail and in person.
Reservations should be made by phone or letter.
Projectors and video analysis equipment can be set up for scholars.
Copies of many of the tapes and films are available for sale and duplication.

Other Materials

Osiris Productions sponsors showings of their collection in Washington and throughout the U.S. and is building a collection of films and video documents on cultural events in Washington, D.C.

Academic Program

85 Gallaudet College

Gallaudet College Television
Model Secondary School for the Deaf
Florida Avenue and 7th Street, NE
Washington, D.C. 20002
(202) 447-0321

Staff

W. Lee Hunter, Director

Program

Gallaudet College, which serves deaf students, has an acitve program of campus television production: news, instruction, and entertainment programs. Gallaudet College Television tapes news and other programs off the air, adds captions, and makes these available to deaf students. Both the College and the elementary and secondary schools which are located on the Gallaudet campus are expanding their use of television.

Note: The International Visual Literacy Association (entry #103) is located on the Gallaudet College campus.

Collection

86 Gallaudet College—Media Distribution

Gallaudet Memorial Library
Florida Avenue and 7th Street, NE
Washington, D.C. 20002
(202) 447-0677

8:00 A.M.-10:00 P.M.   Monday-Thursday
Shorter hours on Friday, Saturday and Sunday

Tom Harrington, Librarian

Eligibility

Open to the public.

Collection

250 titles: the deaf. Thirteen films from the teens and twenties, with explanations in sign language, are from the National Association for the Deaf Collection. Recent programs explore dance, stories, and songs for the deaf. Many introduce sign language and other communication methods to those who can hear. There is a large collection of Gallaudet College Television productions.

Special Collection

A collection of 1,200 videotapes of broadcast television dating from 1974 have, under a special provision of the copyright law, been taped off the air, captioned for the deaf, and made available only to institutions for the education of the deaf.

Catalogue

A descriptive catalogue of films for public distribution is available by mail. A computerized catalogue of the entire collection is in production.

Access

Distribution varies title by title. Film and video free loan and video purchase are available. The materials may be picked up in person or ordered through the mail.

Reservations for free loan should be made six weeks in advance. Materials may be kept for two weeks.

A 16mm projector and video analysis equipment are available for limited use.

Academic Program

87 George Mason University

Department of English
4400 University Drive
Fairfax, Virginia 22030
(703) 323-2220

Faculty

Peter Brunette—Film
S. Eric Molin—Film
Joel Foreman—Film
Fred Grossberg—Video
Karen Walowit—Popular culture

Degrees

Programs for a B.A. in English and an M.A. in English or American Studies are offered.

Courses

Undergraduate courses cover film and popular culture. English and American Studies offer a joint course titled, "Problems in American Culture."

Collection

88 George Mason University—Department of English

4400 University Drive
Fairfax, Virginia 22030
(703) 323-2220

Peter Brunette, Faculty

Eligibility

Scholars may request permission to view the films.

Collection

20 titles: entertainment classics. The collection is split between features, both silent and sound, and short cartoons and comedies. These are used in film study and popular culture courses. Individual topics and titles include Chaplin, Betty Boop, *Potemkin, Birth of a Nation,* Capra.

Catalogue

Call the Department for a list of the titles.

Access

Films do not circulate.
Make reservations to view the films by calling the Department.
A projector and room can be arranged for viewing.

Collection

89 George Mason University—Research Center for the Federal Theatre Project

4400 University Drive
Fairfax, Virginia 22030
(703) 323-2251

8:00 A.M.-5:00 P.M.   Monday, Tuesday, Thursday, Friday
8:00 A.M.-9:00 P.M.   Wednesday

Laraine Correll, Director

The Federal Theatre Project, created in 1935 as a branch of the New Deal Works Progress Administration's arts program, was established to bring good theater to all the people of the U.S. while providing employment for professional theater personnel. Living Newspapers, the New York Negro unit, traveling companies in Wisconsin, and 6,000 radio programs were some of the projects of the F.T.P. The program ended in 1939 and the records were presumed lost until their discovery by two English professors from George Mason University.

Eligibility

The collection is available for scholarly and professional use.

Collection

25 hours of videotape: Federal Theatre Project. These videotapes are part of an oral history collection of recently recorded interviews which supplement the materials generated by the Federal Theatre Project in the 1930s. Designers, writers, performers, directors, and others talk about their experiences working with the Federal Theatre Project. A number of tapes deal with the New York Negro unit.

Catalogue

A descriptive brochure about the entire collection is available by mail. A list of the videotapes is also available, and scholars may write or visit the Center for details of this growing collection.

Access

Reservations to view the videotapes must be made in advance.
The collection does not circulate.
Video analysis equipment can be arranged for.
The Research Center will make copies of their videotapes for a fee.

Other Materials

The Federal Theatre Project collection consists of thousands of recently recovered scripts, designs. photographs, posters, and other materials deposited in the Center by the Library of Congress in 1974. The Center has recorded over 200 oral interviews with those involved in the Federal Theatre Project. Of interest to media scholars are 2,500 radio scripts, designs by Orson Welles, and materials about others who later worked in film and television.

Note: The National Archives (entry #155) has films about the Federal Theatre Project in Record Group 69.

Academic Program

90 George Washington University

2121 I Street, NW
Washington, D.C. 20052
(202) 676-6000

AMERICAN STUDIES
2108 G Street, NW
(202) 676-7489

Faculty

Bernard Mergen

Degrees

B.A., M.A., and Ph.D. programs in American Studies with emphasis on American film are offered.

Courses

"American Cinema," an historical survey, is taught regularly by Professor Mergen. Ph.D. candidates do independent readings with members of the Library of Congress staff.

SPEECH AND DRAMA DEPARTMENT
Lisner Auditorium No. 6
21st and H Streets, NW
(202) 676-6350

Faculty

> Joan Thiel—Television history and style
> Margot Kernan—Film history, Political film

Degrees

> B.A. programs in Radio and TV and in Speech Communication are offered.

Courses

> The programs include courses in broadcast history, analysis, and programming. A new program of inter-disciplinary studies in theater is planned.
> The film program emphasizes the analysis of the medium as a social and political artifact as well as an art form. Screenings are scheduled at the National Archives, American Film Institute Theater, and local commercial theaters. The film courses are all taught at the undergraduate level.

Collection

91 George Washington University—Anthropology Department

> *2112 G Street, NW*
> *Washington, D.C. 20052*
> *(202) 676-6983*
>
> Victor Golla, Chairman

Eligibility

> Scholars should contact Professor Golla to make arrangements to view the collection. Screening facilities are available in the Media Resources Center.

Collection

> 18 titles. The collection is for use in introductory and mid-level classes. All of the films were purchased from commercial distributors.

Catalogue

> A descriptive list is available by mail.

Collection

92 George Washington University—Asian Languages and Literature

> *613 University Library*
> *2130 H Street, NW*
> *Washington, D.C. 20052*
> *(202) 676-7106*
>
> Chung-Wen Shih, Professor of Chinese

Eligibility

Interested scholars should contact Professor Chung.

Collection

50 minutes. This 1977 footage covers historical sites and literary figures in the Peoples' Republic of China.

Collection

93 George Washington University—Media Resources Department

University Library
2130 H Street, NW
Washington, D.C. 20052
(202) 676-6378

8:30 A.M.-10:00 P.M.   Monday-Friday
10:00 A.M.-6:00 P.M.   Saturday
Noon-10:00 P.M.   Sunday

Fay Schreibman, Head

Eligibility

The collection is available for in-house use to all scholars, with priority given to G.W.U. faculty, students, and staff and to members of the consortium of Washington libraries.

Collection

150 titles. Groups of films in the collection focus on special education and such contemporary historical events as the Nixon-Frost interviews, a WTOP series on local history, and the Kennedy assassination. There are several series from public television and a small collection of videotapes from the Peoples' Republic of China. A major expansion of videotape holdings is planned for 1980.

Catalogue

All materials are inter-filed in the main card catalogue and in a card catalogue in the Department.

Access

Materials must be viewed in the Department.

Reservations 24 hours in advance are required for G.W.U. and consortium members. The general public should make reservations at least one week in advance.

Film projectors and video analysis equipment are available, as are individual audio and video carrels and a 74-seat classroom with a complete audiovisual playback system.

Other Materials

Audio materials are primarily musical, but commercial spoken word recordings cover such subjects as education, literature, and the sciences.

In addition the Library's own oral history collection deals with Washingtonia, school integration, and the history of the University.

Collection

94 George Washington University—Television News Study Service

University Library
2130 H Street, NW
Washington, D.C. 20052
(202) 676-7218

8:30 A.M.-10:00 P.M.   Monday-Friday
10:00 A.M.-6:00 P.M.   Saturday
Noon-10:00 P.M.   Sunday

Fay Schreibman, Head

The Television News Study Service was established in 1977 to serve as a reference and research center for scholars, especially those interested in the analysis of television news. The center sponsors seminars, conferences, and workshops.

Eligibility

The center is open to scholars and researchers.

Collection

The Vanderbilt Television News Archives tapes are available through the center, which serves as a borrowing agent for Vanderbilt. The Vanderbilt collection contains mostly network news and news specials: evening news on ABC, CBS, and NBC from August 5, 1968; all Presidential addresses and network commentary since 1970; Democratic and Republican conventions of 1968, 1972, and 1976; and selected news events such as Congressional committee hearings.

The CBS television news collections at the National Archives can be made available at the center by special arrangement.

Catalogue

Television News Index and Abstracts (Nashville: Vanderbilt University, 1972-present) is available in the Library. A special arrangement with Vanderbilt University provides the most recent supplements to the *Index* about two weeks after the broadcast. This publication contains the evening news content abstracted to the nearest 10-second interval and extensively indexed.

CBS News Index (Glen Rock, N.J.: Microfilming Corporation of America, 1975-present) is available. This is a yearly index, with quarterly supplements, of all CBS news and news specials since 1975.

Access

The Service provides assistance in identifying and ordering videotape materials from Vanderbilt and other TV news archives.

The Service uses the viewing facilities of the Media Resources Department, which can be reserved by scholars and researchers. There are booths with video analysis equipment, small group viewing areas, and a 74-seat room with a video system, 16mm projection and slide-tape dissolve equipment.

Bibliography

Adams, William C. and Fay C. Schreibman, *TV News: A Guide to Research* (Washington, D.C.: George Washington University, October, 1978).

Other Materials

Transcripts of CBS TV news broadcasts since 1975 are available on microfiche. The Service maintains a collection of television news analysis studies and books and periodicals related to broadcast journalism.

Academic Programs

95 Georgetown University

37th and O Streets, NW
Washington, D.C. 20057
(202) 625-4932

ENGLISH DEPARTMENT
Lauinger Library
(202) 625-4764

Faculty

Joel Siegel—Sound feature films, especially the musical and the French New Wave.

Courses

Professor Siegel teaches film courses each semester in the Fine Arts Department. The courses are different each semester but the emphasis is on form and cinematic style. Professor Seigel has published a biography of Val Lewton and is at work on a biography of Vincente Minnelli. He is the film critic for *Washington Calendar*.

SOCIOLOGY DEPARTMENT
B-12 Copley Hall
(202) 625-4205

Faculty

Jan Fritz—Sociology, Women's studies, Area Studies (Poland, Sweden)

Courses

Although no courses specifically deal with media analysis, Professor Fritz uses film and video materials extensively in her courses. Students make and then analyze their own videotapes and work with available instructional, entertainment, and documentary films.

THEOLOGY DEPARTMENT
O'Gara Hall
(202) 625-4347

Faculty

Paul L. Cioffi, S.J.

Course

Father Cioffi teaches a course each spring, entitled "The Silence of God and the Films of Ingmar Bergman," which uses the Bergman films from 1955 to 1965.

Collection

96 Georgetown University—Audiovisual Department

Lauinger Library
Washington, D.C. 20057
(202) 625-4123

8:30 A.M.-10:00 P.M.   Monday-Friday
10:00 A.M.-6:00 P.M.   Saturday
1:00 P.M.-10:00 P.M.   Sunday

Mark Cohen, Head

Eligibility

The collection is loaned only to faculty for on-campus use. The public may view the collection in the Audiovisual Department.

Collection

300 titles. The Georgetown collection is rich in films which not only support the academic program but which are fine films in their own right. The films classified under "Bioethics" deal with women, children, war, death and other issues and include the classic documentaries *Night and Fog, Joyce at 34, The Poor Pay More, Titicut Follies,* and *Sixteen in Webster Groves.* There are fine psychology, comparative religion, and fine arts collections and eight films on cities ancient and modern. Biographical films include studies of Chekov, Oldenburg, Einstein, and Teilhard de Chardin. Also in the collection are feature films and the videotape series *Ascent of Man, Civilization, America,* and *Rich Man, Poor Man.*

Catalogue

A descriptive catalogue of the film collection with extensive indexing is available at the Audiovisual Department and elsewhere on campus. The videotape collection is in a card catalogue.

Access

No reservations are required to view videotapes in the Audiovisual Department. The film preview room should be reserved.
A projector and video analysis equipment are available.

Other Materials

The audiotape collection consists of 1,500 tapes of music and 1,600 tapes of the spcken word. There are 150 slide sets.

Collection

97 Georgetown University—Lauinger Library

Special Collections
37th and O Streets, NW
Washington, D.C. 20057
(202) 625-3230

9:00 A.M.-5:00 P.M.   Monday-Friday

George M. Barringer, Special Collections Librarian

Eligibility

Open to the public.

Collection

750 reels of film; 600,000 feet of videotape. A minor archival collection of films covers Georgetown University history and sports. Four hundred reels of uncut footage, some of it by documentarist Emile de Antonio, depict events in the 1968 presidential campaign of Eugene McCarthy, including speeches and rallies. The McCarthy Historical Project Archive also includes 600,000 feet of 2-inch videotape of political commercials and a collection of stills.

Catalogue

The McCarthy film collection is not catalogued. The videotape is well-catalogued but at present there are no facilities for viewing 2-inch videotape.

Access

Film and tapes must be viewed in the Library.
Reservations to view the material should be made by phone or letter.
Projectors are available in the Library.
Copies of some of the material may be purchased.

Other Materials

The Wilfred Parsons, S.J. Collection contains about one foot of correspondence related to the Legion of Decency.
The records of the Georgetown University Radio-TV Forum include audiotapes, transcripts, records, and three TV programs from this public affairs series, which was on the air from 1946 to 1972.

The Quigley Photographic Archives consist of 51,500 black-and-white prints and 4,500 negatives from Quigley Publications, which published the trade journals *Motion Picture Herald* and *Motion Picture Daily.* These journals were published from 1906 until the late 1960s and dealt primarily with film distribution and exhibition.

Academic Programs

98 Howard University

2400 6th Street, NW
Washington, D.C. 20059
(202) 636-6100

RADIO, TV, FILM DEPARTMENT
2600 4th Street, NW
(202) 636-7927

Faculty

Arthur Francis, Chairman
Alonza Crawford—Film production
Oscar Gandy—Mass media content analysis
Abiyi Ford—Film analysis, history, production
Haile Gerima—Third World cinema
Thomas Hardy—Public broadcasting
David Honig—Broadcasting and government
Russ Johnson—Programming on minority stations
Robert Jones—Photography
Leroy Miller—Communications law
Ted Roberts—International broadcasting
Abdulai Vandi—Communications research

Degrees

Undergraduate degrees are offered in Film, Television, Radio Production, and Radio Management.

Courses

There are courses in film history, analysis, and production, with special emphasis on Third World films. The broadcasting courses emphasize programming for and by minorities, content analysis, and a wide range of production techniques. Other courses deal with public media and the legal aspects of broadcasting.

ROMANCE LANGUAGES
Locke Hall
2400 6th Street, NW
(202) 636-6758

Faculty

Francoise Pfaff—Blacks in Films in the U.S. and Francophone Africa, French Films
Karen Smyley—Writers and Filmmakers of Francophone Africa

Professor Pfaff and Abiyi Ford of the School of Communication have produced a film interview with Senegalese filmmaker Ousmene Sembene.

Collection

99 Howard University—Afro-American Studies Resource Center

Founders' Library
P.O. Box 746
Washington, D.C. 20059
(202) 636-7242/7243

9:00 A.M.-5:00 P.M.   Monday-Friday

E. Ethelbert Miller, Director

Eligibility

Student groups, organizations, and members of the community may use the Center.

Collection

350 titles: Afro-Americans, the Third World. This large collection of films and videotapes contains many produced at Howard University where lectures, interviews, and performances are regularly recorded on videotape. The greater part of the collection is purchased documentaries about Blacks in the U.S. and the Third World. Biographies include those of Malcom X, Martin Luther King, Jr., Muhammed Ali, Frederick Douglass, Jesse Owens, Fannie Lou Hamer, and Gary Davis. Films from Africa describe geography, anthropology, medicine, music, and students.

The Black experience in the U.S. is documented in films such as *Anderson Platoon, Weapons of Gordon Parks,* and *A Time for Burning.* Other films explore voting, the Black middle class, and the ghetto through the eyes of Black teenagers. The collection includes features *Nothing But A Man* and *Mandabi* as well as a film on the Black Panthers by Agnes Varda.

The videotape collection focuses on Pan-Africanism, fine arts, and literature. The 15 programs of poetry readings are an outgrowth of the poet-in-residence program. Also included are recordings of the television program *Black Journal.*

Catalogue

A descriptive catalogue is available.

Access

Films must be borrowed in person. Videotapes must be viewed at the Center.

Reservations are recommended for borrowing the films. Videotapes need not be reserved.

There are no facilities for viewing the films at the Center. Video analysis equipment is available.

Other Materials

The Center houses 20,000 books, plus periodicals, slides, and audio-tapes related to the Black experience, including an oral history collection.

Collection

100 Howard University—Center for Learning Systems

265 Locke Hall
2400 6th Street, NW
Washington, D.C. 20059
(202) 636-6737

8:00 A.M.-5:00 P.M.   Monday-Friday

J. Edwin Foster, Director

Eligibility

The collection is intended to serve the faculty and students of Howard University, but community groups may borrow the films.

Collection

300 titles. All films were produced before 1966. About half of the films are instructional, serving the programs in education, computer science, and science. There are a number of network TV documentaries and a 1962 series of biographies of world leaders such as Gandhi, Hitler, and Franklin D. Roosevelt. Some groups of films about Africa and Latin America are narrated in English, while others from France, Latin America, and the USSR have foreign-language soundtracks. The African and Afro-American collections are large. Individual titles and topics include *City of Gold* and a number of films on communism.

Catalogue

A descriptive catalogue is available by mail.

Access

Borrowing is in person only.
    Advanced reservations should be made.
    There are limited viewing facilities.

Collection

101 Howard University—Institute for the Arts and Humanities

Carnegie Hall
Room G-18
Washington, D.C. 20059
(202) 636-7737/7738/7739

9:30 A.M.-5:00 P.M.   Monday-Friday

Harold Burke, Media Specialist

Eligibility

> The collection is open to the public, with priority given to Howard University students.

Collection

> 70 titles (400 hours of videotape): Black history and culture. The collection consists of tapes recorded by the Institute's Media Documentation Unit since 1973. Subjects include events in the performing and visual arts, public affairs, sports, literature, folklore, and religion. Most were taped at Howard University but many events in Washington, Atlanta, and other cities are included. The 6th Pan African Congress in Dar es Salaam in June, 1974, is the subject of 12 hours of tape.

Catalogue

> A descriptive catalogue is available.

Access

> The collection does not circulate.
> Reservations should be made one week in advance.
> Video analysis equipment is available.
> Copies may be available for purchase.

Referral Service

102 Independent Curators, Inc.

1740 N Street, NW
Washington, D.C. 20036
(202) 872-8200

Nina Sundell, Associate Director

Eligibility

> The services of Independent Curators, Inc., are available to museums for a fee. Director Sundell is willing to exchange information with scholars. The main office of Independent Curators, Inc., has moved to New York City.

Referral Aids

> Director Sundell has curated video art shows for museums and has extensive knowledge of video art and artists.

Referral Service

103 International Visual Literacy Association

Center for Visual Literacy
Gallaudet College
Florida Avenue and 7th Street, NE
Washington, D.C. 20002
(202) 447-0381

Clarence Williams, Director

The Center for Visual Literacy serves scholars and publishes a series of articles on visual literacy titled "Provocative Papers." The International Visual Literacy Association is an interdisciplinary organization which promotes research in visual literacy and disseminates information on the theories and practice of visual communication.

Eligibility

Scholars and teachers may use the resources of the Center. They are encouraged to join the Association.

Referral Aids

"Visual Literacy Bibliography" and "A Short Mediography on Visual Literacy" are available. The Association also has over 40 short publications for sale.

Collection

104 Japan Foundation

Suite 570
Watergate Office Building
600 New Hampshire Avenue, NW
Washington, D.C. 20037
(202) 965-4313

9:30 A.M.-5:30 P.M.   Monday-Friday

Masaki Kodama, Director
Debra Billings, A-V Collection

Eligibility

The collection is available to universities, museums, and non-profit adult organizations.

Collection

130 titles: Japan. Most of these films and videocassettes present the arts and crafts of Japan, although smaller collections cover festivals, nature, and history. Within the arts and crafts programs, seven explore architecture and gardens, 42 present artists and craftsmen at work, and 13 are performances of Noh plays, puppet plays, dance, and music. Nature films explore the terrain and wildlife of Japan. Individual titles and topics include *TV Nippon,* the Emperor, the Ainu.

Catalogue

A title list is available by mail.

Access

Borrowing is by mail and in person.
Reservations should be made in advance and must be in writing on

the letterhead of the institution which is requesting the films or video-cassettes.

There are no viewing facilities.

Information on TV rights and purchase of prints is available from the Foundation.

Collection

105 Jewish Teacher Center

Board of Jewish Education
9325 Brookville Road
Silver Spring, Maryland 20910
(301) 589-3180

9:00 A.M.- 5:00 P.M.   Monday-Friday

Judy Kupchin, Librarian

Eligibility

The collection serves teachers in the Washington area but is also available to community organizations.

Collection

138 titles. The collection consists primarily of films provided by the Embassy of Israel. General films depict the people and geography of Israel, recent history, art, archeology, and the events which led up to establishment of Israel. American television, the BBC, and Israeli television are represented by series of documentaries. There are films on Jewish holidays and life in a kibbutz, and a few films especially for children. Individual titles and topics include the Palestinians, the 1967 and 1973 wars, the poetry of Amichai, *The Warsaw Ghetto,* American Jewish history, the Hasidim.

Catalogue

A descriptive catalogue is available by mail.

Access

Borrowing is in person only.

Reservations should be made as far in advance as possible.

A projector is available for use at the Center. Projectors are also available for rent.

For information on TV rights and purchase of copies, contact the Center.

Academic Programs

106 Maryland, University of

Route 1
College Park, Maryland 20742
(301) 454-3311

AFRO-AMERICAN STUDIES
2169 New Social Science Building
(301) 454-5665

Faculty

Al-Tony Gilmore
Micah Tsomondo

Courses

Professor Tsomondo teaches a course in the role of motion pictures in the representation and misrepresentation of Blacks to American society. Professor Gilmore is the author of a forthcoming book on the politics and impact of "Amos 'n' Andy" (1928-1954).

AMERICAN STUDIES
2140 Taliaferro Hall
(301) 454-4661

Faculty

Myron Lounsbury—Film and Cultural History

Courses

A general introduction to film and American culture and a specialized course which changes each semester are offered to undergraduates. Occasionally there is a graduate seminar in film criticism and American intellectual and cultural history. Professor Lounsbury's book, *The Origin of American Film Criticism 1909-1939,* was published by Arno Press in 1973.

ENGLISH DEPARTMENT
1125 Taliaferro Hall
(301) 454-2521

Faculty

Joseph W. Miller—Film

Degrees

A film minor is available in both the B.A. and M.A. programs.

Courses

Undergraduate courses are offered under Special Topics, which have included Hitchcock, Ford, and the Western. There is a basic introductory course.

GOVERNMENT AND POLITICS DEPARTMENT
Social Sciences Building
(301) 454-2246

Faculty

James Glass

Courses

Professor Glass offers a summer workshop on the psychological and cultural aspects of politics and films. A feature film is screened each day during the two-and-a-half week course.

HISTORY DEPARTMENT
Francis Scott Key Hall
(301) 454-2843

Faculty

David Grimsted
Hilda Smith

Courses

Professor Grimsted teaches American social history using feature films as documents. Professor Smith uses a social/historical approach in teaching "20th Century American Women Through Film."

RADIO-TV-FILM DIVISION
2148 C Tawes Fine Arts Building
(301) 454-2541

Faculty

Robert McCleary, Chairman—Television
Kathleen Jamieson—Political media, Age stereotyping
Donald Kirkley—Broadcast history and criticism
Robert Kolker—Film history and aesthetics
Charles Niemeyer—Early film history
Gene Weiss—Film, Television
Marion Weiss—Special topics in film

Degrees

B.A. and M.A. programs in Speech and Dramatic Arts with emphasis in radio and television broadcasting or film are offered.

Courses

Maryland's RTVF division has a strong program in film and broadcasting studies as well as production. Film study includes basic introductions plus specialized offerings in genre, documentary, criticism, and contemporary cinema. The broadcasting courses cover analysis, programming, criticism, and television and politics. Gene Weiss has directed annual national student filmmaking competitions.

SOCIOLOGY DEPARTMENT
Art-Sociology Building
(301) 454-5931

Faculty

Margaret Cussler
Sharon Mayes

Courses

Professor Mayes offers a course in the sociology of art with a focus on film. Margaret Cussler is the director of *Hopi Horizons,* an award-winning film made in 1941. The Small Group Committee of the Sociology Department has research facilities for the use of videotape and plans to acquire a collection of tapes for research and teaching.

Collection

107 Maryland, University of—Anthropology Department

1111 Woods Hall
College Park, Maryland 20742
(301) 454-4154

Elaine Roski, Secretary

Eligibility

Films are available to serious researchers for use in the Department offices.

Collection

36 titles: Anthropology. This educational and research collection is designed primarily to serve basic anthropology courses. *Search for Monaone* was produced by the University. Other individual topics and titles include tools, baboons, archeology, corn, *Dead Birds, The Loon's Necklace,* Cooper and Schoendsack's *Grass.*

Catalogue

A card catalogue is available in the Department office.

Access

Scholars outside of the Anthropology Department must view the films in the Department offices.
Scholars should contact Ms. Roski to make arrangements to view the films.
A projector is available.

Collection

108 Maryland, University of—Audiovisual Services

Room 0101
Annapolis Hall
College Park, Maryland 20742
(301) 454-3549

8:30 A.M.-12:00 P.M.   1:00 P.M.-4:15 P.M.   Monday-Friday

Grace Lewis, Film Librarian

Eligibility

Open to the public. There are some restrictions on the use of the Special Collections off campus.

Collection

> 1,100 titles. About 900 titles are films deposited at the University by the U.S. Department of Agriculture for distribution to the public. Many of these date back to the 1940s and 1950s; others were produced in the last ten years. Agriculture and home economics are the focus of these films.
>
> About 200 titles were purchased for use with courses offered at the University. The sciences and social sciences are represented along with a collection of about 30 animated shorts and a number of classic shorts.
>
> Individual titles and topics include *The City, The Green City, The River, The Twisted Cross* (a compilation film about Hitler), Stephen Foster and *The Great Baltimore Fire.*

Special Collections

Food and Nutrition

> 500 titles. The University is the distribution agent for this collection of films controlled by the Food and Nutrition Information Center of the U.S. Department of Agriculture. Scholars may view these films at the University Audiovisual Services office but information about the films and rental policies is available only from the U.S.D.A. (entry #145).

Business Administration

> 60 titles. This collection of films was purchased by the School of Business Administration for use in its classes. They may be viewed at the Audiovisual Services office by anyone, but only faculty, staff, and students may borrow them for use elsewhere on the campus.

Catalogue

> A descriptive catalogue for about 500 of the films is available in the Audiovisual Services office. The remainder of the films are listed only by title in a card catalogue. Any scholar interested in using the collection of older U.S.D.A. films should do preliminary research at the National Archives Motion Picture Branch (entry #155), which maintains the most complete collection of old U.S.D.A. film catalogues.

Access

> The general collection is available for borrowing by mail and in person.
>
> Reservations one week in advance are suggested but walk-in service is available.
>
> A projector is available for use by one or two scholars. Reservations should be made one week in advance.
>
> No information on TV rights or purchase of copies is available from Audiovisual Services.

Collection

109 Maryland, University of—Educational Technology Center

College of Education
Room 0236
College Park, Maryland 20742
(301) 454-4017

9:00 A.M.-10:00 P.M.   Monday-Thursday
9:00 A.M.-4:30 P.M.   Friday

Doug McCrory

Eligibility

> The collection and the dubbing facilities were created primarily to serve the College of Education. Their needs preempt all other uses. The public may view the collection free and use the dubbing facilities for a fee.

Collection

> 400 titles. This collection is changed each semester to meet the needs of courses in the College of Education. The materials are primarily instructional, but many are of more general interest.

Catalogue

> There is a title list.

Access

> The materials do not circulate.
> Reservations are not necessary.
> Video viewing equipment is available.

Services

> For a reasonable fee the Educational Technology Center can provide duplication of color and black-and-white ½-inch open reel and ¾-inch cassette; editing of color and black-and-white ½-inch open reel and ¾-inch cassette; color film chain; playback on Betamax, ½-inch open reel and ¾-inch VHS cassette; consulting services on video installation and production; and audiocassette duplication.

Collection

110 Maryland, University of—Nonprint Media Services

Undergraduate Library
College Park, Maryland 20742
(301) 454-4723

Peter V. Deekle, Head

Eligibility

> Materials in the Library's nonprint media collection support the University's instructional programs, and cannot be borrowed for use off-campus. Persons not affiliated with the University of Maryland/College Park must contact the head of the Nonprint Media Services department for permission prior to the use of these materials.

Collection

1,500 cassettes. The videocassette collection consists of about 1,000 permanent items and 500 items put on reserve by faculty for use during the semester. The permanent collection, purchased by the Library, includes a number of series distributed by Time-Life, such as *America, Ascent of Man, Civilization* and *Women and the Law.* Emphasis is on Afro-American studies, history, women's studies, music, fine arts, literature and drama.

Current history includes presidential and vice-presidential speeches, 1973–1978, and Watergate-related items such as the hearings of the Senate Watergate Committee and the House Committee on the Judiciary. Also of historical interest are the small collection of film classics and almost 200 newsreel subjects.

Individual items include a 16-part series on human sexuality; a 30-part course in instructional television production; a classic theater series which includes *Three Sisters, Candide,* and *Macbeth;* and a series of such literary classics as *Walden* and Dante's *The Inferno.*

Catalogue

The collection is filed in the U.M. Union Catalogue on the main floor of the undergraduate library. Another card catalogue in the Nonprint Media area includes only title cards. The librarians know the collection and are very helpful.

Access

The collection does not circulate.

Reservations are not required for those affiliated with the University of Maryland/College Park. Others should first contact the head of Nonprint Media Services.

Viewing facilities include video analysis equipment in individual carrels, a 70-seat room equipped with 16mm projection facilities and videocassette playback units, a dial access system for scheduled viewing of videotapes, and audiocassette playback units.

Other Materials

The Nonprint Media Services has more than 10,000 audio cassettes. Half of them are music and half are the spoken word. The International Piano Archives Collection, which will include 10,000 cassettes of recorded music and the papers of many musicians and composers, has just been acquired.

Collection

111 Middle East Institute

Film Library
1761 N Street, NW
Washington, D.C. 20036
(202) 785-1141

9:00 A.M.-5:00 P.M. Monday-Friday

Niecy Armstrong, Film Librarian

Eligibility

Open to the public. The rental fees are $6.00 to schools, $10.00 to colleges and $15.00 to individuals and organizations. Scholars may request to rent films at the lowest rate.

Collection

73 titles: Middle East and North Africa. This collection of acquired documentaries focuses on the history of the region and aspects of contemporary life in individual countries of the Middle East and North Africa. There are films on Islam and Judaism and on the oil industry. Individual films cover Afghanistan, Egypt, the Gulf States, Iran, Iraq, Israel, Jordan, North Africa, Saudi Arabia and Turkey.

The Palestine problem is investigated in four films. Individual titles and topics include *Grass,* a 1924 documentary of the Bakhtiari tribe in Iran; Afghan women; artists; nomads; archeology.

Catalogue

A descriptive catalogue is available by mail.

Access

Borrowing is by mail and in person. Although all mail, phone, and in person queries and reservations should be directed to the Institute, the collection is physically housed at Visual Education, Inc., Suite 424, 1425 H Street, NW, Washington, D.C. 20005. Films must be picked up and returned to that office.

Reservations should be made in advance.

There are no viewing facilities.

Collection

112 Modern Talking Picture Service, Inc.

200 L Street, NW
Washington, D.C. 20036
(202) 659-9234

8:30 A.M.-4:30 P.M.   Monday-Friday

Bradley Steward, Manager

Eligibility

The collection is available to groups, institutions, and schools with some restrictions. Scholars may request permission to view the collection in the Washington office.

Collection

766 titles. All titles are available through the Washington office but some must first be ordered from other libraries in the Modern Talking Picture Service (MTPS) network of 25 libraries. MTPS is a commercial distributor which handles films for many organizations, companies, and governments, providing them free to specific audiences. General cate-

gories within the collection are travel and geography, vocational guidance, business, sports, safety, homemaking, science, and others. The collection includes films from the Embassies of Turkey and the Federal Republic of Germany; U.S. Departments of Energy, Commerce, and the Interior; the Army Corps of Engineers; IBM, Exxon, and ALCOA; and many associations and institutes.

Catalogue

Descriptive catalogues are available by mail. Each of the several different catalogues is aimed at a specific audience: adults, schools, business and industry.

Access

Borrowing is in person and by mail.

Reservations should be made six to eight weeks in advance and can be made up to 11 months in advance. Walk-in service is available but the selection is limited to what is on hand.

A screening room with a projector is available for up to five viewers. Information on TV rights and purchase of copies is available.

Other Materials

Packets of posters, pamphlets, and other materials are available for some films. These must be ordered in advance. Videotape titles are handled by the New York MTPS library. The center in Atlanta handles distribution to television stations and theaters, and spot announcements for television.

Academic Programs

113 Montgomery College—Rockville Campus

Route 355 and Mannakee Street
Rockville, Maryland 20850
(301) 279-5000

ENGLISH DEPARTMENT
(301) 279-5147

Faculty

Gail Forman—Film and Literature

Course

Once a year Professor Forman teaches a comparison of films and their literary sources.

VISUAL COMMUNICATIONS TECHNOLOGIES
(301) 279-5256

Faculty

Carolyn Vurridge—Broadcast journalism
Phil Matin—Early films

Courses

The courses are primarily on film, radio, and television production.

Collection

114 Montgomery College—Rockville Campus—Educational Support Services Department

51 Mannakee Street
Rockville, Maryland 20850
(301) 279-5087 (Film)
(301) 279-5085 (Video)

7:30 A.M.-4:00 P.M.   Monday-Friday

Adolphus Sparks, Film
Betty Sullivan. Video

Eligibility

The collection is open to the public for use in the Department.

Collection

775 titles. The 275 films are primarily instructional. The 500 videotapes include instructional material in the sciences, business and vocational specialties such as firefighting and hotel management, but the bulk of the collection is of more interest to a scholar. The material from network and public television includes news specials such as Presidential debates, televised hearings, and documentaries and series such as *Ascent of Man, World at War, Age of Uncertainty*. There are a few fiction features and a good collection of adaptations from literature and drama. A locally produced series profiles Washington media professionals.

Catalogue

A descriptive catalogue is available in the Department.

Access

Screenings must be scheduled by mail or in person three days in advance.
Television monitors are available in various locations on the campus for viewing tapes which have been scheduled. Projectors are available for viewing films in the Department. There are no facilities for video or film analysis.

Academic Program

115 Montgomery College—Takoma Park Campus

7600 Takoma Avenue
Takoma Park, Maryland 20012
(301) 587-4090

ENGLISH DEPARTMENT
Ext 304

Faculty

John Carrington Cross—American sound films

Courses

Professor Cross teaches films and their literary sources.

Collection

116 Montgomery College—Takoma Park Campus—Learning Resource Center

New York Avenue
Takoma Park, Maryland 20012
(301) 587-4090 ext 289

8:00 A.M.-4:30 P.M.   Monday, Friday
8:00 A.M.-9:00 P.M.   Tuesday-Thursday

LaVerne Miller, Director

Eligibility

The collection is open to the public for use at the Center.

Collection

100 titles. The collection consists primarily of instructional films and videotapes for the nursing, dentistry, and business programs. There are some video documents of speeches and events at Montgomery College.

Catalogue

Descriptive catalogues of the film and videotapes are available at the Center.

Access

The collection does not circulate.
Reservations by telephone are suggested.
Viewing rooms with projectors and video analysis equipment are available.
For information on copies of the in-house produced videotapes, contact the Center.

Academic Program

117 Mount Vernon College

2100 Foxhall Road
Washington, D.C. 20007
(202) 331-0400

COMMUNICATION DEPARTMENT
(202) 331-3509

Faculty

Bill Barlow—Radio and the blues
George Lellis—Film analysis

Courses

Entry-level courses in film history, criticism, and production, and the history and theory of broadcasting are part of a program which includes media internships. Professor Lellis has written about French *cinema verité,* and has recently co-edited *The Film Career of Buster Keaton* with George Wead (Boston: G. K. Hall, 1977).

Collection

118 Narcotics Education, Inc.

P.O. Box 4390
6830 Laurel Street, NW
Washington, D.C. 20012
(202) 723-4774

8:30 A.M.-5:00 P.M.   Monday-Thursday
8:30 A.M.-NOON   Friday

W. Francis Norcott, Film Librarian

Eligibility

The collection is available to the public for rent and purchase. Scholars may apply to use the collection.

Collection

22 titles. The films focus on the use of drugs, alcohol and tobacco. Half were produced by Narcotics Education and the rest were acquired. Some titles are available in several languages, including Swedish and Samoan.

Catalogue

Descriptive lists are available by mail.

Access

Borrowing is by mail and in person.
   Reservations four weeks in advance are suggested.
   A projector and a small screening room are available.
   TV rights are available on in-house productions and all films are available for purchase.

Collection

119 National Association for Foreign Student Affairs

1860 19th Street, NW
Washington, D.C. 20009
(202) 462-4811

9:00 A.M.-5:00 P.M.   Monday-Friday

Mary Ammirati, Secretary to AID Projects

Eligibility

The collection may be rented by the public for a small fee.

Collection

30 titles. Six films were produced by the Association to assist with its efforts to orient and counsel foreign students in the U.S. The rest of the films were acquired for the "Hunger Awareness" and "Population Awareness" campaigns often sponsored by foreign students on American campuses. These films present the facts and faces of hunger and over-population in many parts of the world.

Catalogue

Descriptive lists are available by mail.

Access

Borrowing is by mail or in person.
  Reservations should be made in advance.
  There are no facilities for viewing the films.
  TV rights and purchase of copies is possible for those films produced by the Association.

Collection

120 National Geographic Society—Stock Film Library

Note: The collection of acclaimed National Geographic educational films and TV documentaries is available for rent and purchase only. The prints are not located in the Washington office but a descriptive catalogue, "National Geographic Educational Services," can be picked up at the Washington office or requested through the mail. Call (301) 948-5926.

Stock Film Library
17th and M Streets, NW
Washington, D.C. 20036
(202) 857-7660/7661

9:00 A.M.-5:30 P.M.   Monday-Friday

Betty Kotcher, Film Librarian

Eligibility

The Stock Film Library sells outtakes from National Geographic productions to filmmakers. The footage may be previewed. Scholars who wish to view the footage may apply to use the collection.

Collection

2 million feet catalogued; 2 million feet uncatalogued. The catalogued footage is from the series of documentaries made for television beginning in 1963. The uncatalogued footage is from educational films and films shot on Geographic-sponsored expeditions dating back to the 1910s. The emphasis is on ethnographic and wildlife footage.

Catalogue

"The National Geographic Educational Services" describes the subject matter of the footage available through the Stock Film Library. Ms. Kotcher will answer specific questions about the collection. A visitor to the Stock Film Library may use the card catalogue.

Access

Use of the Stock Film Library is by appointment only.
Film analysis equipment is available.
Detailed information on rights is available.

Collection

121 National Trust for Historic Preservation

Audiovisual Collections
1785 Massachusetts Avenue, NW
Washington, D.C. 20036
(202) 638-5200

9:00 A.M.-5:00 P.M.   Monday-Friday

Note: Until 1979 the National Trust collection of films was available for rent, but budgetary cut-backs have forced discontinuation of the distribution program and the film competition until further notice.

Collection

32 titles. This collection of recent short documentaries on the preservation, restoration, and—in some cases—demolition of old buildings is especially interesting because most of the films are award-winners in the Trust's annual film competition. The competition has categories for both "student" and "independent" filmmakers.

Catalogue

Many of the titles in this collection are available from other sources and are listed in the Trust's publication, *Films, Etc.: Historic Preservation and Related Subjects*. This catalogue is free and available by mail.

Academic Program

122 Northern Virginia Community College—Alexandria Campus

Baileys Crossroads Building
3001 N. Beauregard Street
Alexandria, Virginia 22311
(703) 323-4285

VISUAL ARTS AND ENGINEERING
(703) 323-4332

Faculty

Anne Banks—Visual arts

Courses

Courses on film and media are offered some semesters. A program in pre-production, production, and distribution of film and video is now in the planning stage.

Collection

123 Northern Virginia Community College—Extended Learning Institute

5400 Port Royal Road
Springfield, Virginia
  Mailing address:
8333 Little River Turnpike
Annandale, Virginia 22003
(703) 323-3371

8:30 A.M.-5:00 P.M.   Monday-Friday

Hyman Field, Director

The Extended Learning Institute offers courses at the post-secondary level to students via television, mail, and newspapers.

Eligibility

Videotapes in the library are available to scholars and researchers.

Collection

80 titles. The Institute has four series in its library. They consist of courses in American art history, photography, auto repair, and child growth and development.

Catalogue

There is no list or catalogue of the collection.

Access

> Scholars should contact the Institute for policies regarding the use of materials.
>
> The titles available on cassettes can be viewed on video analysis equipment.

Collection

124 Northern Virginia Community College—Film Collection

> *Note:* The Northern Virginia Community College (NOVA) film collection is shared by the five campuses of the college. Some films are located on each campus but all may be requested and sent to any campus. There is a single catalogue.
>
> *Alexandria Campus Learning Resource Center*
> *3001 N. Beauregard Street, Room 337*
> *Alexandria, Virginia 22311*
> *(703) 323-4226*
>
> *Annandale Campus L.R.C.*
> *8333 Little River Turnpike, Room 410 Godwin Building*
> *Annandale, Virginia 22003*
> *(703) 323-3127*
>
> *Loudoun Campus L.R.C.*
> *1000 Harry Flood Byrd Highway, Room 217N*
> *Sterling, Virginia 22170*
> *(703) 323-4507*
>
> *Manassas Campus L.R.C.*
> *6900 Sudley Road, Room 215*
> *Manassas, Virginia 22110*
> *(703) 368-0184 (toll call)*
>
> *Woodbridge Campus L.R.C.*
> *15200 Smoketown Road, Room 413*
> *Woodbridge, Virginia 22191*
> *(703) 670-2191 (toll call)*
>
> 8:00 A.M.-5:00 P.M.   Monday-Friday
> Hours extended to 9:00 P.M. during school year.

Eligibility

> Open to the public for use within the Center.

Collection

> 950 titles. This large collection of films, all purchased within the last ten years, serves the academic programs at the college. One third is of interest to those in the humanities and social sciences with another third serving science programs and the last third serving the programs in technical fields such as police and fire training, nursing, and electronics. The 13

feature films in the collection include six Russian classics, four German classics and two films by D. W. Griffith. There are 16 experimental films and classic documentaries.

Catalogue

A descriptive film catalogue with elaborate indexing is available at each Learning Resource Center and other locations on each campus. There is a card file for videotapes.

Access

The public may view the collection in any Center. Faculty may borrow the films for on-campus use and the collection is available to the Fairfax County Library System and through inter-library loan.

Reservations are not required but scholars should call ahead to check on the availability of a specific title.

Projectors and video analysis equipment are available.

Collection

125 Organization of American States

17th Street and Constitution Avenue, NW
Washington, D.C. 20006
(202) 331-1010

9:00 A.M.-5:00 P.M.   Monday-Friday

Angel Hurtado, Visual Arts Unit   381-8261
Mercedes Fritzsching, Records   381-8255
Berta Schaefer, Public Information   381-8486

Eligibility

Open to the public.

Collection

70 titles: Latin America. Films at the OAS are handled by three different offices:

Visual Arts Unit.

A fine current collection of 25 titles present the visual arts and well-known artists of Latin America. Individual films include the work of contemporary artists Obregon, Manzur, Mabe, Soto, Otero, Cuevas, and others and the work of pre-Columbian artists. The films are available in English and Spanish and are for sale in 16mm and video cassette. Angel Hurtado runs the film unit and directed 11 of these films.

An archival collection of 33 titles includes films from many sources about Latin America. Little information is available about the films beyond their titles. They appear to be general information films about individual countries and chronicles of the activities of the OAS.

Mr. Hurtado has his own collection of programs produced for National Television of Venezuela. These five titles include a dramatic production of Kafka's *Metamorphosis*. Mr. Hurtado is willing to show all three collections to interested scholars and filmmakers.

Records.

There are seven reels of older films in the archives of the OAS. Four are about the OAS in Honduras, 1969–1972. Two reels are untitled but are 15 to 20 years old.

Public Information.

OAS Today is a new film about the OAS. It is available for borrowing alone or as part of a program which includes a speaker from the OAS. The program is available free to area schools and clubs.

Catalogue

A descriptive catalogue of the visual arts films available for purchase can be ordered by mail. Contact the people listed above for information on the other collections.

Access

Only the public information film may be borrowed. All others must be viewed at the OAS.

Appointments should be made one to two days in advance to view films.

A small screening room with a projector is available.

Information on the purchase of film or videotape copies of the visual arts collection is in the catalogue.

Other Materials

A voice archives with recordings of speeches and events dates back to 1935. There is also a Photographic Lending Library (Carl Headen, 381-8700) with 42,000 photographs.

Academic Program

126 Prince George's Community College

301 Largo Road
Largo, Maryland 20870
(301) 336-6000

SPEECH DEPARTMENT
(301) 322-0926

Faculty

Martin Burke—Structuralism in film

Courses

Introductory courses in film analysis and television production are offered.

Collection

127 Prince George's Community College—Learning Resources Center

301 Largo Road
Largo, Maryland 20870
(301) 322-0475

8:00 A.M.-9:30 P.M.   Monday-Thursday
8:00 A.M.-8:00 P.M.   Friday
9:00 A.M.-5:00 P.M.   Saturday
1:00 P.M.-5:00 P.M.   Sunday

Eligibility

The collection is designed for classroom and student use. The public, with identification (a driver's license), may view the collection at the Learning Resources Center.

Collection

750 titles. The films and videotapes are all purchased and were chosen to accompany courses offered at the college. About one-third are instructional, serving the programs in nursing, business, and foreign language. One-third are more general, with emphasis on anthropology, sociology, science, and education. The most interesting third could be classified as film art and history. There are 13 feature films and over 60 classic short films, both silent and contemporary. Individual titles of interest are *Some to Demonstrate, Some to Destroy,* a film about the 1969 anti-war Moratorium weekend in Washington, D.C., and a 1962 short film by Martin Scorcese.

Catalogue

A descriptive film catalogue is available at the Center. The entire collection is filed in the Library's main card catalogue.

Access

The collection does not circulate to the public.
There are no reservations.
There are projectors and video analysis equipment.

Collection

128 Prince George's County Memorial Library System

Films Division
6532 Adelphi Road
Hyattsville, Maryland 20782
(301) 699-3500

9:00 A.M.-5:00 P.M.   Monday-Friday

Borrowers may arrange to pick up and return films at any of the 18 branches during the hours that the branches are open.

Kent A. Moore, Coordinator

Eligibility

The collection is available to holders of adult library cards from any public library in the state of Maryland. A non-resident card is available for a fee. Films may not be shown where any admission is charged or for fund-raising. Films may not be copied or shown on television. Films may not be borrowed for classroom use in any elementary or high school. Fees range from $1.00 to $4.00.

Collection

2,000 titles. This collection ranks third in the Washington area, after the Library of Congress and the National Archives, in holdings of interest to film scholars. The ease with which one may use this collection and the opportunity to view the films at home and share them with friends and colleagues make this collection a scholar's likely first choice, especially for foreign films, silent films, and documentaries.

The collection offers adults entertainment, information, and a solid collection on the history and art of the motion picture while providing entertainment and fine information films for children and students. As is the case with other public library collections, there are groups of biographies, business films, Canadian travel films, and films about childhood, old age, minorities, women, religion, and art.

The most impressive aspect of the collection is that films appear to have been selected both to fulfill the entertainment and information needs of most library patrons and to enhance the collection of classic features, shorts, and documentaries of interest to serious film viewers. For example, the large collection of animations, a favorite of children, includes 35 theatrical cartoons; Eastern European animations; films about animators Emile Cohl, Norman McLaren, Max Fleischer, and Otto Messmer; and *The Yellow Submarine*. Sports films include Leni Riefenstahl's *Olympia* and Kon Ichikawa's *Tokyo Olympiad*.

American Feature Films

Two-thirds of the 300 feature films were produced in the United States. American silent films include *Greed, The Big Parade, Sunrise,* and a number of features from Chaplin, Keaton, and of course D. W. Griffith. Genre classics from the sound era include *I Walked with a Zombie, Flying down to Rio,* and *Little Ceasar.* There are sociological dramas such as *Grapes of Wrath, Nothing but a Man,* and *The Crowd* and such recent films as *Five Easy Pieces, The End of Summer,* and *Planet of the Apes.* From TV there are *Roots* and *The Autobiography of Miss Jane Pittman.*

Foreign Feature Films

The large collection of British films includes literary adaptations, mysteries, three Beatles films, and examples from the early 1960s including

Kes and *Loneliness of the Long Distance Runner.* Among the more than 20 French features are the classics *Rules of the Game* and *Grand Illusion* and more recent films from New Wave directors: *Hiroshima, Mon Amour, The Wild Child,* and *Weekend.* German films of the 1920s are well represented with horror classics, *The Niebelungs,* and *Joyless Street;* Emil Jannings stars in *Variety, The Last Laugh;* and *The Blue Angel* with Marlene Dietrich. *The White Hell of Pitz Palu* is a later film known for its spectacular photography and scenes with Leni Riefenstahl as a young actress.

Thirteen Russian features include the complete repertoire of Sergei Eisenstein (except for his films about Mexico), *Man with a Movie Camera* by Dziga Vertov, three films by Vsevlod Pudovkin. and Alexander Dovzhenko's *Zvenigora* and *Arsenal. Birth of Soviet Cinema* gives a general view of Soviet film history with clips from many films.

Of equal importance to scholars is the Japanese collection, which includes eight films by Akira Kurosawa ranging from the popular *Seven Samurai* and *Yojimbo* to the more complex *Ikiru* and his first film *Sanshiro Sugata.* There also are five films by Kenji Mizoguchi, three by Yasujiro Ozu, and other directors' works.

Several early films by Ingmar Bergman; four by the Danish filmmaker Carl Drever, including *Ordet* and *Vampyr;* two Italian neorealist films; *Viridiana* by Luis Bunuel, and *Pather Panchali* by Indian director Satyajit Ray are also in the collection.

Silent Films

The silent era is represented by more than 100 feature films and another 100 shorter films. There are collections of some of the earliest films from the Lumière brothers, Thomas Edison, and Georges Méliès; shorts and features by D. W. Griffith; great numbers of comedies with Charlie Chaplin, Buster Keaton, Harold Lloyd, Harry Langdon, and others; and French, German, and Russian features and shorts. The collection presents examples of both the earliest silent films and the height and range to which the form developed with features from the 1920s by Erich von Stroheim, Chaplin and others; early animations; and experimental films from Europe.

Experimental Films

The more than 150 titles which can be described as experimental or art films provides the scholar with films of many schools or movements. The collection includes examples of early French and German experiments; American avant-garde films such as *Meshes of the Afternoon* and *Lot in Sodom;* contemporary abstract films, including *Allures, Cycles,* and *Cibernetics 5.3;* and many others, including *Frank Film, La Jetée,* and *Prelude: Dog Star Man.*

Documentaries

Documentaries in the collection span the length of film history beginning with *The Kiss and Edison Kinetoscopic Record of a Sneeze, January 7, 1894* and *Lumière's First Show* and continuing through to the present with recent additions such as *Georgia O'Keefe* and other titles from the

1977 TV series *The Originals.* Robert Flaherty's *Nanook of the North* represents the 1920s; three of his other films are also in the collection. There are *Berlin: Symphony of a City, Rain,* and *Rien que les Heures,* European city symphonies from the 1920s and a later American addition, *N.Y., N.Y.*

Problem-oriented, poetic films of the 1930s and early 1940s include *The River, The Plow that Broke the Plains, The Land, Power and the Land* and *The City,* a film which used scenes of Greenbelt, Maryland to describe the ideal 1939 community. Joris Iven's *Spanish Earth,* and Leni Riefenstahl's *Olympia* and *Triumph of the Will* (in both 111-minute and 43-minute versions) lead into World War II and the seven films of the *Why We Fight* series, *Listen to Britain* (1942), and a 1945 war documentary with an anti-war view, *Battle of San Pietro,* directed by John Huston.

Highlights of the more recent documentaries in the collection are ten films by Frederick Wiseman, including *Titicut Follies* and *Meat;* another cinema verité film, *Salesman;* and the poetic *City of Gold, Ski the Outer Limits,* and *Pas de Deux.* Recent documentaries which incorporate newsreel and other footage from earlier periods include *Over There, 1914–1918,* and two programs from the *World at War* series.

Just for Fun

There are lots of Laurel and Hardy, *Oklahoma, Flash Gordon Conquers the Universe* in 12 chapters, and the very first Superman cartoon entitled simply *Superman.*

Special Collection

Films for the hearing-impaired include both films with signed speech and films within the general collection which are not dependent on narration or sound effects. Many of these films are described in a Library pamphlet, "Films for Hearing-Impaired Children." The Library also has TTY Service (Telephone, Teletypewriter Service for the Hearing Impaired); the films number is (301) 699-9869.

Catalogue

A descriptive catalogue is available for a small fee at all of the Library branches and from the Films Division. The film catalogue does not reflect the richness of the collection since it does not list films by director, genre, production date, or country of origin in most cases. The description of the collection presented above is exceptionally detailed to compensate for the lack of an adequate index. Future plans include better indexing and individual pamphlets describing parts of the collection of interest to scholars.

Access

Borrowing is in person at the Films Division office or at any of the branch libraries. Loans are for 24 hours or a weekend. Four titles, 90 minutes, or one feature can be borrowed at one time.

Reservations must be made two working days in advance, at the Films Division office between 9:00 A.M. and 5:00 P.M. Long lists should be submitted in writing but most requests can be handled by phone. The staff can be helpful with suggestions and information not contained in the catalogue.

There are no viewing facilities.

Collection

129 Project HOPE

Health Science Education Center
Carter Hall
Millwood, Virginia 22646
(703) 837-2100 (toll call)

9:00 A.M.-5:00 P.M.   Monday-Friday

Steve Kussmann, Director of Information Services

Eligibility

Current films about Project HOPE are available from Modern Talking Pictures (entry #112). Scholars may apply to use the collection of archival films and unedited footage.

Collection

30 titles; 50,000 feet of unedited film. The archival collection contains primarily films which were produced over the last twenty years to chronicle the work of Project HOPE with medical problems and medical education in developing areas throughout the world. The footage in the collection was used in the production of these films.

Catalogue

There is no organized catalogue but the staff is familiar with the collection.

Access

Scholars should contact the Department of Information Services.
A projector is available.
For TV rights and purchase of copies, contact the Department of Information.

Collection

130 Public Broadcasting Service—Public Television Library

475 L'Enfant Plaza
Washington, D.C. 20024
(202) 488-5000

9:00 A.M.-5:00 P.M.   Monday-Friday

Alan Lewis, Manager

Eligibility

The Public Television Library is a collection of programs produced for public television and available for non-broadcast use through both rental and purchase arrangements. The collection is also available to public television stations for broadcast. The comments below apply to the non-broadcast or audiovisual use only. Scholars will have access to the collection through the PBS Archive and Study Center (entry #131).

Collection

2,200 titles. The collection includes programs produced by local public TV stations and broadcast by the Public Broadcasting Service from 1970 to the present, programs produced and broadcast locally, and programs of the Educational Television Service from 1965–1970. The subject index to the collection includes long lists of programs on women, U.S. culture, music, and the arts. Smaller groups of programs include those on alcoholism, American Indian culture, Black American culture, cities, cooking, environment, health care, the legal system, marriage, politics, psychology, sexuality, and U.S. history.

Catalogue

A descriptive catalogue of the audiovisual collection is available by mail.

Access

Borrowing is by mail only. All programs are available on videocassette. Other formats can be made available by special arrangement.

There are no viewing facilities at the Public Television Library. The standard rental fee is charged for previews by mail.

Information on rights, rental rates and purchase price is in the catalogue.

Collection

131 Public Broadcasting Service—Public Television Program Archive and Study Center

475 L'Enfant Plaza
Washington, D.C. 20024
(202) 488-5000

9:00 A.M.-5:00 P.M.   Monday-Friday

Alan Lewis

Work has begun at PBS on the Public Television Program Archive and Study Center but no date has been set for the opening of the Center to scholars. The collection will include public television programming which was distributed nationally by NET (National Educational Television) from 1953–1970 and by PBS since 1970. Classroom-directed materials will not be included, and there are no current plans to include locally produced, locally broadcast materials.

The eventual content of the collection is evident from the entry for the Public Television Library (entry #130).

Collection

132 Public Citizen Visitors' Center

1200 15th Street, NW
Washington, D.C. 20005
(202) 659-9053

9:00 A.M.-5:00 P.M.   Monday-Friday
9:00 A.M.-Noon   Saturday

Martha Monteleone

The Public Citizen Visitors' Center is a Ralph Nader group which provides visitors with tours, information on contacting government offices, film programs, and a calendar of events. If you ask the Washington telephone operator for Ralph Nader, this is the number you will be given.

Eligibility

The public may rent the collection for a small fee. Groups may view films at the Center and individual scholars may request to use the collection.

Collection

44 titles. Consumer education, health issues, the environment, energy, and the city are the focus of this collection of recent documentaries. The titles match such Ralph Nader crusades as unsafe automobiles and alternatives to nuclear power plants.

Catalogue

There is no printed list of the films. Contact the Center for information on the collection.

Access

Borrowing is by mail and in person.
   Reservations to rent films or view the collection should be made one week in advance.
   A projector is available.

Collection

133 Resources for the Future—FOCUS

Carnegie Endowment for International Peace
11 Dupont Circle
Washington, D.C. 20036
(202) 797-6424

9:00 A.M.-5:00 P.M.   Monday-Friday

Lee Harper

Eligibility

Prospective buyers of this series of programs may preview them. Scholars may request to view the series. The distribution of the series is handled by:

Pennsylvania State University A-V Services
University Park, Pennsylvania 16802
(814) 865-6314

Collection

16 titles. FOCUS is a series of videotaped discussions of public policy issues by government officials, journalists, and academics. Topics include energy, environment, and foreign policy. The series was produced in the early 1970s.

Catalogue

A descriptive list is available by mail.

Access

The series is available for rent and sale.
Reservations should be made to preview the series.
Some viewing equipment is available.
For information on TV rights, contact the Endowment.

Collection

134 Special Olympics

1701 K Street, NW, Suite 203
Washington, D.C. 20006
(202) 331-1346

7:00 A.M.-5:00 P.M.   Monday-Friday

Donna Soder, Program Coordinator

Eligibility

Scholars may apply to use the collection. The films are available for rent and purchase.

Collection

14 titles: Special Olympics. Eleven short films and five public service announcements describe the Special Olympics, an event for retarded children.

Catalogue

A descriptive list is available by mail.

Access

Rental is by mail or in person.
Reservations should be made in advance.
There are no facilities to view the films.
Information on TV rights and purchase of copies is available.

Collection

135 Suburban Washington Library Film Service

Alexandria Library Film Service
3600 Commonwealth Avenue
Alexandria, Virginia 22305
(703) 750-6354

Arlington County Department of Libraries Film Service
1015 North Quincy Street
Arlington, Virginia 22201
(703) 527-4777

Fairfax County Public Library Film Service
5502 Port Royal Road
Springfield, Virginia 22151
(703) 321-9166

Montgomery County Department of Public Libraries Film Service
99 Maryland Avenue
Rockville, Maryland 20850
(301) 279-1944/1945

Loudon County Public Library Film Service
52 West Market Street
Leesburg, Virginia 22075
(703) 777-0369 (toll call)

Eligibility

The collections are available to holders of adult library cards of each jurisdiction through their own library. The films at the Montgomery County Library are available to adult library card holders of any library in the state of Maryland. Non-resident cards are available at each library for a fee. Special restrictions apply to groups and institutions.

Collection

3,600 titles. This fine public library collection serves both children and adults with primarily entertainment fare, but a substantial part of the collection might be of interest to scholars. The list of over 120 feature films includes a few foreign classics, such as *Open City* and *The Blue Angel;* silent classics, such as *The General* and *Way Down East;* made-for-TV movies, such as *Brian's Song* and *In This House of Brede;* documentaries such as *Triumph of the Will;* and American comedies, horror films, musicals, and children's films.

The collection includes 53 Disney shorts, 11 after-school TV specials, at least 20 theatrical cartoons, about 50 silent shorts and features including 16 Chaplin films, about 30 compilations or films about film history and another 30 about the making of films. There are Canadian travel films, several hundred films for and about children and youths, student-made films, over 100 films on art, and 60 art films. Hundreds of films cover U.S. and world history and politics.

Catalogue

A descriptive catalogue of the consolidated collections of the five libraries is available at any of the libraries for $2.25. Each library has a title list of its own holdings.

Access

This is a cooperative collection. Adult card holders, usually limited to residents of the county or those who work or own property in the county, may reserve any film in the catalogue and pick it up at their own library. Films may not be shown where admission is charged or for fund-raising. Films may not be used in the classrooms of public elementary and high schools. All rentals are for a 24-hour period with the exception of Saturdays, Sundays, or holidays when the library film service is closed.

The hours and varying regulations are listed below for four of the library film services.

ALEXANDRIA LIBARY FILM SERVICE

9:00 A.M.-5:00 P.M. ˙ Monday-Friday

Reservations should be made two weeks in advance. A single program can be reserved by phone; other requests should be made in writing. Up to 90 minutes or one feature film can be reserved per program.

There are no viewing facilities.

ARLINGTON COUNTY LIBRARIES FILM SERVICE

9:00 A.M.-5:00 P.M.   Monday-Saturday
7:00 P.M.-9:00 P.M.   Monday-Thursday
1:00 P.M.-9:00 P.M.   Sunday

Reservations should be made two weeks in advance. Up to five titles can be reserved by phone; longer lists should be in writing. Up to 90 minutes or one feature film can be reserved per program.

FAIRFAX COUNTY PUBLIC LIBRARY FILM SERVICE

9:00 A.M.-6:00 P.M.   Monday-Friday
10:00 A.M.-2:00 P.M.   Saturday

Reservations should be made in writing two weeks in advance. Up to 90 minutes or one feature film can be reserved per program. Walk-in service is available for the films in the Fairfax County collection and three titles will be checked. Films are available through all 17 branches. There are no viewing facilities.

MONTGOMERY COUNTY LIBRARIES FILM SERVICE

8:00 A.M.-5:00 P.M.   Monday-Friday
9:00 A.M.-5:00 P.M.   Saturday

Reservations should be made two weeks in advance. One program can be reserved by phone but longer lists should be submitted in writing. Up to 90 minutes or one feature film can be reserved per program. Walk-in service is available for the films in the Montgomery County collection. Films are available through four branches.

There is a special archival collection of retired films at the Montgomery County Film Service. Most of the films are too fragile to circulate but a scholar might contact Mrs. Spencer with a special request.

Academic Program

136 Trinity College

Michigan Avenue and Franklin Street, NE
Washington, D.C. 20017
(202) 269-2000

FINE ARTS DEPARTMENT
(202) 269-2272

Faculty

Liliana Gramberg—European film history

Courses

"Introduction to Film" and "American Film" are offered every other year.

Collection

137 UNICEF Information Service

110 Maryland Avenue, NE
Washington, D.C. 20002
(202) 547-0204

9:00 A.M.-4:30 P.M.   Monday-Friday

Ann Wagner

Eligibility

Open to the public.

Collection

23 titles. Not surprisingly, this collection is about and for children. Produced by UNICEF, the films focus on health and nutrition. One 1952 film chronicles Danny Kaye's visit to Asia. The rest of the films are post-1960.

Catalogue

A descriptive list is available by mail.

Access

Borrowing is in person only.
Reservations are suggested.
There are no facilities for viewing the films.
Copies are for sale through Association Films (entry #17).

Collection

138 United Nations Information Centre

2101 L Street, NW
Washington, D.C. 20037
(202) 296-5370

9:15 A.M.-5:00 P.M.   Monday-Friday

Jeanne Dixon, Film Librarian

Eligibility

Open to the public in the Washington metropolitan area.

Collection

100 titles. The films are about the work of the United Nations and such issues as drought, economics, and South Africa. A 30-film series *Man Builds, Man Destroys* explores environmental problems. Another series documents international cooperation. There are eight films about women.

Catalogue

A descriptive catalogue is available by mail.

Access

Borrowing is in person only.
Reservations one week in advance are suggested.
There are no facilities for viewing the films.
All U.N. films are cleared for TV and available for purchase. Details are in the catalogue.

Collection

139 United States Catholic Conference—Campaign for Human Development

Room 324
1312 Massachusetts Avenue, NW
Washington, D.C. 20005
(202) 659-6696

9:00 A.M.-5:00 P.M.   Monday-Friday

Tim Collins, Assistant Director

Eligibility

Open to scholars and teachers.

Collection

60 titles. Fifty public service announcements were produced over the last nine years as part of the Campaign for Human Development. Designed to stimulate the thinking and consciences of television audiences, these PSAs run 20 to 60 seconds each. There are also five short films and slide tapes which explain the Campaign.

Catalogue

This is an informal collection and listed only by title and year.

Access

The collection may be borrowed in person only. Similar collections are available in the Campaign office of each Catholic diocese in the United States.
　　Scholars and teachers should call ahead to make arrangements to borrow the collection.
　　There are no viewing facilities.
　　The collection was designed for use on television. A set of the best of the titles is available for purchase. Contact the Conference office for more information.

Collection

140 United Way of America

801 North Fairfax Street
Alexandria, Virginia 22314
(703) 836-7100

9:00 A.M.-5:00 P.M.   Monday-Friday

Mario Pelligrini, Senior Vice-president for Communication
Ruth Jahoda, Archivist

Eligibility

The current collection is for use by local United Way organizations. Scholars may apply to use this collection and the archival materials.

Collection

About 100 titles; thousands of feet of unedited film. Since 1970 the national United Way organization has produced short promotional films, training films for volunteers, and promotional spots for television. All of the production footage and the finished products are in the archives, as are a few locally-produced films.

Catalogue

Information on the collection is available from the archivist.

Access

All materials must be viewed at the United Way office.
Scholars should contact Mr. Pelligrini, the producer of most of the films, or Ms. Jahoda, the archivist.
A projector is available.
For information on TV rights and purchase of copies, contact the United Way office.

Collection

141 U.S.-China Peoples Friendship Association of Washington, D.C.

Box 40503 Palisades Station
Washington, D.C. 20016
(202) 434-7459

Joe Weichbrod

The U.S.-China Peoples Friendship Association is committed to promoting peace and friendship between the people of the U.S. and the people of China. The Association sponsors seminars, speakers, a newsletter, and study tours. The Washington office serves those in the eastern U.S. from Maine to Virginia.

Eligibility

The films are available to the public for a rental fee of $15.00 to $35.00. Rates are negotiable for scholars.

Collection

40 titles: China. The collection includes six documentaries by Felix Greene and four feature-length entertainment films. Most films in the collection were shot in China, two-thirds of them by foreign film and television units. All are in English or have English subtitles. Of special interest are an illustrated lecture by Dr. Joshua Horn on medicine for the masses; a Japanese documentary about the cultural revolution; documentaries by CBS and NBC; and the film shot during a visit to China

by Shirley MacLaine, *The Other Half of the Sky*. Other individual topics and titles include acupuncture, *Red Detachment of Women*, Tan-Zam Railway, Tibet.

Catalogue

A descriptive list is available by mail.

Access

Borrowing in person is preferred. Borrowing by mail (or package express) is possible.

Reservations should be made by phone or in writing.

There is no viewing equipment available.

For information on TV rights and purchase of copies, contact Mr. Weichbrod.

Collection

142 USER—Urban Scientific & Educational Research, Inc.

2712 Ontario Road, NW
Washington, D.C. 20009
(202) 483-9018

Kim Spencer, Project Director

USER is a non-profit research group with interactive video experience in community planning and social change projects of the federal, state and local governments. They are interested in cooperating with other video groups and willing to share their tapes and experiences.

Eligibility

The collection is available for any non-commercial use.

Collection

70 hours of videotape. Unedited master tapes and finished documentaries which USER has produced for government and private groups concerned with the environment are available. Individual topics include water quality, waste disposal, bicycle safety, toxic waste spills, sleep studies, regional planning, and social change.

Catalogue

All tape is logged and accessible.

Access

Borrowing, viewing, and purchase of tapes are negotiable.

Project

Public Interest Video is a national organization of video producers who distribute their programming live by satellite. *Nuclear Power: The Public Reaction* was their first large project; they have 25 hours of videotape from the anti-nuclear demonstrations in Washington and other locations during the spring of 1979. For more information contact USER or call (202) 232-8032.

Introduction to U.S. Government Entries

A TIME OF TRANSITION

Film and video production and distribution within the federal government have been the subject of a number of studies over the years. The most recent one, conducted by Robert Lissitt for the White House Office of Telecommunications (available from the National Telecommunications and Information Administration, Department of Commerce) was released in April of 1978. It surveyed many government audiovisual activities, describing them in detail and suggesting consolidation and elimination of both libraries and production facilities.

The report was followed shortly by "Management of Federal Audiovisual Activities" (Office of Management and Budget Circular No. A-114), which established procedures for centralizing information on government audiovisual products and facilities. The National Audiovisual Center (NAC) was designated as the central source of information on all government-owned films, video, and other A-V products. NAC is to handle all rental and sale of these products as well as maintain a data file for agencies to consult before authorizing new productions. This file, created to avoid duplication, is a rich and convenient resource for scholars seeking information on government film and video productions post-1978.

As this *Guide* is being prepared many agencies are in the process of consolidating their libraries and production facilities. Each is to designate a contact person who will be responsible for maintaining current information on the location and content of that agency's A-V collections. Many items are being turned over to the National Archives and Records Service (NARS).

Scholars seeking information on government-held materials in the near future may find that the conditions described in this *Guide* have changed drastically. During this time of change it is hoped that previously unlocatable items will be discovered and made available to scholars. Unfortunately, there is also the possibility that stray items, especially acquired productions, may be discarded as the libraries are reorganized.

NARS: A CENTRAL SOURCE

Scholars interested in government film and video should first contact the National Archives and Records Service. Three operations within NARS are excellent centralized sources of both information and the films and videotapes themselves.

The Audiovisual Archives Division (entry #155) is responsible for archival copies of selected films and videotapes produced by or for the government or acquired for government activities. Scholars interested in materials produced before 1970 should begin here. This division also maintains large gift collections which include newsreels and television newscasts.

The National Audiovisual Center (entry #156) is a central source of information on recent productions in all government agencies. It provides rental, sales, and some viewing copies of audiovisual materials as well as information on regional libraries and contact people within each agency.

The National Archives Stock Film Library (entry #157) maintains motion picture stock footage produced or acquired by the government, excluding the Department of Defense.

The recent consolidation requirements have strengthened the NARS collections and the ability of staff members to answer questions about government film and video. Scholars should note that the Library of Congress's vast holdings, although considered a government collection, consist almost entirely of privately-produced motion pictures.

WITHIN EACH AGENCY

The entries which follow describe the film and video collections which are part of each agency's program. Other productions of interest to scholars are films and videotapes produced with funds from one of the many grant programs. These grantee products are the most difficult to locate since many are found in grant offices and the rights are usually held by the grantee. Where they exist, catalogues of program-related products usually include the titles of productions made under grants. These catalogues are fine guides to materials on a particular subject and include the names and addresses of the producers or distributors but do not provide information on the location of these titles in local libraries.

Other collections of film and video within an agency may consist of public information films, training films and tapes, and stock footage. Public information films are generally about the activities of the agency and are distributed by the appropriate public affairs office or one of the commercial free loan libraries. There will be fewer of these films in the future according to the new A-V policy guidelines. Obsolete versions of these public information films will theoretically be held by the NARS Audiovisual Archives (entry #155).

Most large in-house collections of training films and videotapes consist of acquired titles and are subject to rights restrictions. The government-produced titles are usually on videotape. An informal clearinghouse for information on the audiovisual training materials of various agencies has been established through the personal initiative of one enterprising civil servant (entry #158).

Stock film collections are currently found within many production facilities but the recent consolidation efforts should bring these to the NARS Stock Film Library (entry #157).

GENERAL ADVICE

It is wise to call or write ahead. Telephone numbers and office locations will be changing as facilities and libraries are consolidated. Also many government agencies are on "flexi-time," a system of staggering work hours to ease rush hour congestion. These offices are generally open during the hours stated in the entry but the staff member who could be most helpful may not be in at the time you visit the office. Check Appendix X, for a list of Federal holidays.

The staff in each government agency is probably your most important source of information and assistance. Those contacted in preparing this *Guide* were particularly receptive to scholars and their needs. Nonetheless, it is important to make an appointment, arrive prepared with a list of specific questions, and keep in mind that serving scholars is rarely the primary duty of the staff.

Under the Freedom of Information Act the public has a right to see most government documents but that approach should be considered only as a last resort. In most cases agency staff members will gladly provide the materials requested, and the cost and complications of securing materials through the Freedom of Information procedures can be avoided.

FREEDOM OF INFORMATION ACT OF 1974

Those needing to view materials previously or currently restricted in some way should be familiar with the Freedom of Information Act of 1974. Anyone can request information from a government agency as long as the request is specific enough for an employee of that agency to locate the materials being requested. There is no need to explain or justify the need for the information. Requests can be informal, by phone or letter, or in person. If the request is denied there are formal procedures for appealing. Scholars should consult the following organizations and publications for details:

Reporters Committee for Freedom of the Press
Legal Defense and Research Fund
1750 Pennsylvania Avenue, NW
Washington, D.C. 20006
(202) 347-6888

Write for a free copy of their guide.

Freedom of Information Clearinghouse
P.O. Box 19367 (2000 P Street NW, Suite 700)
Washington, D.C. 20036

For a free copy of their guide to the FOI Act, send a self-addressed, stamped envelope.

Collection

143 U.S. ACTION

Creative Services
Room P307
806 Connecticut Avenue, NW
Washington, D.C. 20525
(202) 254-8373

Winnie Kelley

Creative Services is in the process of cataloging all current and past films and videotapes, which will be made available to the public through a media library. Several current films are available through the National Audiovisual Center (entry #156).

The media library will include over 100,000 feet of unedited film, over 100 completed productions, and hundreds of television commercials about ACTION programs. These materials date back to 1963 and focus on the Peace Corps, VISTA, and the Older American Volunteer Programs. Public awareness, recruitment, and training materials are included.

Collection

144 U.S. Agriculture Department

Office of Governmental Affairs, Motion Picture Division
Room 1620, South Building
14th Street and Independence Avenue, SW
Washington, D.C. 20250
(202) 447-2592

8:30 A.M.-5:00 P.M.   Monday-Friday

Buddy Renfro, Chief

The Department of Agriculture (USDA) created the first government-produced motion pictures in 1908. For almost 70 years they produced films for their own information and education programs as well as for other government agencies.

In 1976 the unit was greatly reduced and a small staff today does only short productions for television. The vast USDA stock film library was transferred to the National Archives Stock Film Library (entry #157); current films were sent to the National Audiovisual Center (entry #156); archival films and related materials remained at the National Archives (entry #155) and the distribution system was transferred to film libraries throughout the U.S. (seen entry #108).

Eligibility

Open to the public.

Collection

200+ titles. The collection includes USDA and other government productions. There is an uncatalogued collection of older films in the vault. Individual scholars with specific needs could have access to these collections.

Catalogue

Some old catalogues are available.

Access

Because the staff is small and is involved in current productions there is no formal procedure for assisting scholars. It is best to start at the National Archives Motion Picture Branch (entry #155) or the National Audiovisual Center (entry #156). Mr. Renfro is willing to answer specific questions and requests.

Collection

145 U.S. (Agriculture) Food and Nutrition Information Center

National Agriculture Library, Room 304
Baltimore Boulevard
Beltsville, Maryland 20705
(301) 344-3719

8:00 A.M.-4:30 P.M.   Monday-Friday

Joan Zubres, Library
Robin Frank, Director

Eligibility

Open to the public.

Collection

500 titles: food and nutrition. The collection provides information to preschool age through adult audiences on such general topics as cooking, junk food, and vegetarian diets. Specialized films aimed at institutional food service personnel cover sanitation and management. A few films date back to 1958, and several titles are available in both English and Spanish.

Catalogue

A descriptive catalogue is available by mail.

Access

Borrowing is by mail and in person. Postage is paid by the USDA. The collection is housed at the University of Maryland Audiovisual Services office and may be viewed there (entry #108).

Reservations should be made in advance for borrowing by mail and in person.

There are no films and no viewing facilities at the USDA Food and Nutrition Information Center.

Information on the purchase of copies is available from the Center. For TV rights contact the producer.

Other Materials

Filmstrips and slide-tape packages are also available.

Collection

146 U.S. Central Intelligence Agency

Washington, D.C. 20505
(703) 351-1100

The Office of Public Affairs issued the following statement about their film and video collections:

The CIA motion picture and videotape collection is available for use by analysts in the Agency and Intelligence Community who have appropriate clearances and the need to know.

The collection includes a variety of films and videotapes that deal primarily with foreign political, military and economic matters; many of the unclassified items are available in other film collections. The Agency has released some of the Office of Strategic Services' (OSS) films to the National Archives & Record Service for use by the public; additional items in the collection will be released periodically to NARS and made available to the public through that channel.

Referral Service

147 U.S. Defense Department

Products Division
Directorate for Audiovisual Management and Policy
1117 North 19th Street, Room 601
Arlington, Virginia 22209
(202) 694-1050/4166

Chief, Products Division

Like other government departments, the Department of Defense (DOD) is in the process of centralizing the cataloguing, distribution, and production of films and videotapes. The Directorate for Audiovisual Management and Policy, Products Division, is the best source of information in the Washington, D.C., area on DOD film and videotape collections. This office, which is in touch with the audiovisual managers of each of the services, produces two important keys to DOD audiovisual products.

DAVIS (Defense AudioVisual Information System) is a computerized product file of all DOD audiovisual products. Much like the National Audiovisual Center (NAC) file, DAVIS entries contain the title, production date, producing agency, length, format, status of clearances, a synopsis, and other information. The file can be searched for any of these items of information or any word in the synopsis. Scholars may contact the Directorate or the National Audiovisual Center (entry #156) for access to this file.

The printed "Department of Defense Catalogue of Audiovisual Products" contains entries for 30,000 products, including films, videotapes, and other sound and visual media. The information provided is similar to that in the DAVIS product file and includes a detailed subject index. The catalogue is scheduled for publication in 1980 and will be for sale through the Superintendent of Documents.

These two finding aids provide information on films, videotape, and other audiovisual products currently in use and available through libraries at military installations throughout the U.S. and overseas and a few central libraries. The public may borrow those titles which have been cleared for public exhibition. If a title that you would like to view is not now cleared, you may request that it be cleared for your particular needs. Often security restrictions can be reviewed and in many cases a title is simply not cleared for public exhibition until someone requests that it be cleared.

Acquired titles often have contractual limits on exhibition which cannot be waived. Some of these clearance problems can be avoided by requesting to view materials within a library, which is considered in-house use rather than public exhibition. In all cases, however, military use of materials and facilities takes precedence over public use and local libraries can rarely order films from the large central libraries for visiting scholars. Scholars may request materials from the central libraries and those titles cleared for public exhibition can be sent directly to the requestor.

For more details consult the entries which follow this introduction. The entry for each service lists the audiovisual manager for that service; the central library of current and obsolete materials; the stock film library; the local libraries which serve Washington, D.C.; the historical center, which is often the best first stop for scholars; and those National Archives and Records Service (entry #155) Record Groups which contain films of historical interest from that particular component of DOD.

A Defense Audiovisual Agency (DAVA) is being established at Norton Air Force Base in California. This center will coordinate the activities of all of the DOD film libraries.

Collections

148 U.S. (Defense) Air Force Department

Audiovisual Systems Division, Chief
Headquarters, Air Force (XOODV)
Pentagon
Washington, D.C. 20330
(202) 695-9610

CENTRAL LIBRARY

AIR FORCE CENTRAL AUDIOVISUAL LIBRARY
Norton Air Force Base, California 92409
(714) 382-2394

Victor Tomaso, Chief

This centralized collection of films and other audiovisual products serves base AV libraries and other users within the U.S. Over 52,000 products are available. The collection is included in the DAVIS product file and the DOD catalogue. Titles may be borrowed by mail or viewed at the library. Scholars may request to have titles cleared for public exhibition or for viewing at the library, but the process takes several months.

STOCK FILM LIBRARY

AIR FORCE CENTRAL AUDIOVISUAL DEPOSITORY
Norton Air Force Base, California 92409
(714) 382-2513/2514

Charles Schlofner, Chief

The depository contains 101 million feet of film. The great majority of the footage is record film the use of which is restricted. The archival collections date back to 1908 and include the Wilbur and Orville Wright Field Collection and historical films on World Wars I and II and the Korean and Vietnam Wars. The depository also acquires, analyzes, evaluates, stores, and services original footage of all phases of Air Force activities: research and development of aviation history; documentary, operational, training, and promotional films; and coverage of special missile, space, and aviation studies.

Those outside of the military or the government must request permission to use the collection from the Director of Information Services, Office of the Secretary of the Air Force, Washington, D.C. 20330. There is a fee for research and duplication services.

WASHINGTON AREA LIBRARIES

HEADQUARTERS, USAF AUDIOVISUAL LIBRARY
Pentagon
Washington, D.C. 20330
(202) 695-2517

8:00 A.M.-4:30 P.M.   Monday-Friday

Eligibility

The collection is available to the public. It is located within the Pentagon and there is no escort service for those who do not have access to to the building. The more accessible collection at Andrews Air Force Base is described below.

Collection

782 titles. The library has historical films and films for training, safety education, information, and chaplain's programs.

Catalogue

A descriptive catalogue is available. The titles are also described in the DAVIS products file and the DOD catalogue.

Access

Borrowing is in person only.

Reservations should be made to borrow films and to use the screening facilities in the library. This library does not order films from Norton's central library for non-government use.

Projectors and video analysis equipment is available.

Information on TV rights and purchase of copies is in the catalogues.

AUDIOVISUAL SERVICES, ANDREWS AIR FORCE BASE
Pennsylvania Avenue at Camp Springs, Maryland
Mailing Address:
BAVL, Andrews AFB, Maryland 20331
(301) 981-3541

8:00 A.M.-4:30 P.M.   Monday-Friday

Eligibility

Some organizations and institutions may borrow films which have been cleared for public exhibition.

Collection

550 titles. The holdings of this library are similar to the collection in the library in the Pentagon.

Catalogue

A descriptive catalogue is available at the library. The titles are described in the DAVIS file and the DOD Catalogue.

Access

Borrowing is in person only.

Reservations should be made to borrow films and to use the viewing facilities at the library. This library will order any cleared titled from the Central Library at Norton Air Force Base.

Projectors are available.

Information on TV rights and purchase of copies is in the catalogue.

HISTORICAL CENTER

Scholars may find assistance in using Air Force materials for research purposes at the:

OFFICE OF AIR FORCE HISTORY
Library
Building 5681
Bolling Air Force Base
Washington, D.C.
(202) 767-5088

NATIONAL ARCHIVES AND RECORD SERVICE

Air Force related materials in the Motion Picture and Sound Recordings Branch of the Audiovisual Archives are filed in Record Groups 18, 22, 111, 342.

Collections

149 U.S. (Defense) Army Department

Commander, Army Audiovisual Center
Pentagon
Washington, D C. 20310
(202) 695-7275

CENTRAL LIBRARY

ARMY AUDIOVISUAL RECORDS CENTER
Training Support Center
Tobyhanna Army Depot
Tobyhanna, Pennsylvania 18466
(717) 894-9941/9942

Charles Kohler, Distribution

The Center holds all motion picture, television, and audio materials produced or acquired by the Army, and all outtakes from Army productions. A descriptive catalogue is available by mail. Researchers may go to Tobyhanna to work or may arrange for the Center's staff to do the research for an hourly fee. Ninety-five percent of the current films are cleared for public exhibition and are available by mail.

STOCK FILM LIBRARY

The Tobyhanna collection described above includes the Army Stock Film Library.

WASHINGTON AREA LIBRARIES

AUDIOVISUAL SUPPORT CENTER
5A1058 Pentagon
Washington, D.C. 20310
(202) 695-5320

8:00 A.M.-4:30 P.M.   Monday-Friday

Eligibility

The collection is available to the public but access to the Pentagon is restricted. An escort may be arranged by telephone but in most cases it is more convenient for those who do not have access to the Pentagon to use the Fort Meyer library described below.

The central library at Tobyhanna has prepared a list of 200 free rent libraries on Army bases throughout the U.S. The list is available by mail from Tobyhanna.

Collection

1200 titles. All titles are cleared for public exhibition. Over half are training and chaplain films. Others include individual titles in a number of series: Armed Forces Information Films, often historical or descriptive about the U.S. and foreign countries; Combat Bulletins and Combat Historical Reports, war reports from 1944 through 1953; Defense Civil Preparedness Films; Information and Educational Sports Reels; Professional Medical Films; Research and Development Progress Reports; Recruiting Films; and 160 films in the *Big Picture* series made for television from 1957 to 1971.

Catalogue

A descriptive catalogue is available by mail. The collection is also included in the DAVIS product file and the DOD catalogue.

Access

Borrowing is in person only.

Reservations should be made in advance to borrow films and to view films at the library.

Projectors and video analysis equipment are available.

Information on TV rights and purchase of copies is in the printed catalogue.

FORT MEYER AUDIOVISUAL SUPPORT CENTER
Building 201
Highway 50 and Pershing Road
Arlington, Virginia 22211
(202) 692-8416

7:30 A.M.-4:00 P.M.   Monday-Friday

Eligibility

The titles which have been cleared for public exhibition are available to the public.

Collection

1000 titles. The collection is similar to the Pentagon collection. There are an additional 6,000 titles which are restricted to government use or are further restricted to military use only. Most of these titles are acquired products.

HISTORICAL CENTER

Scholars find it helpful to contact the Army Office of Military History for advice on using Army materials and facilities for research.

U.S. ARMY OFFICE OF MILITARY HISTORY
Room 6B081, Forrestal Building
1000 Independence Avenue, SW
Washington, D.C. 20314
(202) 693-5035

NATIONAL ARCHIVES AND RECORD SERVICE

Army-related materials in the Motion Picture and Recorded Sound Branch of the Audiovisual Archives Division (entry #155) are filed in Record Groups 53, 111, 200, 337; Army Air Force materials are in Record Groups 18, 200, 342.

Collections

150 U.S. (Defense) Marine Corps

Central Audiovisual Manager
Headquarters, United States Marine Corps
Pentagon
Washington, D.C. 20380
(202) 694-8534

CENTRAL LIBRARY

The Naval Photographic Center (entry #153) handles production and prints of all Marine Corps films.

STOCK FILM LIBRARY (See entry #151.)

WASHINGTON AREA LIBRARIES

Since Marine Corps films are produced by the Navy, large Navy libraries have prints of current Marine Corps productions. There is a large film library at the Training Support Center, Quantico, Virginia, but it is not open to the public.

HISTORICAL CENTER

Considering the difficulty in obtaining access to Marine Corps films, the Historical Division of the Marine Corps Museum should be the first stop for scholars. Lt. Col. Wayne Bjork is the one to contact for clearance to use the Stock Film Library and for advice and information on materials held by the Marine Corps.

HISTORICAL DIVISION, MARINE CORPS MUSEUM
Building 58, Washington Navy Yard

Mailing Address:
Marine Corps Historical Center
Washington, D.C. 20380

(202) 433-3447
(202) 433-3840 (Lt. Col. Bjork)

NATIONAL ARCHIVES AND RECORD SERVICE

Marine Corps-related materials in the Motion Picture and Recorded Sound Branch of the Audiovisual Archives Division (entry #155) are filed in Record Groups 24, 127, 200.

Collection

151 U.S. (Defense) Marine Corps Film Depository

Building 2013
Quantico, Virginia 22134
(703) 640-2844 (toll call from Washington)

7:30 A.M.-4:00 P.M. Monday-Friday

D.G. Gordon, Film Librarian
C. Polly Bearor, Researcher

Eligibility

This stock film library is open to the public, with some restrictions. A letter should be sent explaining the nature of the proposed research. There is a fee for research and duplication.

Collection

706 titles; 7 million feet. Hundreds of completed films have recently been added to the depository for reference use only. These information and training films pertain in some way to the Marine Corps.

The stock film collection goes back to 1914, but there is very little pre-1927 footage. About one fourth is from World War II and includes much color footage from the Pacific campaign. Combat, peacetime maneuvers, ceremonies, and personalities are the subject of most of the footage.

Catalogue

The reference collection of films is listed by title only. The stock footage is elaborately catalogued in a card file.

Access

All film must be viewed at the depository. The stock footage is for sale to the public.

Scholars and filmmakers should initially contact the depository to determine whether there is any relevant footage. A letter of explanation should then be sent to Marine Corps Headquarters and an appointment made to visit the depository.

Film analysis equipment is available.

Purchase of footage and rights is negotiated case by case. Because of the research fee, this collection could be beyond the means of scholars. For assistance contact the Historical Center (entry #150).

Collections

152 U.S. (Defense) Navy Department

Central Navy Audiovisual Manager
Chief of Naval Operations (OP-O9BP)
Pentagon
Washington, D.C. 20350
(202) 696-4844

CENTRAL LIBRARY

The central film depository for the Navy is part of the Film Depository Division of the Naval Photographic Center. Most completed films are only in preprint form, without viewing copies. The depository serves the Marine Corps installations and the two lending libraries listed below. Copies of Navy films may be purchased through the National Audiovisual Center (entry #156).

STOCK FILM LIBRARY (See entry #153.)

WASHINGTON AREA LIBRARIES

Neither the film library at Naval Photographic in Washington nor the Marine Corps library at Quantico, Virginia, which holds many Navy films, is open to the public. The Eastern part of the U.S. is served by the library at Norfolk, Virginia and the western part of the U.S. is served by the library at San Diego, California.

FILM LENDING LIBRARY
Commanding Officer
Naval Education and Training Support Center (Atlantic)
Building W313, Fleet Branch
Norfolk, Virginia 23511

FILM LENDING LIBRARY
Commanding Officer
Naval Education and Training Support Center (Pacific)
San Diego, California 92132

HISTORICAL CENTER

Scholars may find it helpful to contact the Naval Historical Center for advice on doing research within the Navy.

NAVAL HISTORICAL CENTER
Building 76 (Naval Museum), Washington Navy Yard
Washington, D.C.

Mailing Address:
Building 220, Washington, D.C. 20374
(202) 433-2765

NATIONAL ARCHIVES AND RECORDS SERVICE

Navy-related materials in the Motion Picture and Recorded Sound Branch of the Audiovisual Archives Division (entry #155) are filed in Record Groups 24, 38, 78, 80, 111, 200.

Collection

153 U.S. (Defense) Naval Photographic Center

Film Depository Division
U.S. Naval Station (near Bolling Air Force Base)
Washington, D.C. 20374
(202) 433-2115

7:15 A.M.-3:45 P.M.   Monday-Friday

Carl Carlson, Head

Eligibility

This stock film library is intended primarily to serve the Navy but the public may search the files, view footage, and purchase copies. There is an hourly research fee. Scholars should call or write to Mr. Carlson for information on the content of the collection and the procedures for its use.

Collection

45 million feet of 16mm film; 18 million feet of 35mm film. The collection, dating from 1956, focuses primarily on Navy hardware, personnel, and installations. It also includes footage of Vietnam, scenes of Washington, D.C., and pictures of famous people. It dates from 1956 to the present.

Catalogue

The footage collection is elaborately indexed in a card file with more than 450 main headings. The research fee is charged for the time spent searching the file.

Access

Copies of the stock footage are for sale.
Since the service to the public is low priority for this stock film library, arrangements should be made well in advance and delays should be expected.
Film analysis equipment is available.
Purchase of footage and rights are negotiated case by case.

Collection

154 U.S. Energy Department

Office of Public Affairs
Forrestal Building
1000 Independence Avenue, SW
Washington, D.C. 20585
(202) 252-5000 (DOE Operator)

8:30 A.M.-5:00 P.M.   Monday-Friday

Jack Moser, Audiovisual Branch

The Department of Energy (DOE) Film Library is located in Oak Ridge, Tennessee. It handles the films included in the DOE free loan catalogue and maintains an archival collection. (See Appendix III.) Information on the collection and access to it can be obtained from the Office of Public Affairs. Some titles are available in the Washington office.

Collection

155 U.S. (GSA) National Archives and Records Service

Audiovisual Archives Division
Stack Office 18E
Pennsylvania Avenue between 7th and 9th Streets, NW
Washington, D.C. 20408
(202) 523-3010

8:45 A.M.-5:00 P.M.   Monday-Friday

James Moore, Director
Richard Myers, Assistant Director
Jane Lange, Librarian

Eligibility

Open to the public. Appointments are recommended. In visiting the National Archives, the first step is to obtain a "Researcher Identification" card from the Central Research staff in Room 200B. Applicants identify themselves, register, and then may proceed to the research areas.

Collection

The National Archives and the Library of Congress are the primary sources of film and video available for research in the Washington, D.C., area and rank among the top four or five research collections in the United States. Located within the Audiovisual Archives Division of NARS are motion pictures on over 100,000 subjects, including titled productions, series of newsreels, and unedited footage dating back to 1894; over 3,000 videotapes, mostly network news and news specials dating from 1974; over 5 million still pictures, including photographs, posters, and photographs of paintings; 104,000 sound recordings dating from the turn of the century; and over 5 million feet of 16mm stock footage. The stock film collection is described separately (entry #157).

The collection includes materials created for and acquired by the government as well as gift materials from private sources that relate to the history of the United States.

Materials are arranged by Record Groups (RG). Each numbered group contains the records of a single government agency or subdivision. The National Archives Gift Collection of non-government donations is in RG 200.

The motion picture and videotape collections are described by Record Group, with an index at the end of the descriptions. Information on the other audiovisual materials will be found at the end of this entry.

Paper records relating to government audiovisual products often present problems for the researcher since they are generally stored outside of the Audiovisual Archives Division. The Archives staff can assist researchers in locating these materials. Historian David Culbert, in his essay "A Note on Government Records" (Appendix VII), describes his own odyssey through these collections of paper records.

MOTION PICTURES AND VIDEOTAPE

Motion Picture and Sound Recording Branch
Office 20E
(202) 523-3267

William Murphy, Chief, Motion Pictures
Donald Roe, Reference Specialist—Motion Pictures, Video, Audio

Eligibility

The collection is open to the public and may be viewed free of charge. Because of limited audiovisual facilities, reservations are strongly recommended. No reservations are needed to use the card catalogues but an initial consultation with one of the reference staff can provide valuable guidance on the impersonal though often remarkable card catalogues.

A limited number of videotapes, including those films which have been transferred to videotape, can be viewed outside of Washington in the Presidential libraries and the NARS regional archives, which have video playback facilities. These centers, listed at the end of this entry, will order tapes upon request. The CBS News tapes may be ordered from the National Archives through the inter-library loan programs.

Collection

103,000 subjects. The following description is an update of the 1972 publication, "Motion Pictures in the Audiovisual Archives of the National Archives," by Mayfield S. Bray and William T. Murphy. The volumious information quoted directly from that publication has been supplemented by notes on materials added to the collection between 1972 and 1979.

The Motion Picture and Sound Recording Branch holds some paper records related to the films in its collections. These range from a few vague notes to boxes of scripts and production files. Brief descriptions of these paper records have been added to the descriptions of relevant record groups.

RG 4: U.S. Food Administration, 1917-18. 2 reels.

Films of supporters of the Food Control Act, Senators George E. Chamberlain and Willard Saulsbury, Representatives Champ Clark and Asbury F. Lever, and Food Administrator Herbert C. Hoover.

A film on wartime farming in France. Animated cartoons dramatizing the need to conserve food.
Some paper records are available.

RG 9: National Recovery Administration, 1933. 3 reels.

One short film done by Warner Brothers for the NRA, *The Road is Open Again.*

RG 12: Office of Education, 1940-55. 16 reels.

Fight for Life, a 1940 documentary about obstetrical training and practice in the Chicago slums, written and directed by Pare Lorentz. Films, 1944-45, intended for use in supervisory training and a film on the industrial skills of the blind. A filmed address of President Dwight D. Eisenhower to the White House Conference on Education, November 28-December 1, 1955.
Some paper records are available.

RG 15: Veterans Administration, 1919 and 1946. 27 reels.

Films pertaining to the work of the Bureau of War Risk Insurance, 1919. A film explaining the organization of the Veterans Administration, 1946. Several documentaries explaining and illustrating the educational, financial, medical, and rehabilitation services of the Veterans Administration.

RG 16: Office of the Secretary of Agriculture, 1928-55. 404 reels.

Films illustrating Federal farm programs and films serving the educational or informational needs of agricultural communities, 1928-55. *Power and the Land,* produced in 1940 by the U.S. Film Service for the Rural Electrification Administration and directed by Joris Ivens.

RG 18: Army Air Forces, 1912-49. 6,132 reels.

World War II training films illustrating the coordination of the various operational units of the American 8th Army Air Force and the combined efforts of these units in preparing and completing a bombing mission; and World War II training films instructing in flight and gunnery and the maintenance and use of planes, helicopters, airfield tractors, forklift trucks, spray painting equipment, and the like.

Air Transport Command briefing films consisting of aerial and ground views of terrain, flight routes, and landing facilities in the South Atlantic, North Atlantic, Europe, India and China, the Caribbean, South America, Africa, and the Pacific, the British Isles, Alaska, the Canal Zone, and the United States. Animation for the briefing films shows particular flight routes, locations of landing strips, radio beams, and the principal geographic configuration of specific areas.

Outtakes from *Thunderbolts,* a 1946 William Wyler production documenting activities of the 12th Army Air Force in Europe, June 1944-

April 1945. Combat footage made in all theaters of operation in World War II concerning activities of the USAAF and containing camera records on all other aspects of the war, including such things as land and sea battles; amphibious operations; civilian and military leaders of the Allied Powers attending conferences and visiting troops; entertainers; war correspondents; Red Cross activities; rest and recreation activities; native peoples and their customs and participation in the war; captured enemy spies and saboteurs; Allied and Axis prisoners of war and prisoners-of-war camps; internees and internee camps; concentration camps; Axis atrocities; V-E and V-J Days; the occupation of Germany and Japan; atomic scientists; the A-bomb blast over Nagasaki; and damage to Nagasaki and Hiroshima.

Films concerning the development and use of lighter-than-air craft, 1925-35. A film made by the Air Corps of the 1933 Arkansas flood. A Coast Guard training film on swimming through burning oil and in surf. A film entitled *Last Rites of the Battleship Maine,* made by the Selig Corp. in 1912.

Color footage shot by the Army Air Force during the closing months of the war in France and Germany, March-June, 1945.

Paper files with digest sheets and caption sheets are available.

RG 21: District Courts of the United States, 1903 and 1927. 8 reels.

Films filed as plaintiff's exhibits in a copyright case brought before the U.S. Circuit Court for the Eastern District of Pennsylvania, *American Mutoscope and Biograph Company v. Sigmund Lubin,* October, 1903. Films from the records of the U.S. District Court for the Western District of Washington of the Demsey-Tunney heavyweight boxing match held at Soldiers Field, Chicago, September 22, 1927, and of the Dempsey-Sharkey fight held at Yankee Stadium, New York City, July 21, 1927.

RG 22: Fish and Wildlife Service, 1915-37. 13 reels.

Films made by the Bureau of Fisheries in the 1920's concerning cooperative fish culture in the United States and pearl culture in Japan. A film relating to an inspection trip to Alaska made by Bureau officials, including Commissioner Henry O'Malley, ca. 1929.

Department of Agriculture films instructing in the control of pests such as rats, prairie dogs, and porcupines, 1915-16. A film on life in a Boy Scout camp, ca. 1937, and a film illustrating aerial bombing techniques of the Air Service, 1921.

Some paper records are available.

RG 24: Bureau of Naval Personnel, 1917-27. 101 reels.

Films made or collected by the Bureau of Naval Personnel or its predecessor, the Bureau of Navigation, relating to naval air activities during World War I in the Atlantic and at the Key West Naval Station, including submarine patrol, convoy escort, rescue operations, and ground operations; ship launchings and maintenance at the Newport News Naval Shipyard; submarine maneuvers; Marine training; torpedo manufacturing and firing; and minelaying in the North Sea from a base in England.

Films of Liberty loan drive activities, patriotic celebrations, parades, ceremonies, and armistice celebrations in New York City, Washington, D.C., Pittsburgh, and London. Persons participating include President Woodrow Wilson, Secretary of the Navy Josephus Daniels, Secretary of War Pershing and Alexander B. Dyer, Lt. John Philip Sousa, Gov. Charles S. Whitman of New York, and Mayor John F. Hylan of New York City.

News coverage of President Wilson's second inaugural and films of his first visit to Europe following the armistice, including his departure aboard the transport *George Washington,* the arrival of the convoy in Brest, and the welcoming procession in the streets of Brest.

Films depicting war damage to Rheims, France, and Ostend, Belgium, and to other towns and the countryside of both France and Belgium. Films of German prisoners of war, captured German armament, and a U-boat. Newsreel films of postwar Volendam, Holland, and the gardens at Versailles.

Films of American leaders, including Secretary of the Navy Daniels, Secretary of State Robert Lansing, Adms. William S. Sims, William S. Benson, Roger Welles, Albert Gleaves, and Hugh Rodman, with foreign dignitaries on visits to the United States and aboard U.S. Navy vessels. Dignitaries include Prince Exel of Denmark, King Alfonso and Queen Victoria of Spain, and King George V of Britain. Films of the dedication of an American Expeditionary Forces monument at St. Nazaire, France, with U.S. Ambassador Myron T. Herrick, Marshal Ferdinand Foch, and General Pershing participating; and of President and Mrs. Warren G. Harding aboard the Presidential Yacht *Mayflower,* ca. 1921.

Films of the 1924 transatlantic flight of the airship *Los Angeles* (ZR-3), of rescue operations by lighter-than-air craft, and of a demonstration of aerial mapping techniques at Miami, Florida.

Films of postwar Navy training in seamanship, first aid, and the repair and maintenance of electrical equipment, machinery, dirigibles, and airplanes aboard ships, at several Navy yards and bases, and at the Naval Academy and the Great Lakes Naval Training Station.

News coverage and Navy films of League of Nations, Red Cross, and U.S. Navy activities relating to the removal of Armenian and Greek refugees from Turkey to Greece, ca. 1921, and films of the rescue of personnel from grounded and burning ships.

Films of recreation aboard ships and of sightseeing all over the world. Many scenes of U.S. Navy ships in harbors, at sea, on maneuvers, and so forth, and of ships of the Italian, British, and Turkish Navies.

A film about the newly-acquired Virgin Islands, ca. 1918.

RG 25: National Labor Relations Board, 1938. 1 reel.

A film of the complete assembly of Ford automobiles.

RG 26: United States Coast Guard, 1918-55. 84 reels.

Films, 1918-38 and 1945-55, about the peacetime activities of the Coast Guard, including rescue work at sea and in inland disaster areas,

cooperation with the Fish and Wildlife Service in the whaling and fur
seal industries, waterfront and harbor protection and law enforcement,
enforcement of ship safety regulations, beach and off-shore patrols
against smuggling, icebreaking and lighthouse duties in the Great Lakes,
iceberg patrol, lighthouse and light buoy construction and maintenance,
navigation assistance to ships in U.S. coastal waters and abroad, weather
observation, training and education at the Coast Guard Academy and
at other institutions, and recreation. Films relating to domestic activities
during World War II, including dock and harbor patrol, ship inspection,
investigations of ship sinkings, firefighting, weather observation, and
beach patrol (including a film showing FBI agents posing with German
spies captured by the Coast Guard); and films concerning Coast Guard
overseas activities during the war, such as amphibious operations in all
theaters, transportation of troops and war materials, rescue at sea,
submarine patrol, and convoy escort. Films of a yacht race and of
activities of U.S. political and military leaders, ca. 1938.

Some paper records are available.

RG 28: Post Office Department, 1921-57. 69 reels.

Films depicting activities and facilities of the Department, including the
Dead Letter Office; mail handling and delivery; transporting mail by
air, land, and water; parcel post; manufacturing and repairing mailbags;
printing and issuing stamps; protecting the mails from use in defrauding
mail users; and post office buildings and the construction and dedication of the New Post Office, Washington, D.C., 1931-34. The films include footage of persons such as Presidents Herbert C. Hoover and
Frankin D. Roosevelt, Postmasters General Harry S. New, Walter F.
Brown, and James A. Farley, and aviatrix Amelia Earhart.

A scenic film about Mount Ranier National Park.

German propaganda films. 1939-40, including *Baptism of Fire,* which
depicts the conquest of Belgium, Holland, France, and Poland. Ad-
dressed to the German consul in New York, the films were impounded
as undeliverable mail shortly after the United States entered the war.

Some paper records are available.

RG 29: Bureau of the Census, 1937-39 and 1960. 16 reels.

Films seeking public cooperation in the National Unemployment Census
of 1937 and in the 1940 census. Training films for enumerators for the
1940 census. A National Educational Television series on the 1960
census illustrating the work of the Bureau, presenting the history of
census-taking in the United States, and explaining the kind of information sought in the 1960 census and the uses to which it can be put.

Some paper records are available.

RG 31: Federal Housing Administration, 1935-36. 10 reels.

Films of a series entitled *Better Housing News Flashes* relating to the
construction, renovation, and modernization of homes, farm buildings,
and commercial properties under the Administration and to the effect of

the FHA and its government-insured loan program on the building in-dustries. Also a film on the construction of low-cost housing in Bethesda, Maryland.

Some paper records are available.

RG 33: Federal Extension Service, ca. 1913-70. 589 reels.

Films made or collected by the Department of Agriculture, relating chiefly to the educational activities of the Extension Service, including assisting and advising farmers and ranchers in methods of cultivation, soil conservation, the use of farm machinery, crop storage and market-ing, plant and animal breeding, plant and animal pest and disease con-trol, the care and feeding of animals, livestock butchering and market-ing, farmyard sanitation, and home improvement and modernization; home economics instruction, including such topics as canning, nutri-tion, child care, housekeeping, sewing, and bookkeeping; sponsorship of and cooperation with 4-H Clubs, American Farm Bureau Federations, the National Grange, and state farm organizations and extension ser-vices; work with the land-grant colleges in agricultural education; and cooperation with the Federal Emergency Relief Administration in estab-lishing and operating cooperative farm communities.

Films, 1913-47, on the history and organization of the Department of Agriculture; Department facilities, including the buildings in Washing-ton, D.C., and the Research Center at Beltsville, Maryland; and Secre-taries, Department personnel, and other prominent persons. Films on the role of the Department in enforcing the Pure Food and Drug Act, 1920-32 and 1959, in conducting agricultural explorations of other lands for plants that could be grown in the United States, 1928-32 and 1952, and in inspecting imported seeds and plants, 1922 and 1932. Also the role of the Department in both World Wars and a 1924 film on its motion picture making activities.

Films illustrating activities of the Forest Service, including the regu-lation of lumbering and grazing in national forests, fire prevention and fighting, pest and disease control and wildlife conservation. Films illus-trating the work of the Bureau of Public Roads, 1915-37. Films relat-ing to national parks in all areas of the United States. Films explaining the work of the Weather Bureau. Films covering highlights of the Coo-lidge and Hoover administrations and depicting activities of well-known persons and news events, 1925-39.

Paper records which are available include U.S. Department of Agri-culture caption sheets.

RG 35: Civilian Conservation Corps, 1933-43. 2 reels.

Motion pictures on the role of the CCC in erosion control and on work and recreation during one day in a CCC camp.

RG 38: Office of the Chief of Naval Operations, 1941. 1 reel.

A film of the testing of Higgins amphibious tanks by the Board of In-spection and Survey.

Some paper records are available.

RG 39: Bureau of Accounts (Treasury), ca. 1935. 1 reel.

A film illustrating the accounting system of the Treasury Department and showing President Franklin D. Roosevelt addressing Congress on the public works program.
Some paper records are available.

RG 43: International Conferences, Commissions, and Expositions, 1936-68. 1,040 reels.

A film illustrating power resources in the United States, 1936. A 70mm films entitled *Us,* which was shown at the U.S. Federal Pavilion at the 1968 Hemisfair in San Antonio, Texas, and 1,000 reels of color outtakes depicting many aspects of American life. Films used at the Seattle World's Fair, 1962.
Some paper records are available.

RG 46: United States Senate, 1936-38. 4 reels.

Newsreel footage received from a subcommittee of the Senate Committee on Education and Labor of the 1936 San Francisco dock strike, the 1937 Republic Steel strike in Chicago, and the 1938 Stockton, California cannery strike.

RG 47: Social Security Administration, 1936-40. 34 reels.

Films on procedures for obtaining old age and survivors insurance, disability insurance, and unemployment benefits. Newsreel footage covering activities of President Franklin D. Roosevelt, Secretary of State Cordell Hull, Governor Alfred M. Landon, and others.
Some paper records are available.

RG 48: Office of the Secretary of the Interior, 1929-62. 179 reels.

Films, 1935-37, relating to the overall activities of the Department, including the activities of the Office of Indian Affairs, the Bureau of Reclamation, the National Park Service, the Division of Territories and Island Possessions, and the Bureau of Mines. Films of President Harry S. Truman signing the Defense Production Act of 1950 and of Secretary of the Interior Oscar L. Chapman speaking, ca. 1950.
A film about the operation of the Alaska Railroad, 1962.
Films made by or for the Office of Indian Affairs, 1933-36, about the origin and history of American Indians and their contemporary customs and ways of life.
Films made or collected by the Bureau of Mines, ca. 1936, relating to volcanic action and resultant geological formations, mountain building, and geological problems in mining and structural engineering, and Texas and its industries and geography.
Films from the 1930s made by or relating to National Park Service activities, including films of scenes, work, and recreation in national and state parks and at national monuments and national historic sites all over the United States and in the territories.

Films made by the Bureau of Reclamation or relating to Bureau activities, 1934-38 and 1952, concerning conservation in general, the history of the westward expansion of the United States and the depietion of natural resources, activities of the General Land Office and the Geological Survey, activities of the Civilian Conservation Corps, and reclamation projects and their impact on communities.

Films made or collected by the Division of Territories and Island Possessions of the 1929 Carpenter-Whitney Expedition to Alaska and films about the Katmai National Monument, n.d. Films concerned mainly with sugarcane growing and refining in Hawaii, 1937, and films of scenery, tourist activities, and agricultural and other work on St. Thomas, St. John's, and St. Croix Islands in the Virgin Islands, 1935-36.

Films depicting activities of agencies other than the Department of the Interior, including a film made by the Public Buildings Administration of the Federal Works Agency of a housing project for married enlisted men at Fort Jackson, S.C., 1941, and a few films, 1935-36, on the creation and development of the Tennessee Valley Authority.

Some paper records are available.

RG 53: Bureau of the Public Debt, 1914-18. 4 reels.

Films dramatizing several heroic acts of World War I infantrymen, produced by the Treasury Department to promote the fourth Liberty loan drive. Films of the Salvation Army Congress in London, 1914.

Some paper records are available.

RG 56: Department of the Treasury, 1941-75. 169 reels.

Incentive films and advertising spots used in connection with defense and Victory bond promotional drives by the Savings Bonds Division and covering aspects of World War II, Korea, and Vietnam, as well as peacetime defense needs.

A savings bond promotional TV spot entitled *The Uncle Sam Caper,* 1975.

RG 59: Department of State, 1911-65. 206 reels.

Films made by the Department, its subsidiary agencies, other government departments, and private companies reflecting Department of State activities and policies and illustrating the history of the U.S. role in world affairs.

Films of the construction of the Panama Canal and views of the surrounding countryside and native life, 1911-13.

News coverage of British Foreign Secretary Arthur J. Balfour's visit to Washington, D.C., 1917.

A film showing President Calvin Coolidge with members of his Cabinet, 1925.

A 1926 film of the U.S. Legation in San Salvador and a 1929 film of La Paz, Bolivia, Bolivian cities and towns, the Bolivian countryside, and U.S. Minister David E. Kaufman with Bolivian President Hernando Siles.

A Fourth of July celebration in Shanghai, 1924.

The Notre Dame Boys Choir singing Christmas hymns, 1933.

A 1938 film in the *March of Time* series entitled *Uncle Sam—The Good Neighbor.* The film illustrates U.S. Foreign Service activities, with several officials of the Service and the Department of State and several ambassadors participating. A film of discussion by Assistant Secretary of State Sumner Welles about Nazi infiltration in South America and of the Presidents of Brazil, Argentina, and Uruguay meeting to confer on the problem.

Films of activities aboard the Swedish Red Cross ship *Gripsholm* in New York harbor as it prepares to repatriate Japanese citizens and to deliver packages to American prisoners of war in Japan, 1943.

Documentaries and newsreels produced by the Office of War Information reporting on World War II activities at home and in the combat theaters; covering a visit to the United States by Madame Chiang Kaishek, 1943; and reenacting the sinking of the freighter *Delia B* by a German submarine and the sinking of the submarine by a B-24. Documentaries about life in America from the *American Scene* series made during the war by the Office of War Information for distribution abroad.

A film illustrating Office of Strategic Services Operations during the Allied invasions of Sicily and Italy, 1944.

A film made by the Foreign Liquidation Commission in Italy illustrating procedures for disposing of surplus property and reconstruction work, 1946.

A film about the work of the United Nations Educational, Scientific, and Cultural Organization in assisting students from all over the world, 1947.

A film showing a U.S. military cemetery in Margraten, Holland, and scenes and life in Limburg Province, ca. 1950, presented to the U.S. Ambassador to the Netherlands by the Association of Netherlands Coal Mines.

Films illustrating reconstruction and economic development made possible by Marshall plan aid to Italy, Greece, and Great Britain, 1950-51; and films on efforts to improve the quality of life in Mexico and South America under the Point 4 Program, 1951.

Films reviewing international events from 1945 to 1951; covering the proceedings of the Japanese peace treaty conference held in San Francisco in 1951; depicting the plight of Arab refugees from Israel in the Gaza Strip and Jerusalem, 1950; showing refugees from East Berlin, 1951; covering the Korean War; and relating to youth activities in East and West Germany, 1950-51.

A film biography of General Dwight D. Eisenhower to the time he was appointed commander of the North Atlantic Treaty Organization, 1951.

Films showing the construction of the U.S. pavilion at the Brussels World's Fair, the opening ceremonies of the fair, and films shown as exhibits in the U.S. pavilion, 1958.

Films, mostly from television shows, of speeches, interviews, and discussions featuring Secretaries and Assistant Secretaries of State and others, including Dean Acheson, Christian Herter, Dean Rusk, George Ball, Douglas Dillon, and W. Averell Harriman, 1950-65, relating to U.S. foreign policy and world conditions.

Two public affairs documentaries, one describing the work of the U.S. mission to the U.N. under Arthur Goldberg and the other a film about U.S. aid to Ecuador to combat communist ideology and insurgency.

Some paper records are available.

RG 64: National Archives and Records Service, 1936-70. 58 reels.

Films of the first meeting of the National Archives Council, June 10, 1936, and of a luncheon meeting of the National Historical Publications Commission, June 17, 1958. Films of ceremonies at the National Archives marking the opening of the exhibit of the Japanese surrender documents, 1945; concerning historical documents in the Library of Congress; and of the transfer of the Declaration of Independence and the Constitution from the Library to the National Archives, 1952. Films of tests conducted at the National Bureau of Standards on the burning characteristics of nitrate motion picture film, 1936-38. A film entitled *Your National Archives*, 1953. A film of the voyage of the U.S.S. *Skate* under the North Pole, 1958.

And That's the Way It Was, T.V. News 1947-1968, a series of 19 programs which were shown at the Archives and then donated to the collection. Events include the Cuban missile crisis, the Bay of Pigs, the U-2 incident, civil rights, the Nixon-Khrushchev debate and many others.

Some paper records are available.

RG 65: Bureau of Investigation, 1936. 3 reels.

A motion picture entitled *You Can't Get Away with It* which portrays FBI activities in detecting and arresting criminals.

Some paper records are available.

RG 69: Works Projects Administration, 1931-39. 105 reels.

Films produced or distributed by the Motion Picture Record Division or its successors relating to WPA activities, including flood, drought, and hurricane relief and rehabilitation; dam, road, park, airport, and public building construction; slum clearance; development of recreation facilities; projects for promoting children's welfare; public education; women's work projects; and "white collar" work projects, including the Federal theater project and the Federal art project, 1935-39. Films illustrating WPA programs in particular areas of the country and in Alaska, 1935-37.

Instructional films in the *Physical Science* and *Bringing the World to the Classroom* series, 1931-36.

Films illustrating activities of the Civilian Conservation Corps and the National Youth Administration, 1936.

RG 70: Bureau of Mines, 1913-55. 238 reels.

Firms relating to mining methods, processing, refining, manufacturing, and products; uses of nickel, silver, lead, iron, copper, aluminum, magnesium, sulfur, clay, asbestos, carborundum, and sillimanite, 1919-38 and ca. 1943; coal mining methods, 1919-38, drilling oil wells and quarrying sandstone, granite, and limestone for Portland cement, 1915-31; automobile, manufacture and assembly, including explanations of the principle of the internal combustion engine and of the lubrication of a car, 1926-36; manufacturing, testing, and uses of dynamite, electric detonators, electric meters, safety glass, spark plugs, steel, storage batteries, valves, and watches, 1922-38; applications of steam, water, and electric power, 1922-28 and ca. 1943; and demonstrations of the uses of the oxyacetylene torch, 1922 and 1938.

Films used in the Bureau's safety and health education programs, 1913-17; gas, fires, dust explosions, equipment handling, and digging in coal mines, 1914-30; shoring, blasting equipment handling, and ore loading in metal mines, 1914-30; fires in oil wells and general safety in the oil industry, 1923-24; carbon monoxide gas poisoning, 1928; rescue and first aid, 1915-31; traffic safety, 1924 and 1937; and sanitation practices in mining towns.

Films on the natural resources and beauty of Arizona and Texas and films on the national parks, including Yellowstone, Yosemite, Grand Canyon, Rocky Mountain, and Shenandoah, 1925-55.

News coverage of the Royalton, Illinois, mine disaster, 1914,; testing of railway guns at Fort Story, Virginia, 1929; and the arrival of the U.S.S. Houston at Cartagena, Columbia, with President Franklin D. Roosevelt aboard, 1934.

Some paper records are available.

RG 75: Bureau of Indian Affairs, 1908-21. 13 reels.

Films made by the Rodman Wanamaker Historical Expeditions to the North American Indians, 1908-20. The films depict the life, religious customs, dances, and methods of warfare of North American Indians; the adoption of Marshall Ferdinand Foch by the Crow; the groundbreaking ceremony for an Indian memorial in New York State, with President William Howard Taft and his Cabinet in attendance; the declaration of allegiance made by the tribes on becoming American citizens; and the adoption of Joseph M. Dixon, leader of the expeditions, into the Wolf Clan of the Mohawk Nation, Iroquois Confederacy.

A film made by the Office of Indian Affairs during a trip by the revenue cutter *Bear* from the Aleutian Islands to Siberia showing many arctic scenes, including icefields, Eskimos and their homes, and animals, especially reindeer, 1921.

Some paper records are available.

RG 78: Naval Observatory, 1930. 1 reel.

A film of an astronomical expedition to Samoa to study solar eclipses.

RG 79: National Park Service, 1930-36. 15 reels.

Films, 1930-36, illustrating tourist activities, Park Service work, park facilities, and the people who lived in the Shenandoah and Great Smoky Mountains National Parks before the parks were dedicated. A film depicting a typical day at Camp Roosevelt, a Boy Scout camp at Willows, Maryland, ca. 1930.

RG 80: Department of the Navy, 1925-65. 8,568 reels.

Films made or collected by the Navy and used in training during World War II relating to the history of naval aviation, ships, submarines, airplanes, training of personnel, and mail delivery; kamikaze attacks; the battles of Midway and the Marianas; invasions of the Solomon Islands, Eniwetok, Saipan, and Guam; preparations for the invasions of the Ryukyus and Okinawa; bombing raids over Japan; and Japan and the Japanese people.

Outtakes and camera records, 1942-65, from the central motion pictures files of the Navy showing experimental equipment, aircraft in flight, aircraft crashes, and flight deck operations; ship movements; Pacific engagements and landings during World War II and the Korean War; the Japanese surrender ceremonies; the Allied occupation of Japan; returning prisoners of war; ceremonies, reviews and disasters at sea.

News outtakes and clips relating to World War II and the Korean action.

A *Combat Bulletin* film on the Japanese surrender showing President Harry S. Truman announcing the surrender, celebrations in the United States, and the surrender ceremonies aboard the U.S.S. *Missouri,* 1945.

Captured enemy films relating to naval activities during World War II.

British and American films of the Atlantic Conference between President Roosevelt and Prime Minister Churchill aboard the U.S.S. *Augusta,* 1941.

News coverage of the wreckage of the Navy dirigible Shenandoah (ZR-1), 1925.

A *March of Time* film about medical training in the United States, 1938.

Some paper records are available.

RG 82: Federal Reserve System, 1937. 1 reel.

A film made at the dedication ceremonies opening the Federal Reserve Building, Washington, D.C., with President Franklin D. Roosevelt making the dedicatory remarks.

Some paper records are available.

RG 86: Women's Bureau, 1928-38. 6 reels.

Dramas concerning the role of women in industry and the impact of labor laws and union activity on working conditions for women.

Some paper records are available.

RG 87: United States Secret Service, 1939. 1 reel.

A motion picture entitled *Know Your Money,* containing instructions on

detecting counterfeit bills and coins and the action to be taken when counterfeit money is received.
Some paper records are available.

RG 90: Public Health Service, 1924-50. 49 reels.

Films in a series entitled *Science of Life,* produced in 1924 and designed for use in the life sciences and personal hygiene instruction for young men and women. Films pertaining to the causes, treatment, and control of malaria, syphilis, other communicable diseases, and cancer, 1924-50.
Some paper records are available.

RG 91: Inland Waterways Corporation, 1932. 1 reel.

A film of the christening of the packet boat *Mark Twain* at Jefferson-ville, Indiana, including film of an animated map of the inland water-ways routes in the Mississippi River region from Minnesota and Lake Michigan to New Orleans.
Some paper records are available.

RG 96: Farmers Home Administration, 1936-37. 11 reels.

Documentaries produced by the Rural Settlement Administration and the Farm Security Administration under the direction of Pare Lorentz. The documentaries include *The Plow That Broke the Plains,* a film that illustrates the history of the Plains from the era of the open range through the coming of the "dirt farmer," the dirt farmer's exploitation of the soil, and the drought and winds that stripped the topsoil from the area; *The River,* a pictorial history of the part the Mississippi River played in the history of the United States from frontier days to the flood of 1937, emphasizing the erosion and floods that occur as a result of careless use of the land.
  Miscellaneous films about migratory labor camps; agricultural and industrial cooperatives in Russia, England, Sweden, Finland, and Scot-land; and the construction of different types of houses and barns.
Some paper records are available.

RG100: Bureau of Labor Statistics, 1938. 1 reel.

A motion picture film entitled *Stop Silicosis,* illustrating the causes and prevention of the disease.
Some paper records are available.

RG 102: Children's Bureau, 1919-26. 11 reels.

Films on prenatal, infant, and child care and diseases.
Some paper records are available.

RG 103: Farm Credit Administration, 1936-37. 4 reels.

A film promoting the cooperative marketing of wool. Films of President Franklin D. Roosevelt at his desk in the White House, of Gov. William

I. Myers of the Farm Credit Administration in front of the FCA Building, and of several other buildings in Washington, D.C.

Some paper records are available.

RG 104: Bureau of the Mint, 1940. 1 reel.

A film dealing with minting coins and casting medals at the Philadelphia Mint.

RG 106: Smithsonian Institution, 1903-49. 49 reels.

Films, 1931-41, from Bureau of American Ethnology records illustrating the preparation of an anthropological exhibit at the Smithsonian and of diggings and surrounding areas made in the course of archaeological explorations in New Mexico, Arizona, Tennessee, Colorado, Yucatan, and Honduras. Films, ca. 1930-31, illustrating the making of a dictionary of intertribal sign language of the Great Plains Indians and depicting the theory, history, and practice of the sign language.

Films, 1929 and 1950, pertaining to the history of the planning and development of Washington, D.C.

Films pertaining to the history of flight from 1903 through 1927 and films, 1927-32, of important events in the life of Charles A. Lindbergh, from his transatlantic flight to the kidnapping of the Lindbergh baby, and of a glider exhibition and contest.

RG 107: Office of the Secretary of War, 1941-45. 191 reels.

Films from the Bureau of Public Relations documenting American military activities in all theaters of operation during World War II and activities of the Allied military governments in Europe and in the Far East. Some captured German films for the same period.

RG 111: Office of the Chief Signal Officer, 1909-54. 18,801 reels.

Pre-World War I films concerning the development of flight, the construction of the Panama Canal, 1910-14, President William Howard Taft on an inspection tour of the Canal, ca. 1912, and the Mexican Punitive Expedition, 1916. Most of these are from the Historical (H) series.

Films of the World War I period depicting activities of the American Expeditionary Forces in France; homefront activities, such as mobilization and training and industrial production; U.S. Navy activities, submarine warfare, and convoys carrying troops overseas; British, French, Russian, and Italian participation in the war; the war in the Near East; peace celebrations in Paris and in America; and President Woodrow Wilson's two trips to France and the signing of the Treaty of Versailles. Most of these are from the H and Miscellaneous (M) series.

Films made between the wars relating to all phases of Regular Army, Army Reserves, ROTC, Citizens Military Training Corps, and West Point training, education, and maneuvers; Army activities in the territories and in other countries; military medicine; ordnance manufacturing, testing, and demonstrations; installing and maintaining communications systems; the history of flight, including Air Service activities, early parachute jumps, and air races; civil projects of the Army, such as river and harbor improvements and disaster relief; sports and recreation, such as the Olympic games, national rifle matches, and Army-Navy football games; and Army participation in parades and celebrations, in various funeral ceremonies, and in the burial of the Unknown Soldier. Coverage of news events, such as Charles A. Lindbergh's transatlantic flight, President Franklin D. Roosevelt's first and second inaugurations, the *Hindenburg* disaster, and volcanic eruptions. These films are in the M series.

Films of the Second World War period relating to all aspects of the conflict, including the Allies and the Axis Powers and their conduct of the war in all theaters; the Italian invasion of Ethiopia, 1935; the Spanish Civil War, 1937; the Japanese invasion of China, 1937; American homefront activities and war production; mobilization and training; the roles of women, Negroes, and Nisei in the war effort; entertainment for troops; the atom bomb; the end of the war; the Cairo, Teheran, Yalta, Quebec, and San Francisco Conferences; Allied military governments in Germany and Japan; postwar problems in Europe and Asia; and war crimes trials in Germany and Japan. The films are from the M, Army Depository Copy (ADC), Training Films, Combat Reports, Engineering Board Film Digest, Educational Films, Film Bulletins, Historical Reports, Staff Film Reports, Orientation Films, Army-Navy Screen Magazine (SM), Special Bulletins, Team 21, and War Film series.

Films relating to the Korean action and covering all aspects of the conflict and the peace negotiations, from the Combat Bulletins, ADC, M, and SM series.

Films of the inaugural ceremonies and parades of Presidents Harry S. Truman, 1949, and Dwight D. Eisenhower, 1953, from the M series.

Films made by other government agencies, including the Navy Department, the Bureau of Mines, and the War Relocation Authority. Films from private sources such as the Red Cross and newsreel companies, and films made in Germany, Japan, Italy, Finland, Great Britain, France, Russia, and Canada.

There are 19 boxes of paper records for this group of films which include production files from 1942-54 and training film digest sheets from 1930-45.

RG 117: American Battle Monuments Commission, 1937. 8 reels.

A motion picture entitled *America Honors Her War Dead*, showing excerpts from dedication ceremonies of American war memorials and chapels in Europe, August and October 1937.

RG 119: National Youth Administration, 1937-42. 56 reels.

Motion pictures illustrating the functions of the Administration, including the work and student programs, recreational activities, programs for Negroes, and activities at resident centers; and dramatizations of the problems of unemployed youth and NYA assistance given them.

Two films made by NYA personnel, one of the visit of King George VI and Princess Elizabeth of England to Washington in 1939, and the other of the inauguration of President Franklin D. Roosevelt in 1941.

RG 121: Public Buildings Service, 1940-43. 2 reels.

Films of President Franklin D. Roosevelt speaking at the dedication of the Washington National Airport, 1940, and of the site clearance and construction of the War Department Building (the Pentagon), 1940-43.

RG 126: Office of Territories, 1939-41. 97 reels.

Films covering all aspects of the Byrd Antarctic expedition of 1939-41.

RG 127: United States Marine Corps, 1939-45. 21 reels.

Training films used during World War II and films of combat in the South Pacific.

RG 128: Joint Committees of Congress, 1965 and 1969. 2 reels.

Films of the inaugurations of Presidents Lyndon B. Johnson, 1965, and Richard M. Nixon, 1969, made under the direction and authority of the Joint Congressional Committee on Inaugural Ceremonies.

RG 129: Bureau of Prisons, n.d. 1 reel.

A film entitled *Protecting the Public.*

RG 130: White House Office, ca. 1923-32. 5 reels.

Films relating to the informal activities of President Calvin Coolidge, ca. 1923-29, and activities of President Herbert C. Hoover, 1929-32, including a fishing trip Hoover made and a plea by him to the nation for relief aid. Films of the 1932 Republican National Convention.

RG 131: Office of Alien Property, 1930s. 36 reels.

Films from the records of the Hamburg-American Line—North German Lloyd concerning travel in Germany and other countries. Japanese dramas from the records of Haruta & Co., Inc.

RG 145: Agricultural Stabilization and Conservation Service, 1941. 31 reels.

A film entilted *The Land,* directed and photographed by Robert Flaherty for the Agricultural Adjustment Administraiton, and concerned with the reclamation and conservation of farmland exhausted or eroded by poor agricultural practices.

RG 146: United States Civil Service Commission, ca. 1921. 26 reels.

A film illustrating the career possibilities afforded by the merit system.

RG 170: Bureau of Narcotics and Dangerous Drugs, 1928-37. 14 reels.

Films relating to drug traffic and the enforcement of narcotics laws in Egypt, China, and the United States. A British instructional film on the cultivation of the poppy plant.

RG 171: Office of Civilian Defense, 1941-45. 57 reels.

Films used in training civilian defense workers in mobilization, rescue, firefighting and prevention, child care, defense against poison gas attacks, smoke concealment, air raid defense operations, and various defense equipment and its use. Films of London under aerial attack.
Films promoting victory gardens and food conservation.

RG 174: Department of Labor, 1940-68. 100 reels.

Films the Labor Department made or collected relating to its history and its activities in areas such as discrimination in hiring, employment for youth and the elderly, enforcement of labor legislation and regulations, civil rights, and foreign trade, 1940-68.

Television documentaries, interviews, and panel discussions, 1960-68, aired by American Broadcasting Company news. Columbia Broadcasting System's "Face the Nation" and "Washington Conversation," National Broadcasting Company's "Today Show" and "Meet the Press," and National Educational Television programs. The documentaries include *Harvest of Shame*, a 1960 Columbia Broadcasting System documentary about the living conditions of migrant workers in the United States; *A View from the Cabinet*, featuring some of President John F. Kennedy's Cabinet members and President Lyndon B. Johnson discussing the Kennedy administration; and other films that present the Secretaries of Labor, other Cabinet members, the Vice Presidents, and various Congressmen and labor leaders discussing labor and economic conditions and the labor policies of the Kennedy and Johnson administrations.

Television spot announcements in support of Labor Department policies and featuring such persons as Secretaries of Labor Willard Wirtz and Arthur Goldberg and Vice President Hubert H. Humphrey.

RG 178: United States Maritime Commission, 1924-45. 75 reels.

Films depicting the history of the merchant marine from Revolutionary times through World War II, including its activities during the Revolutionary War, the War of 1812, and the Civil War; peacetime shipping and passenger service on the Great Lakes and at sea; rescue work; and convoy duties in all theaters of operation during World War II.

Films illustrating recruiting, training, and other activities of the Maritime Commission at training schools and stations, at a convalescent center, and aboard sailing vessels and steamships, 1938-44.

Films concerning the manufacture of all types of merchant vessels during World War II and of President Franklin D. Roosevelt, Henry J. Kaiser, the Dionne quintuplets, and others participating in ship launchings. Films illustrating the principles of the steam turbine engine; relating to the repair and renovation of ships for the Victory Fleet; and showing the manufacture of World War II material, including train axles and wheels, B-24 bombers, and tanks.

Miscellaneous films of Richard E. Byrd and Clarence Chamberlain participating in an early airmail flight from the deck of a ship, 1928; of the work of the Coast Guard in keeping shipping lanes open and safe, 1929; and of British coastal fortifications, 1940.

RG 179: War Production Board, 1940-44. 15 reels.

Films produced to stimulate war production concerning the conduct of the war in several theaters. Films of Allied and Axis military and political leaders and films about the manufacture and transportation of war material, how war material is damaged, and how it is repaired.
Films instructing in good telephone manners.

RG 182: War Trade Board, ca. 1919. 1 reel.

A film of Board members and of the War Trade Board Building, with a large number of employees in front of the building.

RG 188: Office of Price Administration, 1943-46. 15 reels.

Films created to enlist the cooperation of the public in OPA programs, concerning the necessity for price controls and rationing both during and immediately following the war, explaining the role of the consumer in enforcing regulations, and warning against participation in the black market because of the inflationary results.

RG 200: National Archives Gift Collection, 1896-present. 53,539 reels, 3,000 videocassettes.

Newsreels, 1919-1967. Chiefly unbroken series of Paramount News, October 1941-March 1957; Movietone News, January 1957-October 1963; *News of the Day*, October 1963-December 1967; and Universal newsreels, including material used in released newsreels and some out-takes, 1946-48 and 1950-67. Newsreels produced by Movietone, Pathé, Fox, International, Paramount, and Telenews covering selected news items, including the Big Four at the Paris Peace Conference, 1919; the Navy's transatlantic flight from the Azores to Lisbon, 1919; activities of Presidents Calvin Coolidge, Franklin D. Roosevelt, Harry S. Truman, and Dwight D. Eisenhower; the 1924 Republican National Convention; events leading to and occurring during World War II; and the 1959 swearing-in ceremonies of the first Senators from Alaska and the first Congressmen from Hawaii.
Recent additions to the newsreel collections include a 1940 *News of the Day* on Wendell Willkie; a 1918 Hearst-Pathé Newsreel; six issues of Universal-International Newsreels, 1920-21; and a short composite film of newsreel clips, 1895-1975.
A recent fire in the National Archives nitrate film vaults destroyed 75% of the outtakes from Universal Newsreels from the 1930s and 1940s. The outtakes from 1951-1967 are on safety film and still in the collection.
Paper records include the production files of Universal Newsreels.

The March of Time, 1939-51. Documentary films relating to U.S. history, culture, social problems, science, education, mental health, and international problems; to government agencies, such as the FBI, the Secret Service, and the Post Office Department; to wartime and postwar activities of private institutions, such as the American Red Cross; and to the effect of World War II on one small American town.

The March of Time, 1935-51 Stock Film Library. 15.000 reels of unedited footage dating from 1935 that relates to the subjects listed above.

World War I films, 1917-19. Films made behind German lines by Jacob Berkowitz; the *Official War Review* series on land and air battles, maneuvers, and training, distributed by the Films Division of the U.S. Committee on Public Information; the National Aeronautics Committee's film on the celebration at Hollywood, California, of Air Memorial Day, 1919; a documentary on World War I, produced in 1956 by the National Broadcasting Company and entitled *The Great War* and a large quantity of footage collected by the Columbia Broadcasting System from sources all over the world in producing the documentary entitled *World War I.*

A recent addition is a 1918 film on the training of soldiers produced by the Committee on Public Information, George Creel, Chairman.

World War II films, 1940-45. Films produced by Warner Brothers, Paramount Pictures, Inc., and Columbia Pictures Corp., under the technical supervision of the armed services, and several films distributed by the War Activities Committee of the Motion Picture Industry. The films concern activities of the Army Air Corps, the Navy, the Marine Corps, and the Coast Guard, including officer training programs and homefront aspects of the war effort. Also documentaries compiled from newsreels, one on events leading up to the war entitled *The World in Flames,* and one by Paramount concerning resettlement of Jewish refugees in the Dominican Republic; a re-release of the National Film Board of Canada of a World War I Charlie Chaplin film promoting the sale of war bonds; pictures of German air raids on London, presented to the National Archives by the British Library of Information; a Finnish Relief Fund film about the Russo-Finnish War; films relating to the training of Dutch troops in exile and to the liberation of Greece; a collection of German newsreels covering the early stages of the war, presented to the National Archives by Lt. William F. Rope; and an Army Air Forces film of the ceremonies attending the placing of the German surrender documents on exhibit in the National Archives.

Recent additions include *The Negro Soldier,* produced by the Army; *You, John Jones,* produced by the War Activities Committee of the Motion Picture Industry; *Which Way This Time,* produced by the Office of Price Administration; and an RKO-Pathé film *Here Come the Yanks.*

Ford collection, 1914-56. 1,500 reels. The *Ford Animated Weekly,* 1914-21, consisting of short news features, films about cities, and general interest films; the *Ford Educational Weekly* and the *Ford Educational Library,* 1916-25, consisting of short features and unedited film on agriculture, civics and citizenship, industrial geography, regional geography, history, nature study, recreation and sports, sanitation and health, and technical subjects; the *Ford News,* a series of newsreels shown at Detroit area theaters during 1934; and films on agriculture and conservation, charities, education, geography, sports and recreation, and presenting dramas and news. Films of the informal activities of the Ford family and family's philanthropies and films relating to personal projects of Henry Ford, including the *Dearborn Independent* newspaper, the Ford farm, and the Henry Ford Museum and Greenfield Village. Films illustrating the activities of the Ford Motor Company, including activities of domestic and foreign branches, 1928-54; non-manufacturing activities, 1914-54, and plants and the major manufacturing activities, 1906-56; and war-related activities during both World Wars and the Korean action. Also several films made by producers other than the Ford Motion Picture Laboratories and not produced for the Ford Motor Company, including advertisements for companies other than newsreels, personal films, propaganda films, public service features, technical features, and travelogs.

Harmon collection, 1930-51. 1,400 reels. Films produced by the Harmon Foundation on many aspects of the history and accomplishments of minority cultures in the United States and on the cultures of Asia, Africa, and other developing areas.

League of Nations collection, 1920-46. 56 reels. This collection was presented to the National Archives by the United Nations. It consists of films of the first and last meetings of the League; of meetings and activities concerning such problems as the Greco-Bulgar incident, 1925, the Sino-Japanese conflict, 1932, and the Italo-Ethiopian conflict, 1936; of health and disarmament conferences; and of League delegates and officials.

Washington Debates of the Seventies, 1970-73. 40 reels. Filmed recordings of televised discussions and seminars relating to public affairs, including U.S. policy in the Middle East, the role of Congress in foreign policy, the Presidency, consumer protection, national health insurance, social security, defense, civil disobedience, tax reforms, Vietnam, and the "Nixon Doctrine." Sponsored by the American Enterprise Institute.

National Councils of Churches, 1970-72. 26 reels. Discussions and interviews with writers, theologians, scientists, and public leaders about peace, violence, racism, justice, and other issues that affect the moral life of the nation.

AFL-CIO collection, 1952-71. 32 reels. A gift of the AFL-CIO, this collection includes films about public issues affecting the American worker. The films were produced or acquired by the AFL-CIO and used in its educational library loan service.

Other educational and documentary films, 1915-76. A series by Eastman Teaching Films, Inc., 1927-35, on history, geography, industry, conservation, recreation, agriculture, and sports; two series produced by Warner Brothers Pictures, Inc., 1934-35, entitled *See America First* and *Our Own United States*, concerning U.S. history, industry, occupations, recreation, scenery, and ethnic groups; a series, *The Washington Parade*, by Columbia Pictures, Inc., on scenes and activities of various federal agencies, chiefly at Washington, D.C.; and a Columbia Broadcasting System series, *Eyewitness to History*, 1959-60, with pictorial summaries of President Dwight D. Eisenhower's trips abroad, Nikita Khrushchev's visit to the United States in 1959 and to France in 1960, and Charles de Gaulle's visit to the United States in 1960; and a TV series, *Longines Chronoscope,* about public affairs with interviews and discussions, 1951-55.

Also documentries, dramas, and television news specials and stock footage received from individuals, motion picture companies, and other organizations. These films are on American history; political parties; the administrations of Presidents Calvin Coolidge, Franklin D. Roosevelt, Dwight D. Eisenhower, and John F. Kennedy; the 1959 funeral services for John Foster Dulles and Adm. William F. Halsey; the development of motion picture equipment, radio broadcasting, the telephone, aviation, atomic energy, and space flight from Robert H. Goddard's experiments in the 1920s and 1930s to Col. John H. Glenn's orbital flight in 1962; Donald McMillan's expedition to Greenland, 1925; Sir Ernest Shakleton's 1922 Antarctic expedition, Adm. Richard E. Byrd's 1927 transatlantic flight and his Antarctic expeditions of 1926, 1928-30, 1933, and 1947-48, and Lincoln Ellsworth's 1936 Antarctic expedition; a 1915 congressional visit to the Philippines and Hawaii; the 1947 Texas City disaster; and activities of the American Red Cross and the National 4-H Club Foundation. The films also cover other topics as diverse as poverty in the Tennessee hill country, whaling and walrus and bear hunting in the Arctics, integration in Atlanta, Georgia, charting ocean winds, and many other social problems, ranging from venereal diseases to the need for city planning. There are also films relating to events and conditions outside the United States and its territories, including life in East Africa in 1924, the eruption of Paricutin in Mexico in 1943, communism in Russia and Cuba, nazism in Germany, the history of Austria from the Hapsburgs to the end of World War II, the National Archives of India, and the state funeral of Sir Winston Churchill in 1965.

Recent additions include films from the 1920s on naval torpedoes, Hopi and Pueblo Indians and the swearing-in ceremony for President William Howard Taft. Recent documentaries: *March on Washington,* about a 1969 anti-war demonstration, *No Vietnamese Ever Called Me Nigger,* and *The Unquiet Death of Julius and Ethel Rosenberg.* A group of films made by Congressman Richard H. Poff to communicate with his constituency. Films of national parks and Indians, 1941-46. Included also are the first and second generation copies of the 8mm motion picture film taken by Abraham Zapruder showing the assassination of President Kennedy, November 22, 1963.

Historical commercial films productions, 1896-1943. Prints of motion picture productions presented to the National Archives as having historical or research interest incidental to the dramatic presentation. They include two collections presented by Thomas Armat, consisting of penny-in-the-slot and nickelodeon shows produced by the Edison, Pathé, Méliès, and Urban companies, 1896-1910; *The New York Hat,* 1912, and *Birth of a Nation,* 1916, both directed by D. W. Griffith; Selznick International Pictures' *Gone with the Wind;* Paramount Pictures' *The Biscuit Eater;* Warner Brothers' *Mission to Moscow* and a shortened version of *Black Legion;* and Theatre-on-Film, Inc.'s *Journey to Jerusalem.* Also eight films (*The Man I Married, Man Hunt, They Dare Not Love, Night Train, Confessions of a Nazi Spy, Dispatch from Reuter's,*

Underground, and *Foreign Correspondent)* that were studied by a sub-committee of the Senate Interstate Commerce Committee investigating the dissemination of anti-Nazi propaganda before the United States entered World War II.

Television Newscasts, April 1, 1974-present. The National Archives holds licenses to record the evening network news from ABC and NBC. The collection includes ABC evening news, daily except Sunday, from April 11, 1977 and NBC evening news, daily, from July 19, 1976. CBS has deposited their evening, morning, and midday news, daily, from April 1, 1974 (see RG 330 for TV news excerpts).

Microfiche copies of the transcripts of CBS news broadcasts dating from January 1, 1974 are available.

Television News Specials, April 1, 1974-present. All CBS News Specials from April 1, 1974-present and selected specials from ABC and NBC from 1976-present are part of the National Archives collection. These include state of the Union addresses, the impeachment hearings, the Democratic and Republican conventions in 1976, and the Carter inauguration.

Additional televised news specials in the collection include the PBS coverage of the Judiciary Committee hearings, July 24, 1974 to July 30, 1974, and the Daniel Schorr controversy. Individual documentaries made for television may be found elsewhere in Record Group 200 and in other record groups.

Microfiche copies of the transcripts of "Face the Nation" and "60 Minutes" are available.

RG 207: Department of Housing and Urban Development, 1948-69. 165 reels.

Documentation of the creation of the Department, President Lyndon B. Johnson's appointment of Robert C. Weaver as its first Secretary, several ceremonies relating to the establishment of the Department, and early Department activities. Footage produced by the Department for use in the film *Open Space;* fair housing television spots; and "instant rehabilitation" renewal project materials. Completed films on urban and community planning, discrimination in housing, urban poverty, housing codes, and home construction.

A few films on housing and planning in the Soviet Union, Great Britain, and Latin America.

A recent acquisition is a small group of films on housing and urban planning acquired by HUD.

RG 208: Office of War Information, 1941-45. 661 reels.

Informational, propaganda, and documentary films covering all phases of homefront activities, including farming, industry, housing, education, manpower needs, the roles of women and Negroes in the war effort, and Japanese relocation; urging citizen support for and participation in the war effort on the homefront, including participation in conservation, preventing inflation, war bond drives, and safeguarding military information; illustrating the Social Security system and its benefits to the working man; covering lend-lease activities; reporting on all aspects of the war, from training of the armed forces to the fighting fronts in all theaters; depicting the Allied peoples, customs, and contributions to the war effort; and concerning the Axis Powers and their conduct of the war, military strength, and ambitions.

A film, narrated in Chinese, of the Chungking memorial service for President Franklin D. Roosevelt, 1945.

Newsreels, including "United News," sponsored by the OWI, 1941-45, most narrated in English, with samples narrated in Portuguese, Arabic, French, Chinese, Afrikaans, and Japanese; "Fox Movietone News," covering the period 1942-45; "News of the Day," 1937-43; Free French newsreels, 1945; "Indian News," released in India in 1945; "Russian News," made in Russia, 1942-45; and "War Pictorial News," produced in England, 1943.

RG 210: War Relocation Authority, 1942-43. 4 reels.

Films about the activities of the WRA, life in relocation camps, and the training and record of Nisei soldiers in World War II.

RG 218: United States Joint Chiefs of Staff, 1942-46. 9 reels.

Motion pictures relating to the development of radar, radio, guided missiles, and other equipment.

RG 220: Presidential Committees, Commissions, and Boards, 1957-70. 19 reels.

Records of the President's Committee on Employment of the Handicapped, consisting of films of the 1957 annual meeting, the life story of Glen Cunningham, and training for the handicapped. Also one-minute television spots featuring President Dwight D. Eisenhower and Roy Campanella.

Records of the President's Commission on Campus Unrest consisting of six films of Kent State University and the city of Kent, Ohio during the period of protest and shooting, May 1-4, 1970. Films were taken by NBC, CBS, and private citizens.

RG 223: Office of the Bituminous Coal Consumers Counsel, 1943. 2 reels.

Films entitled *Coal for Victory* and *Know Your Coal,* illustrating methods of coal conservation.

RG 226: Office of Strategic Services, 1942-45. 235 reels.

Films about the industry and people of Pearl Harbor prior to World War II and the Japanese attack of December 7, 1941. Films describing the social structure and behavior patterns of the Japanese and the geography and natural resources of Japan.

Films depicting the Allied landing in Sicily, 1943.

Recent acquisitions include a film of the North Africa campaign, in color; *Mission to Yenan,* which shows the training of the Chinese and their leaders Mao Tse-tung and Chou En-lai; films on the geography and wartime action in the China-Burma-India theater; and a film of the Yugoslav partisans.

RG 227: Office of Scientific Research and Development, 1943-44. 203 reels.

Films by Divisions 8, 9, 10, 11, and 12 of the Office as illustrations for reports on the development of high explosives and rocket propellants; insecticides and protective chemicals for clothing and equipment; aerosols, gas mask absorbents, filters, and screen smoke; incendiary devices and hydraulic fluids; and amphibious vehicles.

RG 229: Office of Inter-American Affairs, 1941-45. 45 reels.

Informational and propaganda films dealing with the peoples and cultures of Latin America, inter-American cooperation, Latin American minerals and archaeological treasures, a study of an ancient Inca city, and war activities of the United States.

RG 234: Reconstruction Finance Corporation, 1943-47. 29 reels.

Films relating to a U.S. Commercial Company survey of the economy, geography, and sociology of the Micronesian Islands, 1945-47; and films of cinchona plantations, natives, and the countryside of Guatemala, taken in connection with the activities of the U.S. Commercial Company in developing sources of quinine, 1943-44.

Films of plantations, natives, cities, and the countryside of Brazil made in connection with activities of the Rubber Development Corporation, 1943-44.

RG 235: Department of Health, Education, and Welfare, ca. 1963. 1 reel.

A film illustrating language teaching techniques.

RG 237: Federal Aviation Administration, 1957. 3 reels.

Films illustrating the functions and activities of the Administration.

RG 238: National Archives Collection of World War II War Crimes Records, 1921-45. 76 reels.

Films used as evidence at the war crimes trials of Axis leaders before the International Military Tribunal, Nuremberg, 1945-46, and before the International Military Tribunal for the Far East, Tokyo, 1946-48, consisting of German films documenting the Nazi rise to power and triumphs in Europe, 1921-44. the entry of Germany into Austria, 1938, the political and industrial activities of the Krupp family and company officials, 1930-40, the construction of the No. 1 Hermann Goering steel plant, 1939-41, and the Nazi Supreme Court trial of the 20th July 1944 conspirators against Adolf Hitler. Films of concentration camps taken by American and Russian forces as they advanced through Germany, 1945. Also a Japanese film entitled *Japan in Time of Emergency.*

RG 242: National Archives Collection of Foreign Records Seized, 1941-, 1916-1950. 2,276 reels.

German documentaries and newsreels covering World War I land and sea battles and the life of Paul von Hindenburg. Leni Riefenstahl's film entitled *Triumph of the Will,* made at the 1934 Nazi Party rally at Nuremberg, and coverage of the 1936 Olympic riding competition from her film entitled *Olympiad.* A feature film that was used in anti-Semitic indoctrination entitled *The Jew Suss.* The personal film collection of Eva Braun, ca. 1939-40. German films on the history of the Nazi Party in Germany, many aspects of World War II on all fronts, war materiel manufacture and weapons development, German culture, and the training of Hitler Youth and of political leaders for administrative posts in occupied countries.

Italian documentaries and newsreels covering World War II on several fronts, including the Ethiopian and Greek invasions and the North African campaign.

Japanese documentaries and newsreels, 1932-44, relating to the fishing industry, travel in Japan, the invasion of China, and many aspects of the war in the Pacific.

French newsreels made in 1944 about World War II and films made ca. 1950 about the campaign against the Vietminh in Indochina.

Russian newsreels, educational films, documentaries, and feature films on subjects such as the natural sciences, technology, agriculture, transportation, housing, travel in the Soviet Union, and Russian culture and history. Films on the death of Nikolai Lenin, 1924; the fall of Berlin at the end of World War II and the meeting of Russian and Western Allied troops at the Elbe; Hungary; the socialization of several republics of the Soviet Union; Soviet cooperation with other Communist countries; and North Korea of 1950. Also several anti-American dramas.

North Korean films about the 38th parallel and of American prisoners at Pyongyang.

Chinese Communist anti-Nationalist propaganda films made during the postwar period and before the removal of Chiang Kai-shek to Taiwan.

American films relating to civilian victims of war, 1942, and to the escape of American prisoners of war from the Island of Palawan in the Philippines.

German films of rocket experiments at Peenemunde, 1942-45, with some footage in Agfacolor.

RG 243: United States Strategic Bombing Survey, ca. 1944. 11 reels.

Captured German films relating to American incendiary bombs and bombing methods and to German war industries.

RG 252: Office of the Housing Expediter, 1946. 1 reel.

A film about housing for veterans.

RG 269: General Services Administration, 1971. 2 reels.

Films entitled *Partners in Progress* about minority businesses and *Clear Skies, Clean Air* about the use of natural gas-powered automobiles.

RG 272: President's Commission on the Assassination of President Kennedy, 1963. 15 reels.

Films collected in the course of the investigation. These films are held by the Judicial and Fiscal Branch of NARS.

RG 274: National Archives Collection of Records of Inaugural Committees, 1965-73. 6 reels, 2 videocassettes.

Films entitled *1965 Inaugural Parade, The Inaugural Story 1973,* and *Inauguration Ceremony and Parade—1973.* The 1969 inaugural concert at Constitution Hall is on videotape.

RG 286: Agency for International Development, ca. 1955. 2 reels.

Films of the International Cooperation Administration, consisting of a report to the American people on technical cooperation and illustrating U.S. assistance to India, Libya, Ecuador, Indochina, Sudan, Ethiopia, Paraguay, Thailand, Indonesia, and Afghanistan in improving educational, agricultural, medical, and other techniques. Films concerning U.S. military assistance programs and cooperation in RIO, NATO, and SEATO.

RG 291: Property Management and Disposal Service (GSA), ca. 1957. 1 reel.

A film concerning the processing of nickel ore at the Defense Materials Service Nicaro Project in Cuba.

RG 305: Bonneville Power Administration, 1949. 2 reels.

The Columbia and *Hydro* were films made by BPA in 1949 using the songs of Woody Guthrie for the sound track. The films described the benefits of public ownership of electric power facilities. All copies were ordered destroyed in the 1950s, but a janitor rescued these prints.

RG 306: United States Information Agency, 1932-68. 40,000 reels.

Documentaries produced or acquired by the Agency for distribution abroad about many aspects of life in the United States; the lives of famous Americans; the history of aviation; World War II; peacetime uses of atomic energy; U.S. foreign relations, including treaties, the Marshall plan and reconstruction in Europe, visits of foreign heads of state to the United States, cultural exchange, international trade, the Berlin airlift, and international sporting events; and life in South America, Europe, North Africa, and the Soviet Union. Many instructional films that were used in technical assistance programs on such subjects as farming, poultry raising, swimming, child care, training of nurses and teachers, medicine, rehabilitation of the blind and of veterans, apprentice training, civilian defense, and industry.

Welt im Film, a German language newsreel which was produced jointly by the British and American military governments and shown in the British and American zones of Germany, Austria, Vienna, and Berlin from 1945 to 1952. The newsreels were part of the "denazification" efforts.

The USIA collection (the agency is now called the International Communication Agency) is the largest one within the Motion Picture and Recorded Sound Branch. It contains about 2,000 titles. Use is restricted to representatives of the media, members of Congress, scholars and research students.

RG 310: Agricultural Research Service, 1939-49. 11 reels.

Films illustrating methods of cultivating and harvesting sugar beets.

RG 326: Atomic Energy Commission, ca. 1964. 203 reels.

Films about AEC's contribution to the peaceful uses of atomic energy. Seventy-nine films produced by the atomic energy agencies of the USSR, France, Italy, India, and Canada and shown at the Third International Conference on Peaceful Uses of Atomic Energy, Geneva, 1964. Both technical and public information films are included. Also 121 reels of unedited film.

Some paper records are available.

RG 330: Office of the Secretary of Defense, 1961-75. 619 reels.

Films of the inaugural ceremony and parade of President John F. Kennedy.

Kinescopes of excerpts from television newscasts, 1965-75, which dealt with the Vietnam War and other stories of interest to the Department of Defense such as arms limitation and foreign relations. The excerpts were taped off the air for internal use but now are available to researchers. Some typed summaries are available.

RG 337: Headquarters Army Ground Forces, 1942. 2 reels.

A film entitled *Speed with Power and Traction,* demonstrating the uses of the MG-2 high-speed tractor.

RG 341: Headquarters United States Air Force, 1950-67. 20 reels.

Films received by the USAF during the official investigation into the existence of unidentified flying objects filmed by military personnel and civilians. Two television documentaries about UFO's are included.

RG 342: United States Air Force Commands, Activities, and Organizations, 1900-67. 4,670 reels.

Films made or collected by the Air Force on the history of the development of flight, including activities of the Wright brothers from 1900 on, such as their demonstration flights in France, Italy, and the United States, and on the development of airplanes, gliders, balloons, dirigibles, autogiros, helicopters, rockets, jets, satellites, aeronautical oddities, parachutes from the 1930s on, ballistic cameras, and radar.

Films about early air races, airshows, and distance and altitude records; the flight by Richard E. Byrd and Floyd Bennett to the North Pole, 1926; the Hindenburg crash, 1937; Finne Ronne's Antarctic Expedition, 1946-48; the dedication of the New York International Airport, 1948; and people prominent in the history of flight, including Wilbur and Orville Wright, Edward V. Rickenbacker, Billy Mitchell, Charles A. Lindbergh, Richard E. Byrd, Floyd Bennett, Igor Sikorsky, and Wiley Post.

Films reflecting noncombat activities of the Air Force and its predecessors, 1920s to 1964, including the airmail service; rescue and assistance missions in natural disaster areas at home and abroad; hurricane hunting; the Berlin airlift; training and maneuvers; airbase construction; the opening of the Air Force Academy, 1955; participation in the preparations for and activities of the International Geophysical Year, 1953-59; A-bomb tests in the Pacific and elsewhere; and research and development work in the fields of guided missiles, remote-control weapons, supersonic flight, and space technology.

World War I films illustrating the activities of the Army Air Service in France.

Films made in all theaters of operation during World War II concerning the activities of the Army Air Forces and all other aspects of the war, including the AAF at home; women in the AAF; Axis concentration and prisoner-of-war camps and atrocities; Allied bombing missions over Europe and Africa and in the Pacific area; the defense of Britain and Moscow; the effects of bombing raids on Japan, including the atomic bombing of Hiroshima and Nagasaki; the surrender of Germany and Japan; and the customs, religion, industry, black market, and Allied occupation of Japan.

Films on aerial aspects of the Korean action and the truce-signing ceremonies.

Television news release prints on the war in Vietnam.

Films on the inauguration of Presidents Franklin D. Roosevelt and Harry S. Truman. Films relating to the Presidency of John F. Kennedy, including his inauguration, his activities as President, and worldwide memorial services and tributes to him. Films of the funeral of Gen. John J. Pershing, 1948.

Films of the 1952 Olympic games.

Captured German films depicting the war in Poland and covering research and development of planes, gliders, helicopters, jets, rockets, and ballistic missiles, 1912-44. Captured Japanese films relating to preparations for the Pearl Harbor attack and World War II combat. A Russian film of the 1949 May Day celebration.

Many military and civilian leaders appear in these films, including Theodore Roosevelt, Dwight D. Eisenhower, Fiorello La Guardia,

Winston Churchill, Richard M. Nixon, Chiang Kai-shek, Syngman Rhee, Paul von Hindenburg, Josef Stalin, and V. M. Molotov.

Unedited footage of the USAF Thunderbirds and their audiences in the U.S., Europe, and Latin America, 1958-67.

Training films with approved War Department and DOD doctrine showing Air Force procedures, equipment, and World War II combat. These films were used between 1942 and 1963.

RG 362: Agencies for Voluntary Action Programs, 1961-71. 144 reels.

Films created, commissioned, or acquired by Peace Corps, VISTA, Foster Grandparents Program, and other voluntary action programs which document the work of these programs, show conditions in other countries, or prepare volunteers for their assignments. Films produced by the governments of Botswana, Mexico, India, Indonesia and others.

Some paper records are available.

RG 374: Defense Atomic Support Agency, 1954-62. 20 reels.

Classified and unclassified training films used by the Nuclear Weapons School to instruct in the care, handling, storage, and operation of atomic weapons.

RG 381: Office of Economic Opportunity, 1964-72. 654 reels.

Films produced and acquired by OEO for its social welfare programs to combat poverty and racism. Films showing the OEO workers among Indians, Chicanos, blacks, and whites.

Films and unedited footage from an experiment in police-community relations in Washington, D.C., which was never released because of the negative image it showed.

Unedited footage of the Cuban missile crisis, Lady Bird Johnson and Robert Kennedy.

Most of the 37 short films produced in Farmersville, California, for a project in self-help through visual communication patterned after the "Challenge for Change" project tried in Canada by its National Film Board.

Some paper records are available.

RG 397: Office of Civil Defense, 1952-60. 66 reels.

Documentaries produced by predecessor agencies of the OCD depicting nuclear bomb explosions, flood damage, and all phases of civil defense.

RG 452: American Revolution Bicentennial Administration, 1976. 10 reels.

Films produced for the Bicentennial entitled *Project Civic*.

Subject Index

References are to Record Group numbers.

Catalogues

Twenty per cent of the collection is uncatalogued. However, individual films can be located by the reference staff. Scholars should also note that the collection has traditionally been of more interest to those making films than those studying them, so the cataloguing system is closer to that of a stock film library than a university library. For example, there are as many cards in the Main Card Catalogue for Herbert Hoover as there are for ice skating.

Card Catalogues

The Main Card Catalogue has productions and footage catalogued by record group, title, and credits if known. There is an elaborate subject index based on Library of Congress subject headings.

The Ford Film Collection Catalogue has a key word index.

The Army Air Forces Combat Subjects/Signal Corps Army Depository Film Catalogue has a subject index.

The Universal Newsreel Catalogue has an elaborate subject index.

The Air Force Miscellaneous Series has no subject index.

The other Air Force catalogues (Various Series) have no subject index.

The Army Air Forces Special Film Projects Catalogue subject index is in process.

The Navy Catalogue subject index is available elsewhere.

The Atomic Energy Commission Catalogue is a subject catalogue.

Other Finding Aids

The *Ford Film Guide,* available for purchase, is an overview. This NARS publication was compiled by Mayfield Bray in 1970.

Television News Index and Abstracts is a detailed breakdown of network news programs, August 1968-present. This series of publications is available at the Archives but it has been published since 1972 by the Vanderbilt Television News Archive in Nashville, Tennessee, and is available in many libraries. (See Appendix III.)

The *CBS News Index,* published annually by CBS and available from Microfilming Corporation of America, Glen Rock, New Jersey, lists alphabetically by name and subject all stories which have appeared in CBS newscasts and news specials since 1975. The *Index* is available at the Archives and at many libraries.

Also available are Universal Newsreel Summary Sheets and shelf lists of uncatalogued films.

Special Publications of the Audiovisual Archives Division

Copies of these publications are available free:

Special List #14, List of World War I Signal Corps Films, 1957.
Audiovisual Records in the National Archives Relating to World War II, 1971.

Audiovisual Records in the National Archives Relating to Black History, 1972.
Audiovisual Records Relating to Indians in the National Archives, 1972.
Audiovisual Holdings of the Presidential Libraries, 1972.

There are also a number of unpublished lists on specific subjects.

Access

As stated above, most films and videotapes must be viewed at the National Archives. Some videotape collections and films which have been transferred to videotape may be requested through regional archive branches to be viewed in those facilities. The CBS News collection is available through inter-library loan. (Also see entry #94.)

Appointments should be made in advance to request materials and to reserve viewing facilities.

Film and video analysis equipment is available.

Most of the government materials are in the public domain and copies are available for a fee. Many items in the Gift Collection (RG 200) are also in the public domain. Some films and most of the videotapes are encumbered by copyright or other restrictions.

Other Materials

Sound Recordings

Motion Picture and Sound Recording Branch
Office 20E
(202) 523-3267

Donald Roe

The 104,000 items in the collection are described, much as the motion pictures and videotapes are described above, in "Sound Recordings in the Audiovisual Archives Division of the National Archives," 1972. That publication is free and available by mail. It is elaborately indexed by the name of the speaker and the title of the programs or series.

The Gift Collection (RG 200) contains the ABC Radio Collection of ABC network radio broadcasts from 1943-71. A separate description of this collection is available.

Available subject matter guides include "Sound Recordings: Voices of World War II, 1937-1945," "Captured German Sound Recordings," and "The Crucial Decade: Voices of the Postwar Era 1945-1954."

Copies of the recordings are available subject to copyright and other restrictions.

Still Pictures

Still Pictures Branch
Office 20
(202) 523-3054

Joe Thomas Chief
William Leary, Archivist

The over five million still picture items in the collection are also described in much the same way as the motion pictures and videotapes described above. The descriptive publication, free and available by mail, is "Still Pictures in the Audiovisual Archives Division of the National Archives," 1972. There is a subject index.

Available subject matter guides in the "Select Audiovisual Records" series include "Pictures of the American West 1848-1912," "Pictures of the Civil War," "Pictures of United States Navy Ships 1775-1941," and "Negro Arts from the Harmon Foundation."

Copies of the photographs and photographs of posters and artworks are available subject to copyright and other restrictions.

Regional Archive Branches

Lyndon B. Johnson Library
2313 Red River Street
Austin, TX 78705
(512) 397-5137

John F. Kennedy Library
Federal Archives and Record Center
380 Trapelo Road
Waltham, MA 02154
(617) 223-7250

(Atlanta area)
1557 St. Joseph Avenue
East Point, GA 30344
(404) 763-7477

(Boston area)
380 Trapelo Road
Waltham, MA 02154
(617) 223-2657

(Chicago area)
7358 South Pulaski Road
Chicago, IL 60629
(312) 353-0161

(Denver area)
Denver Federal Center
Denver, CO 80225
(303) 234-5271

(Fort Worth area)
4900 Hemphill Street (building)
P.O. Box 6216 (mailing)
Fort Worth, TX 76115
(817) 334-5515

(Kansas City area)
2306 East Bannister Road
Kansas City, MO 64131
(816) 926-7271

(Los Angeles area)
24000 Avilla Road
Laguna Niguel, CA 92677
(714) 831-4220

(New York area)
Building 22-MOT Bayonne
Bayonne, NJ 07002
(201) 858-7245

(Philadelphia area)
5000 Wissahickon Avenue
Philadelphia, PA 19144
(215) 951-5591

(San Francisco area)
1000 Commodore Drive
San Bruno, CA 94066
(415) 876-9001

(Seattle area)
6125 Sand Point Way NE
Seattle, WA 98115
(206) 442-4502

Collection

156 U.S. (GSA) National Archives and Records Service—National Audiovisual Center

8700 Edgeworth Drive
Capital Heights, Maryland

Mailing Address:
Washington, D.C. 20409
(301) 763-1896 (Reference)

8:00 A.M.-4:30 P.M.   Monday-Friday

The National Audiovisual Center serves as the central source of information on Federal audiovisual materials and provides distribution services for these materials through sale and rental programs.

Eligibility

Information and distribution services are available to the public.

Collection

10,000 titles. Over 90% of the titles are films and videotapes. The concentration is in medical, dental, technical, vocational, and science materials, but over 2,000 titles fall within the humanities and social sciences. The large history collection covers classic government documentaries and many military and aviation history subjects. There are other groups of titles focusing on civil rights, communism, democracy, international relations, and NATO, with some dating back to the 1930s. Most of the films and videotapes are recent productions since the purpose of the collection is sales and rentals. For older materials, contact the Motion Picture and Sound Recording Branch of the National Archives and Records Service (entry #155).

Catalogue

A Reference List of Audiovisual Materials Produced by the United States Government is a descriptive catalogue of 6,000 of the NAC titles with extensive indexing. It is available for $5.75 from the Superintendent of Documents, U.S. Government Printing Office, Washington, D.C. 20402 (stock number 052-003-00497-6).

Access

All films for which there are preview prints may be viewed at the Center. Preview prints are available by mail only to those who have the funds and authority to purchase prints. All items in the catalogue are for sale and many of the films can be rented for a fee.

Those wishing to view films at the Center should contact the Reference Section to ask if prints are available.

Small screening rooms with projectors, video analysis equipment, and an auditorium which seats 60 are available.

For information on rights and restrictions, contact the producing agency. For purchase of copies, contact the Center.

Referral Aids

NAC Data File

The National Audiovisual Center has been designated ". . . to serve as a central information source to the public and Federal agencies concerning the availability of audiovisual products produced for and by the Government." (OMB Circular A-114, Attachment D, April 13, 1978). After July 1, 1978 all government agencies must report information on their audiovisual activities for inclusion in the NAC Data File. Security materials, in-house specialized training materials, and products with a useful life of less than one year or which cost less than $1,500 are exempt.

As of June, 1978, the NAC Data File included the six thousand titles that are listed in their catalogue and an additional four thousand titles of products that are older or specialized. Each entry includes the title, technical information, the producing agency, the date of production, and a synopsis. This computerized file can be accessed by any of these categories and by any word in the synopsis. Scholars with specific questions and needs may request a search of the File.

Defense Audio-Visual Information System (DAVIS) File

The NAC staff also has access to the DAVIS File and can search it for scholars who have specific questions and needs. See entry #147 for more information on the DAVIS File.

Government Collections

NAC can provide information on the location of other audiovisual collections within the government. Many agencies have free loan programs and libraries located throughout the U.S.

Collection

157 U.S. (GSA) National Archives and Records Service Stock Film Library

1411 South Fern Street
Arlington, Virginia 22202
(703) 557-1114

8:00 A.M.-4:30 P.M.   Monday-Friday

The Stock Film Library, a part of the Audiovisual Archives Division of the National Archives and Records Service, is a depository for the storage and preservation of motion picture stock footage produced and acquired by the federal government. It serves government as well as private film producers. Scholars are welcome to use the facility.

Eligibility

Open to the public.

Collection

5 million feet of 16mm film. The collection dates back to 1957, with the majority of the footage from the National Aeronautics and Space Administration (NASA). Other government agencies which have contributed to the collection include:
Agency for International Development
Department of Agriculture
Department of Commerce—U.S. Travel Service
Department of Energy—Atomic Energy Commission
Department of Health, Education and Welfare—Administration on Aging
Department of the Interior—U.S. Fish and Wildlife Service
Department of State
Department of Transportation—Coast Guard, Federal Aviation Administration, Federal Highway Administration
Environmental Protection Agency
National Science Foundation (Antarctica)
Postal Service
The footage is mostly a combination of trims and outtakes and evidential footage. There are some completed NASA productions.
The collection of the Stock Film Library will grow and broaden considerably under the recent federal regulations which require that federal agencies submit all stock footage to this depository. The Department of Defense is exempted from these regulations.

Catalogue

The NASA collection is filed in a card catalogue organized under a highly classified scheme. The rest of the collection is arranged in another card catalogue by direct and specific entry.

Access

Viewing prints of over 95% of the footage are available at the library. They do not circulate.

Advance notice is recommended so that viewing facilities may be scheduled.

Film analysis equipment is available.

With very few exemptions, all footage is in the public domain.

Other Materials

Documentation exists for most of the NASA footage and for some of the footage from other sources.

Collection

158 U.S. Health, Education and Welfare Department

Office of Public Affairs
Humphrey Building, Room 645F
200 Independence Avenue, SW
Washington, D.C. 20201
(202) 245-6221

Maurice McDonald, Audiovisual Director

Within the Department of Health, Education and Welfare (HEW), there are two large collections of film and videotape: the National Library of Medicine (entry #159) and the Captioned Films for the Deaf program (Appendix III). Smaller collections are distributed by the National Institute on Drug Abuse and the National Institute on Alcohol Abuse. These collections are available through the National Audiovisual Center (entry # 156).

HEW-produced films not in the above collections are generally placed with one of three free loan distributors: Modern Talking Pictures (entry #112), Association Films (entry #17), or R.H.R. Filmedia, 1212 Avenue of the Americas, New York, New York 10036. They are also available for sale through NAC. After a title is retired from a free loan program, it is often available for rent and sale from NAC. More than half of the films funded by HEW are produced under grants and distributed by the grantee. Some offices which administer grants have random collections of films and/or publish guides to audiovisual products on particular subjects.

Public service announcements for television are produced by many components of HEW. There is no central collection of these short films, which are most often handled by the public information office of the respective components.

Videotape is generally used only for research or in-house training programs. There are large training collections at the Social Security Administration in Baltimore, Maryland, the Public Health Service, and the National Institutes of Health (NIH). At the NIH training office, Pete Eddy has set up a remarkable informal exchange system which includes a catalogue of the audiovisual training materials held by 25 government training offices. Government training officers interested in the cooperative lending arrangement which is part of this system should contact Mr. Eddy at (301) 496-2146.

NAC is the best place to begin searching for current films from HEW and the government in general, but there are individuals within HEW who are in touch with media activities in the individual components of the department. Don Jordon, (202) 472-5955, is the Audiovisual Coordinator for the Office of Education. Walter Clark, Assistant Chief of the Mental Health Education Branch of NIMH, can be reached at (301) 443-4573.

Collection

159 U.S. (HEW) National Library of Medicine

Reference Services Branch
8600 Rockville Pike
Bethesda, Maryland 20209
(301) 496-6095

8:30 A.M.-9:00 P.M.   Monday-Friday
8:30 A.M.-5:00 P.M.   Saturday

Alvin Barnes, A-V Librarian

Eligibility

Open to the public.

Collection

6,000 titles: medicine. This collection of audiovisual materials includes sound recordings and slide tapes but consists primarily of videotape and film products. Its purpose is to serve medical professionals, but many titles may be of interest to scholars in the social sciences and humanities. There are groups of anthropological and sociological films; materials on malpractice and the legal and ethical aspects of medicine, and chronicles of the history of medicine, including interviews with many individuals. The collection does not contain patient or public education films.

Catalogue

An annual catalogue is available at the library and by mail from the Superintendent of Documents. *The National Library of Medicine Audiovisual Catalogue,* DHEW #NIH78-1102, contains entries for all films in the Library of Medicine collection. The catalogue is based in the

AVLINE file which is part of the MEDLARS computerized system. The terminal in the Reference Services Division can be used by the staff to answer questions about the collection.

Access

The collection does not circulate. Some of the titles are available for sale and rent, many through the National Medical Audiovisual Center, 1600 Clifton Road, NE, Atlanta, Georgia 30333, (404) 633-3351.

Reservations to view the collection are not necessary.

Viewing facilities include projectors and video analysis equipment.

Information on TV rights and purchase of copies is available from the Reference Services staff.

Referral Service

160 U.S. Housing and Urban Development Department

Office of Public Affairs
Room 4272
451 7th Street, SW
Washington, D.C. 20410
(202) 755-6073

Charles Cogan, Chairman, Communication Review Board

The Department of Housing and Urban Development is in the process of gathering information on film and videotape collections within the Department. Information now available indicates that both current and out-of-date films have been turned over to the National Audiovisual Center (entry # 156) and the Audiovisual Archives Division of the National Archives (entry #155).

Current films are also available for free loan from RHR Filmedia, 1212 Avenue of the Americas, New York, NY 10036.

Collection

161 U.S. (Interior) National Park Service

Harpers Ferry Center
Harpers Ferry, West Virginia 25425
(304) 535-6381 (toll call from Washington)

9:00 A.M.-5:30 P.M. Monday-Friday

Thomas Gray, Chief, Pictorial Services

Until the mid-1960s there was no centralized film production facility for the National Park Service. Each park produced its own films and many of the parks have archival collections of these films and others acquired for historical purposes. Films produced by the Harpers Ferry media facility are all available from the National Audiovisual Center (entry #156). Only a stock footage collection is available in Harpers Ferry, and much of the older footage has been transferred to the National Archives Stock Film Library (entry #157).

Eligibility

Open to both scholars and filmmakers by appointment.

Collection

Stock footage. This collection of thousands of feet of stock footage serves the production needs of the Park Service. The footage is from Park Service productions and includes scenes of the parks, wildlife, vegetation, and historical material.

Catalogue

The footage is not catalogued but is listed by park and production title.

Access

All footage must be viewed at the Harpers Ferry Center.

Scholars and filmmakers should contact the Center with their specific needs and make an appointment to view the stock footage. Park Service and other government staff take first priority.

Film analysis equipment is available.

Copies of the footage may be purchased.

Collection

162 U.S. International Communication Agency

Television and Film Service
Room 2406, 601 D Street, NW
Washington, D.C.

Mailing Address:
Washington, D.C. 20547
(202) 376-7731

8:45 A.M.-5:30 P.M.   Monday-Friday

Cooki Lutkefedder, Special Assistant to the Director

Eligibility

The International Communication Agency (ICA), formerly the U.S. Information Agency, is restricted by Congress from disseminating its program materials within the United States and its territories and possessions. ICA materials are produced and acquired for distribution overseas through the U.S. foreign service posts. Exceptions are made for representatives of the media, members of Congress, scholars, and research students. Scholars may apply to view ICA films and television programs at the agency's offices in Washington or New York.

Collection

2,000 titles. ICA products are used with foreign audiences to explain foreign policy and American culture—the people, their art, history, industry, politics. This impressive collection of films and videotapes includes well-known documentaries and fiction films acquired by ICA and their own productions, which use the talents of some of America's finest documentary filmmakers.

Catalogue

Active Films and Television Programs is a computer printout which describes the two thousand titles currently in use and indexes them according to subject. *Master Retired List* is a title list of four thousand films and television programs produced since 1952 and no longer used by the agency. About half of these titles are in the National Archives.

Access

ICA products are not distributed in the U.S.

Scholars wishing to view films and television programs should contact Ms. Lutkefedder to request permission and make appointments to view materials in Washington or New York.

Films are viewed in a screening room. Video analysis equipment is available for those programs on cassettes.

Information on rights for ICA-acquired titles is available.

Other Materials

ICA also produces exhibits and magazines. It includes the Voice of America. For information on these other offices within ICA contact the Congressional and Public Liaison office (202) 724-9103.

Collection

163 U.S. Justice Department

Constitution Avenue between 9th and 10th Streets, NW
Washington, D.C. 20530
(202) 633-2000

Hours vary from office to office. Appointments are suggested since access to some offices is restricted.

A large collection of films is distributed by the Law Enforcement Assistance Administration (entry #164). Smaller collections are briefly described below.

DRUG ENFORCEMENT ADMINISTRATION
1405 I Street, NW
(202) 633-1230 (Prevention Programs)

The Prevention Programs Section of the Office of Public Affairs distributes about 20 films on drug abuse prevention. These films are also available from Drug Abuse Prevention Centers throughout the United States.

FEDERAL BUREAU OF INVESTIGATION
Pennsylvania Avenue between 9th and 10th Streets, NW
(202) 324-3691 (Press Office)

The Press Office has a few films about the FBI. There is a large collection of training films at the FBI Academy in Quantico, Virginia. Contact Ed Kenney at the Learning Resources Center, 273-0700 (toll-free from Washington). The collection of 354 films consists primarily of acquired films about law enforcement likely to be of little interest to scholars. Those who are interested may apply to use the collection.

IMMIGRATION AND NATURALIZATION SERVICE
425 I Street, NW
(202) 633-2942 (Public Affairs)

The Public Affairs Office has produced a number of public service announcements for television.

Collection

164 U.S. (Justice) Law Enforcement Assistance Administration

TV and Motion Pictures Branch
633 Indiana Avenue, NW
Washington, D.C. 20531
(202) 724-5884

9:00 A.M.-5:00 P.M.   Monday-Friday

Vincent Williams, Film Library

Eligibility

Open to the public.

Collection

110 titles. The focus of the collection is crime, crime prevention, and the duties of a police officer. Much of the collection was produced on grants from LEAA. Other titles were acquired from private and government sources.

Catalogue

A descriptive list is available by mail.

Access

Borrowing is by mail and in person.
Reservations to borrow the films and to view them at the library are suggested.
A projector is available.
Some information on TV rights and purchase of copies is available.

Referral Aids

> *Criminal Justice Audiovisual Materials Directory*, January, 1978, is a guide to films and videotapes within the categories of courts, police techniques, prevention, prisons, and public edification. It is for sale by the Superintendent of Documents, U.S. Government Printing Office, Washington, D.C. 20402 (Stock No. 027-000-00629-9).

Collection

165 U.S. Library of Congress—Motion Pictures, Broadcasting and Recorded Sound Division

Thomas Jefferson Building, Room 1053
2nd Street and Independence Avenue, SE
Washington, D.C. 20540
(202) 287-5840

Note: The address and telephone number will change in 1980.

8:30 A.M.-5:00 P.M.   Monday-Friday

Erik Barnouw, Chief
Paul Spehr, Assistant Chief
Patrick Sheehan, Barbara Humphrys, Emily Sieger, J. R. Smart, Reference Staff

FILM AND TELEVISION

Eligibility

The collection does not circulate. Titles for which there are reference prints may be viewed for scholarly study and research. Undergraduate students must provide letters from their professors endorsing their projects. The facilities are not available to high school students.

Many serious researchers find that the Library of Congress (LC) collection is the best and only source of the motion pictures in which they are interested. (It should be noted that the term "motion picture" is used to describe all moving picture film and videotape in the LC collection.) It is one of the largest archival collections of commercially-produced films and TV in the world. The staff is sincerely interested in helping researchers use the collection and has the knowledge to offer substantial guidance to those who have done their own preliminary research.

For some researchers, the LC collection may not be the best or most convenient source of motion pictures. This huge collection of 75,000 motion pictures is not subject indexed. Information on each motion picture is in the Shelf List, a card catalogue arranged by title. To determine whether a specific motion picture is in the collection and whether there is a viewing or reference print, it is absolutely necessary to first have established the exact title.

The staff is knowledgeable and the reference library in the Motion Picture and Television Reading Room does help a researcher discover the titles of the motion pictures which might be of interest. However, this initial title search is often best done before coming to the Library of Congress. Any large public library, a university library, or the American Film Institute Library (see entry #6) has the resources to help a researcher produce a list of titles.

Even if the motion pictures you wish to view are included in the LC collection, prints may be more conveniently available elsewhere. This is especially true for scholars interested in documentary or educational films produced in the last 20 years. The Washington, D.C., area public library film services have surprisingly rich collections of both documentaries and entertainment features. Countless sources provide free loan films by mail. Area universities and community colleges have large collections of films and videotapes which can be viewed in their libraries. The indexes at the back of this volume suggest alternate sources for various categories of motion pictures.

Collection

75,000 motion pictures. Describing this vast collection presents many problems since it is neither logically reducible to convenient increments nor served by a subject index. The motion picture holdings do include the Copyright Deposits Collection and special collections of groups of titles added through gifts, purchases, or placement by other government agencies, and this rough existing breakdown has been adhered to in the descriptions which follow.

Each of these large collections is described with information on how the collection was acquired by the Library of Congress, the production dates, approximate numbers of titles, and a list of finding aids. These finding aids include both card catalogues available only in the office of the Motion Pictures, Broadcasting and Recorded Sound Division and published works available in large libraries throughout the U.S. Detailed descriptions of the finding aids are in the "Catalogue" section of this entry.

Note: The alphabetical designations applied to each collection have been created solely for indexing this *Guide* and do not reflect any Library of Congress system.

A. Copyright Deposits Collection

40,000 titles: 1942—present. Since 1942 motion pictures have been selected from those registered for copyright to form a collection which includes feature-length and short entertainment films; educational, scientific, religious, and business-sponsored films; and ten thousand entertainment, documentary, and educational television programs. Guidelines for selection include both diversity and quality, with additional emphasis on sociological and historical importance. At present all entertainment features (about 200 titles each year) and almost all television documentaries registered for copyright are selected. Many other nontheatrical productions and some instructional films are added to the collection each year. The selected titles average about 60% of those registered for copyright. That statistic is a bit misleading since almost any motion picture released in the U.S. and registered for copyright that a researcher would want to view is likely to be among those selected under the current policy.

Motion pictures produced before 1942 are also found in the LC collection. The special collections described below include copyright deposits which were preserved on paper and later re-photographed to form the Paper Print Collection of productions released between 1894 and 1915. Between 1912 and 1942 copies of motion pictures submitted for copyright were not selected for the permanent collection, but special collections and individual titles added to the Library's holdings in recent years have begun to fill that 30-year gap.

Synopses, continuities, publicity materials and other print items were submitted as part of the registration for copyright from 1912 to 1942. Similar materials exist for some post-1942 submissions. This collection is described under "Other Materials."

Reference prints for motion pictures are generally available in this collection.

There is no single finding aid which includes a complete listing of just this collection. In the Shelf List and Television Productions File the copyright deposits are interfiled with every other motion picture in the collection. The two Library of Congress publications which are available in many libraries do not describe the LC collection but can be useful in compiling a list of titles to be looked up in the Shelf List. *Catalog of Copyright Entries: Motion Pictures* lists materials registered for copyright but does not indicate which titles were selected for the collection. *Library of Congress Catalog—Films and Other Materials for Projection* contains cataloging information on motion pictures of general interest to libraries, schools, and individuals but is not related to the copyright process or to the LC collection.

B. Paper Print Collection

3,000 titles: 1894-1915. In 1893 W. K. L. Dickson, an assistant to Thomas Edison, submitted a paper print of a strip of sample images from an early Edison Kinetoscope production. Until 1912, film producers submitted this same kind of positive photographic image on rolls of paper to register their work for copyright. These rolls were re-photographed frame by frame in the 1950s by Kemp R. Niver and his assistant, producing the existing projection prints of these early films. The re-photographed prints include over 300 short films by pioneer director D. W. Griffith, dating from 1909 to 1912, and 30 films by French filmmaker George Melies, copyrighted in 1903 and 1904.

Reference prints are available for most of these titles.

The Paper Print Collection is described and indexed in Kemp R. Niver's *Motion Pictures from the Library of Congress Paper Print Collection, 1894-1912,* edited by Bebe Bergsten. Individual titles are all included in the Shelf List and some are also in the card catalogues which index silent films in the LC collection.

C. American Film Institute Collection and the United Artists Collection

14,000 titles: emphasis on years 1912-1942. The American Film Institute (AFI) collects films and deposits them in the Library of Congress. These efforts have begun to fill the 30-year gap during which prints were not selected from motion pictures submitted to the Library for copyright. Through a cooperative arrangement with the AFI, the Library has received nitrate original negatives and other materials from RKO

Radio Pictures, Hal Roach Studios, Columbia Pictures, and Universal Pictures. There also are films from many individuals; independent producers from the teens and twenties; and sound shorts of operas, minstrel shows, vaudeville acts and speeches. Within the collection are groups of Yiddish films from the 1930s and 1940s and feature and short films produced during the same decades which had all-black casts.

From United Artists came the Warner Brothers films made prior to 1949, including 700 sound features and eighteen hundred sound shorts, Looney Tunes, and Merrie Melodies cartoons. Non-Warner Brothers materials include early Vitaphone shorts, Monogram features and the pre-1948 Fleischer Studios/Paramount Pictures Popeye cartoons.

Reference prints are available for only a small part of the AFI collection. Reference prints for the United Artists collection, related manuscript material, and the complete business records of United Artists up to 1950 are in the collection of the Wisconsin Center for Film and Theater Research (Appendix III).

The AFI Collection and the United Artists Collection are listed by title in the AFI publication *Catalog of Holdings of the American Film Institute Collection and the United Artists Collection at the Library of Congress*. The collections are also included in the Shelf List and many of the titles have been added to both the Directors File and the card catalogues which index silent films in the LC collection.

D. George Kleine Collection

456 titles: 1898-1926. George Kleine was a pioneer in the American motion picture industry. He manufactured motion picture equipment, was the K of the Kalem Company which distributed European films, and later joined Thomas Edison and others in the Motion Picture Patents Company. His private film collection and his business papers were purchased by the Library of Congress. The collection includes a range of comedy, drama, documentary, educational, and serial films over half of which were produced by Edison between 1914 and 1917. Of special interest are over 50 films produced by foreign film companies Gaumont, Pathé, Cines, and Ambrosio and released in the U.S. by Kleine. These were among the first feature-length films shown in the U.S.

Reference prints are available for all of these titles. The Kleine Papers are in the LC Manuscript Division described later in this entry. Pressbooks and other printed materials which relate to specific titles are available in the Motion Picture and Television Reading Room.

An LC pilot cataloguing project resulted in a computer file of this collection with subject indexing. A published print-out by title is available for use in the Reading Room. A published catalogue is being prepared. The individual titles are in the Shelf List and many of the titles have been added to both the Directors File and the card catalogues which index silent films in the LC collection.

E. Theodore Roosevelt Association Collection

375 titles: 1909-1930s. This collection of early news films was received from the Theodore Roosevelt Association through the National Park Service. The collection covers President Roosevelt's life from his Rough Rider days through his later life, with emphasis on the period 1909-

1919. The footage includes major political events, family members, celebrities, and Roosevelt's funeral and posthumous tributes to him.

Reference prints are available for most titles in this collection.

The collection is described and indexed by subject, date, place, and name in a catalogue which will be published by the Library. The collection is described in "Theodore Roosevelt on Film," in the *Quarterly Journal of the Library of Congress.*

F. Mary Pickford Collection

100 titles: 1909. This collection, a gift to the Library of Congress from Mary Pickford, includes silent shorts and features which span the career of this silent film star and follow her into the first years of sound films. The collection includes early Biograph shorts and features produced by Famous Players and United Artists.

Reference prints are available for most of these titles.

The collection is included, title by title, in the Special Collections card catalogue and in the Shelf List. Most of the titles are also included in both the Directors File and the card catalogues which index the silent films in the LC collection.

G. German Newsreels and Films

3,000 titles: 1919-1946. After World War II this group of German films was confiscated by the U.S. government and transferred to the Library of Congress. A 1963 agreement with the German government gave the copyrights back to the original owners but allowed the Library screening privileges and the permanent custody of the prints. The collection includes about a thousand feature films produced between 1919 and 1946, the majority of which were produced between 1935 and 1944, and over a thousand newsreels, including extensive runs of *Die Deutsche Wochenschau* (1934-1944). The numerous educational, entertainment, documentary, and propaganda shorts are all in the original language.

Reference prints are available for most of the newsreels, 80% of the features, and 60% of the shorts. Over 100 boxes of non-film materials which accompany the collection are available in the Division offices.

The collection is listed, title by title, in the Shelf List and in the German Collection card catalogue. The feature films are indexed by director and release date.

H. Italian Newsreels and Films

500 titles: 1930-1943. This group of Italian films was confiscated by the U.S. government after World War II and transferred to the Library of Congress. In 1963 the copyrights were returned to the original owners while the Library maintained permanent custody of the prints and screening rights. The collection, all with Italian soundtracks, includes documentary, newsreel, feature, education, and propaganda films.

Reference prints are available for most of the 275 *Instituto Luce* newsreels (1938-1943), 100 *Luce* shorts (1930-1943), and several of the 40 features (1934-1940). There are fact sheets for most of the newsreels.

The collection is listed, title by title, in the Italian Collection card catalogues and the Shelf List.

I. Japanese Newsreels and Films

1,400 titles: 1933-1945. Like the German and Italian film collections described above, the Japanese films were confiscated after World War II and transferred to the Library of Congress. In 1962 the copyrights were returned to the original owners while the Library maintained permanent custody of the prints and the rights to screen and copy the films for official use. Newsreels include *Asahi News* (1935-1939), *Yomiuri News* (1936-1940) and *Nippon News* (1940-1945). There are 200 feature films and 700 education, documentary, and propaganda shorts.

Untranslated reference prints of most of the titles and descriptive sheets for many of the titles are available.

The collection is listed, title by title, in the Japanese Newsreels card catalogue.

J. *Meet the Press* Collection

1000 telecasts: 1949-1975. Lawrence Spivak and the National Broadcasting Company donated a large collection of materials related to the public affairs program, *Meet the Press*. Most of the paper materials are in the Lawrence Spivak Papers in the Manuscript Division, photographs and cartoons are in the Prints and Photographs Division, and the audiotapes are held by the Recorded Sound Section of the Motion Picture, Broadcasting, and Recorded Sound Division. For the 1000 telecasts which span the years 1949 to 1975, the Library has videotapes, kinescope negatives, or kinescope prints.

There are reference prints for 100 of the telecasts. The published *Meet the Press* transcripts (1957-71) and the guest roster (1956-1971) are available in the Division.

The programs are indexed by title and surname of the guests in the Television Holdings File and are included in the Shelf List.

K. *Original Amateur Hour* Collection

567 telecasts: 1948-1968. The *Original Amateur Hour* Collection of papers, audiotapes, audio discs, and kinescopes was donated to the Library of Congress in 1969. This popular talent show was broadcast on radio from 1935 and on television from 1948. Most of the telecasts in the LC collection are from the late 1950s and 1960s.

Reference prints are available for most telecasts.

The collection is listed by date in the Shelf List. Additional information can be found in the papers which were included in the gift.

L. Smaller Special Collections

A number of small collections include silent films and early documentaries. The Edison Laboratory Collection of 75 miscellaneous titles, transferred to the Library by the National Park Service, reflects early experiments in motion picture technology by Thomas Edison and his assistants, including films shot in his studio, the Black Maria, and the picture portions of some early sound experiments. The collection also includes newsreel clips of Edison in the 1920s and promotional films for Edison Industries.

Other small collections are the Allen Collection which contains 75 silent films; the Cowling Collection of 25 documentaries from the 1930s; the Dunstan Collection of 50 titles, which includes some westerns; the Fleming Moore Collection of 40 silent films from the teens and twenties; and the 40-title Ernst Collection, which includes some Krazy Kat cartoons.

Reference prints are available for most of these titles.

These motion pictures are filed by collection, with an entry for each title in the Special Collections card catalogue.

Catalogues

The following finding aids are located only in the Motion Pictures and Television Reading Room:

The Shelf List, although not 100% dependable, has an entry, by title, for each non-nitrate motion picture in the LC collection and is the best finding aid available. Entry cards may include release date, production company, director, a synopsis, credits and notes on the availability of a reference print, and pre-print materials.

The Television Holdings File is a card catalogue with entries by both series title and episode title for each TV production in the collection. The holdings are also indexed by "content descriptors," 41 categories of genre and subject descriptors. This file is a recent addition and greatly improves the access to TV holdings in the LC collection.

The Special Collections Card Catalogue is arranged by collection and has an entry for each motion picture in those collections.

The following card catalogues are "in progress" and therefore reflect only part of the LC collection. Nonetheless, they can be quite helpful for a researcher putting together a list of titles:

The Directors File is a card catalogue containing entries for about 2,000 directors of feature length films. It is arranged alphabetically by the name of the director. Each entry lists titles of films by that director which are in the LC collection.

The Silent Films Files index silent features, theatrical shorts, and non-theatrical shorts by title, date, and production company. The files are not complete.

The following published finding aids are available in many libraries:

Catalog of Copyright Entries (Washington, D.C.: Copyright Office, The Library of Congress, various dates), is a multi-volume cumulative catalogue of works in all media registered for copyright. The "Motion Picture" catalogue volumes are *1894-1912, 1912-1939, 1940-1949, 1950-1959, 1960-1969,* and semi-annual issues beginning in 1970. Works in these catalogues are arranged alphabetically by title. Each entry includes basic credits, copyright claimant, and copyright number. An index to each catalogue provides access by the names of the copyright claimant and others.

Since the largest part of the LC collection consists of copyright deposits, these catalogues can be helpful, but they contain no indication as to which titles were selected by the Library for its collection. Also, of course, they do not list those titles selected for the collection that were never registered for copyright. Nontheless, the catalogues can be useful in putting together a list of titles.

Library of Congress Catalogs—Film and Other Materials for Projection (Washington, D.C.: U.S. Library of Congress, various dates), is a multi-volume listing of items by title, beginning in 1948. The volumes provide cataloguing information for libraries and are produced by the Audiovisual Section of the Descriptive Catalog Division. The volumes do not describe the LC motion picture holdings *per se* although some titles are in the collection. The catalogue has been subject indexed since 1953 and thus is a valuable tool for locating titles of educational and documentary motion pictures.

Catalog of Holdings, The American Film Institute Collection and the United Artists Collection at the Library of Congress (Washington, D.C.: The American Film Institute, 1978), includes listings for 14,124 motion pictures by title and provides the production date, producer, an actor, and notes on the availability of a reference print and pre-print materials. Like any published description of a working collection, it was out-of-date before it was published, but it is a valuable and handy guide to a large part of the LC collection. It can be helpful in compiling a list of titles and as a reminder that there are no reference prints for many of the titles.

Motion Pictures from the Library of Congress Paper Print Collection, 1894-1912, by Kemp R. Niver, edited by Bebe Bergsten (Berkeley: University of California Press, 1967) describes the collection by type of motion picture, e.g., advertising, comedy, documentary. The index provides access to the collection by a few subjects and by title.

The *Quarterly Journal of the Library of Congress* has featured individual articles describing various parts of the LC collection of motion pictures.

Scheduled for publication by LC are three catalogues relating to specific collections: *The Theodore Roosevelt Memorial Association Catalog; The George Kleine Film Collection Catalog;* and *Television Programs in the Library of Congress: Programs Available for Research as of December 1979.*

Access

The collection is archival, does not circulate, and is not intended for projection.

Reservations for using the viewing facilities should be made in advance. A minimum of 24 hours notice is required for ordering motion pictures. Three feature-length films or the equivalent may be viewed each day. Usually there is a wait of a few weeks to use the viewing facilities, so reservations should be made well ahead.

Film analysis equipment is available. At the present time the viewing machines may only be used in real time, that is, they cannot be run in fast forward. This can add considerably to the amount of time that a researcher must spend viewing films.

The Shelf List does not contain information on the status of rights for each title. Those wishing to purchase copies must determine whether there are any copyright or donor restrictions. A further complication in purchasing copies of LC motion pictures is the lack of printing materials for some titles. Details on the costs for reproductions are available from the reference staff.

Other Materials

Copyright Descriptions. Within the Division are copyright descriptions for each motion picture registered for U.S. copyright since 1912. The material may include a synopsis, a continuity, a press book, or other descriptive materials. For a film registered for copyright between 1912 and 1942 this material may be the only source of information.

Non-film Card Catalog. This file contains information on non-motion picture materials within the Division. This catalogue is arranged by title of the related motion picture, and some entries list available stills, reviews, publicity materials, and other documentation.

Descriptions Files. Folders are arranged alphabetically by title and contain documentation in many forms and from many sources.

Office of War Information (OWI) Materials. During World War II thousands of films, primarily Hollywood feature films, were evaluated by the Office of War Information. The materials generated by this project are found in various places within the Division.

SOUND RECORDINGS

Eligibility

The collections are available for serious research. Those wishing to listen to recordings should make an appointment at least one week in advance.

Collection

One million sound recordings, both published and unpublished. The Armed Forces Radio Service broadcasts include domestic radio broadcasts and shows which the Service produced in Los Angeles with the help of many celebrities; German speeches and broadcasts, 1930-1945; *Arthur Godfrey Time* broadcasts from the 1950s and 1960s; McGregor Transcription Service recordings of plays recorded for broadcast, 1940-1977, including the Salvation Army's *Heartbreak Theater;* and 100,000 recordings from the Office of War Information, 1942-1945.

The *Original Amateur Hour* and *Meet the Press* collections include radio recordings and are described with the motion picture special collections above. Recordings of music and commentary from the Voice of America's music branch date from 1943. Recordings of National Public Radio programming are deposited regularly. Additional collections include Damrosch Family, Jessica Dragonet, General Foods, H. Voss Greenough, Wally Heider, Dr. A. F. R. Lawrence, NBC Radio, National Press Club, Wilfred Pelletier, Edward Rickenbacher, and the recordings of the newscaster Raymond Swing.

In 1979 the House of Representatives began to record its floor proceedings on audiotape and videotape and to transmit the signals live to television and radio systems across the U.S. The audiotapes become part of the LC collection after 30 days. For more information see Appendix I.

There are a number of sound recordings which are the spoken word but not radio broadcasts. These include the U.S. Marine Corps Combat Records, about 2,500 recordings, 1943-45, from Guam, Okinawa, Saipan, Iwo Jima, and other locations in the Pacific, consisting in part of interviews with men returning from combat and eyewitness accounts of battles.

Catalogue

Much of the collection consists of recordings of music, which are fully catalogued. The voice recordings, including radio recordings, are accessible but not catalogued. The best source of published information on radio materials in the Library collection is *A Guide to Special Collections in the Library of Congress* by Annette Melville, to be published in 1980. It describes in detail 20 of the significant radio collecticns.

Such finding aids as lists and card files are available, but it is best to consult the reference staff.

RELATED MATERIALS IN OTHER LC DIVISIONS

Prints and Photographs Division
Thomas Jefferson Building, Room 1051
(202) 287-6394

8:30 A.M.-5:00 P.M.   Monday-Friday

Jerry Kearns, Reference Librarian

Motion picture stills and publicity photos are generally held by the Motion Pictures, Broadcasting, and Recorded Sound Division. Prints and Photographs Division holdings include photographs of motion picture production, devices, and personalities, as well as a fine collection of movie posters, theater announcements, and a few movie stills.

For those interested in photographs in general, this is probably the largest and most comprehensive collection in the country. There are six million photoprints and five million original negatives, acquired primarily through gift and copyright deposits. The collection provides a pictorial record of American and world political, social, and cultural history from 1860 to the present. The history of photography, from the first daguerrotypes to contemporary portfolios, is found in the master photographs collection. Thirty-five hundred original images by noted photographers illustrate the technical and artistic development of the medium.

The fine print collection, 110,000 items, includes woodcuts, engravings, etchings, lithographs, and other print media by artists throughout the world. The holdings date back to the 15th Century. The more than 40,000 historical prints include lithographs, woodcuts, and other original prints of 18th and 19th century life in America and Europe. There are many political cartoons, advertisements, and sentimental pictures. Sixty-thousand American and foreign posters advertise motion pictures, theatrical performances, circuses, and art exhibitions. There are war, propaganda, travel, and art nouveau book and magazine posters, as well as groups of Austrian and German expressionistic posters, silk screen display posters produced by the Works Projects Administration, 1936-1941, and the work of contemporary poster artists.

The Division has the most comprehensive architectural archives in the United States. It includes the photographic records of the Historic American Buildings Survey, the Historic American Engineering Record, the Pictorial Archives of Early American Architecture, the Carnegie Survey of the Architecture of the South, and a fine collection of original architectural drawings.

The reference staff performs limited searches, and copies of non-restricted materials can be ordered. Researchers are invited to use the card catalogues in the Reading Room. Much of the collection is indexed by subject, photographer or creator, and collector. Shirley L. Green, a free-lance picture researcher familiar with the collection, has written *Pictorial Resources in the Washington, D.C. Area* (Washington, D.C.: Library of Congress, 1976), which describes in some detail this collection and those of many other government and private institutions. Ms. Green's excellent book is a necessary companion to this *Guide* for those interested in non-print research resources.

Manuscript Division
Manuscript Reading Room
Thomas Jefferson Building
(202) 287-5387

8:30 A.M.-5:00 P.M.   Monday-Friday

John Broderick, Chief
Ronald Wilkinson, Specialist in American Cultural History

The Manuscript Division has collections related to the history of motion pictures and television, including the papers of author James M. Cain, Huntington Cairns, Elmer Davis, Will Durant, Lillian Gish, Ruth Gordon, John Hays Hammond, Jr., William S. Hart, inventor Frederick E. Ives, Garson Kanin, film pioneer George Kleine, actor Arnold Moss, Vladimir Nabakov, Eric Sevareid, and Lawrence Spivak, and the records of the DuMont Laboratories. These collections are described in the *National Union Catalog of Manuscript Collections* (NUCMUC).

Other collections of interest but not included in NUCMUC, are the papers of actors Hume Cronyn and Jessica Tandy, 1934-1960, which include 23,800 items; Groucho Marx, 352 items; Clarence E. Mulford, 1904-1941, 16,000 items; Henry Pringle, 1944-1946, 14,000 items; May Robson, 1882-1942, 350 items; cinematographer Harold Sintzenich, 1912-1973, 61 items; Miriam Cooper Walsh, 1915-1974; Mae West, 1926-1928, scripts. Collections which have not yet been organized for reader use include the papers of Rod Serling, Vincent Price, and agent Lucy Kroll.

The Reading Room is open to researchers, with some restrictions. Finding aids for many of the collections describe the contents of the boxes and folders. It is possible to obtain most materials shortly after requesting them.

Collection

166 U.S. National Endowment for the Arts—Media Arts

Archives
2401 E Street, NW
Washington, D.C. 20506
(202) 634-6300

9:00 A.M.-5:30 P.M.   Monday-Friday

Maria Goodwin, Archives and Evaluation

Eligibility

Copies of films, videotapes, and audiotapes produced under grants are in the NEA archives but are not available for viewing. Viewing copies of productions from 1974 to the present are available at the Library of Congress (entry #165).

Collection

200 titles. Grants have been awarded for the production of films, videotapes, and radio programs since 1970. Copies of some of the early productions are on deposit in the NEA archives. Since 1974 all grantees have been required to deposit copies of their productions with the archives and the Library of Congress.

The productions treat film and video as art and include short documentaries, fiction shorts, and experimental films. Films and video about American art cover dance, music, drama, and crafts.

Catalogue

No catalogue is available, but specific questions will be answered by the Media Arts program staff.

Access

The collection is archival and cannot be viewed.

Other Materials

Grantees' final reports, a few scripts, and brief descriptions of the productions are available. Information on the holder of rights or the distributor is also available. Those wishing to use these files should call or write to make an appointment.

Collection

167 U.S. (Smithsonian) Anacostia Neighborhood Museum—Center for Anacostia Studies

Research Department
2500 Martin Luther King Jr. Avenue, SE
Washington, D.C.
   Mailing Address:
Washington, D.C. 20560
(202) 381-6635

9:00 A.M.-5:30 P.M.   Monday-Friday

Louise Daniel Hutchinson

Eligibility

Scholars may apply to use the collection.

Collection

Oral history collection of four videotapes and 100 audiotapes. The project, begun in 1972, recorded interviews with Anacostia residents whose recollections covered the period 1890-1935. The interviews have been transcribed, indexed, and supported with a documentation collection.

Catalogue

The collection is indexed and the book which was a result of the study, *The Anacostia Story* (Washington, D.C.: Smithsonian Institution Press, 1977), is available by mail.

Access

The collection does not circulate.
Viewing and listening facilities can be arranged.
For TV rights and purchase of copies, contact the Center.

Collection

168 U.S. (Smithsonian) Anacostia Neighborhood Museum—Education Department

2405 Martin Luther King Jr. Avenue, SE
Washington, D.C.

Mailing Address:
Washington, D.C. 20560
(202) 381-6731

10:00 A.M.-6:00 P.M.   Monday-Friday
1:00 P.M.-6:00 P.M.   Saturday, Sunday

Zora M. Felton, Director of Education

Eligibility

Open to the public.

Collection

10 titles. The collection consists of three films about Kwanza and seven television documentaries, including a *Reasoner Report,* and three other programs on the role of Blacks in the opening of the West.

Catalogue

A descriptive catalogue is available in the education office.

Access

> Borrowing is in person only.
> Advanced reservations should be made.
> A projector is available. Call to reserve.

Collection

169 U.S. (Smithsonian) Anacostia Neighborhood Museum—Outreach Program

2405 Martin Luther King Jr. Avenue, SE
Washington, D.C. 20020
(202) 381-6731

8:45 A.M.-5:15 P.M.   Monday-Friday

Education Office

Eligibility

> Open to the public.

Collection

> 150 titles. This collection of videotapes documents neighborhood events, museum programs, and events related to the history of the area. Individual subjects include crafts, drugs, African games, Williamsburg, dance.

Catalogue

> A descriptive list is in production and will be available by mail.

Access

> The collection does not circulate.
> Reservations should be made to view the material.
> Video analysis equipment is available.
> For information on purchase of copies, call the Museum.

Collection

170 U.S. (Smithsonian) Archives of American Art

National Portrait Gallery
8th and F Streets, NW
Washington, D.C.

Mailing Address:
Washington, D.C. 20560
(202) 381-6174

8:45 A.M.-5:15 P.M.   Monday-Friday

Arthur Breton, Manuscripts
Nancy Zembala, Manuscripts

Eligibility

The motion pictures and videotapes are archival copies; there are no viewing prints. The rest of the collection is available to scholars. Much of the collection is on microfilm and available at regional centers in New York, Boston, Detroit, and San Francisco.

Collection

30 items. These films and one videotape are part of manuscript collections from American artists. They cannot be viewed at this time and have been described by the Curator as ". . . home movies from artists, with a few of professional quality."

Other Materials

The thousands of photographs available for study are primarily photographs of paintings and sculpture, but portrait photographs of artists and the work of a few artist/photographers are also included.

Referral Service

171 U.S. (Smithsonian) Hirshhorn Museum

8th Street and Independence Avenue, SW
Washington, D.C. 20560
(202) 381-6771

8:45 A.M.-5:15 P.M.   Monday-Friday

Barbara Coleson, Film Programmer

Eligibility

Open to scholars.

Referral Aids

Ms. Coleson plans the Hirshhorn film series and is willing to share her collection of catalogues of art film and video with scholars.

Program

See Appendix IV for details on the Hirshhorn film events.

Collection

172 U.S. (Smithsonian) Museum of History and Technology

12th Street and Constitution Avenue, NW
Washington, D.C. 20560

8:45 A.M.-5:15 P.M.   Monday-Friday (for researchers)

Access

The following information applies to all collections within the Museum of History and Technology. Details are found under the listings of the individual divisions.

Materials do not circulate.

Advanced reservations should be made to view the materials not on display in the Museum.

There are no viewing facilities in the individual divisions but arrangements might be made for researchers to view film and videotape in the production facilities.

Duplication and TV rights vary item by item. Most of the film and video held by the Smithsonian is for research purposes only. In some cases information about copyright holders can be provided.

Note: The alphabetical designations applied to each Division have been created solely for indexing this *Guide* and do not reflect any Museum of History and Technology system.

DEPARTMENT OF CULTURAL HISTORY

A. DIVISION OF COMMUNITY LIFE
(202) 381-6133/5652

Richard Ahlborn—Ethnic and regional studies
Carl Scheele—Popular culture

Eligibility

Scholars may request to use the collections.

Collection

6 titles. Composite films have been put together for exhibits on entertainment and sports. Individual items cover ironwork, baskets, Protestant revivals, and news broadcasts by satellite.

Other Materials

There are a collection of over 2,000 phonograph records of American popular music and a photograph collection which includes thousands of stills on the history of labor, entertainment, education, and sports.

B. DIVISION OF GRAPHIC ARTS
(202) 381-6297
Elizabeth Harris, Curator

Eligibility

The film collection is currently inaccessible. The videotapes are part of the permanent display in the Museum.

Collection

300 titles. A very small collection of clips from television news programs is shown on TV sets in the Museum. The film collection consists of half-hour travelogues produced during the 1950s and early 1960s by enterprising filmmakers who traveled around the world getting foreign governments to finance films which were then offered free to American distributors. Most of these are 35mm.

Catalogue

> There is a list of the travelogues. The prints are uncatalogued and in storage outside the Museum.

DEPARTMENT OF NATIONAL HISTORY

C. DIVISION OF POLITICAL HISTORY
(202) 381-5532

Margaret Klapthor—White House, First Ladies
Herbert Collins—Presidents, political campaigns
Edith Mayo, Assistant Curator

Eligibility

> Scholars may request to use the collections.

Collection

> 100 titles. Most of the materials are presidential campaign media. The largest collection includes 57 videotapes from the campaign of Jimmy Carter, produced by the Rafshoon Agency. Other campaign materials include scattered commercials, video documents of events, and televised debates from campaigns from the early 1960s to the present. There are also a few composite documentaries produced for television using the collections of this division of the Smithsonian. A group of records of campaign music going back to the campaign of Thomas Jefferson was produced by the Westinghouse Broadcasting Corporation.

Catalogue

> Film and videotape titles are filed in the Campaign Subject File located in the Division.

Other Materials

> Audio recordings include speeches by candidates that go back to 1895. Many are inaccessible because there are limited playback facilities in the Division.
> The Division holds an outstanding collection of campaign materials—buttons, posters, newspapers, photographs.

DEPARTMENT OF HISTORY OF SCIENCE

D. DIVISION OF ELECTRICITY AND MODERN PHYSICS
(202) 381-4067

Bernard Finn, Curator
Elliot Sivowitch, Museum Specialist (Radio)

Eligibility

> Scholars may request to use the collection.

Collection

45 titles. The collection is primarily about the technical aspects of broad-casting, telephone, telegraph, and wire photos. Six films dealing with television are from the Allen DuMont collection and include commercials from 1953 and a 1954 lecture on the potential of color television.

Catalogue

There are rough indexes to the collections.

Other Materials

The large George Clark (RCA Radio Historian) Collection focuses on the technical history of radio.

The Allen DuMont Collection, which deals with TV technology and the DuMont network, includes 50 to 100 stills from TV commercials of the mid-1940s.

E. DIVISION OF EXTRACTIVE INDUSTRIES
(202) 381-5582/6215

John Hoffman, Curator
Terry Sharrer, Assistant Curator

Eligibility

The collection is open to scholars.

Collection

330 titles. Over 300 of the films are the *Industry on Parade* series which was shown on television during the 1950s and 1960s. Others are technical and deal with petroleum, coal, and agriculture.

Catalogue

A title list for the TV series and a guide to the Warshaw Collection described below are available.

Other Materials

A large collection of stills covers all phases of the food industry. The Warshaw Collection is of American product advertising and labels from the turn of the century.

F. DIVISION OF PHOTOGRAPHY
(202) 381-5295

Eugene Ostroff, Curator
David Haberstich, Assistant Curator

Eligibility

The collection is open to scholars.

Collection

> 25 titles. The small collection includes seven William S. Hart westerns, *Birth of a Nation* and some Chaplin shorts. These films can be viewed at the Library of Congress.

Catalogue

> There are card catalogues for the films, hardware, and the still photographs.

Other Materials

> The division has a major collection of motion picture and still hardware. It includes the original Biograph camera and projector. The small collection of posters and memorabilia from the silent era includes the boots and gun of William S. Hart, an uncatalogued collection of several thousand movie posters from the 1940s and 1950s, and over one million photographs.

Collection

173 (Smithsonian) National Air and Space Museum

Room 3100
6th Street and Independence Avenue, SW
Washington, D.C. 20560
(202) 381-6591

8:45 A.M.-5:15 P.M.   Monday-Friday

Catherine Scott, Librarian
Dick Crawford, Film Reviewer

Eligibility

> Scholars and researchers may apply to view the collection.

Collection

> 2,000 reels of film. The aeronautics collections of historical films have been donated by government agencies, aerospace manufacturers, trade and professional associations, and individuals. The astronautics and astronomy collection consists primarily of films produced by the National Aeronautics and Space Administration (NASA).
>
> The collection is documentary with the exception of an episode from "Star Trek" and *The Spirit of St. Louis* (1957). Many of the films are from the 1920s and 1930s. There are films of early rocketry in the U.S. and Germany, and one early film which shows pre-1903 flying machines.

Catalogue

> In progress is a computerized listing of the collection indexed by title (abstract and key word descriptors), producer, running time and date.

Access

The materials do not circulate.

Questions regarding the content of the collection, permission to view the films and viewing facilities will be answered by phone or by mail.

This is not a stock film library or a distribution service. Those interested in TV rights or purchase of copies should contact the National Archives and Records Service (entries #155, 156, 157) and the Department of Defense stock film libraries (entries #148, 149, 150, 151, 152, 153).

Other Materials

The museum library has a collection of over 800 audiotapes and a few videotapes which includes oral history tapes of personalities in aerospace history, speeches of notable persons in the field, and sounds of aircraft and rockets. The collection is being catalogued and its use is restricted to scholars and researchers.

Collection

174 U.S. (Smithsonian) National Anthropological Film Center

L'Enfant Plaza, Room 3210
Washington, D.C.
  Mailing Address:
Washington, D.C. 20560
(202) 381-6537

9:00 A.M.-5:00 P.M. Monday-Friday

E. Richard Sorenson, Director

The name of the Center may be changing soon to better describe the multidisciplinary purposes it is meant to serve. Scholars in many fields are taking advantage of the potential of the visual media to explore and reveal the range of human qualities and behavior. The Center is collecting older films and research projects with emphasis on recording the human activity in vanishing and changing ways of life and culture.

While the greatest resources are being devoted to adding to the collection of visual data, the Center is working in several ways to eventually make these materials accessible through a system designed for research. The Center is also preparing a National Union Catalogue which will include ethnographic films and other materials chosen for their research value in the humanities and sciences. A tentative title is "National Union Catalogue of Visual Data on the Human Condition."

To date the Center has developed visual data resources in Afganistan, Paqua-New Guinea, Western Tibet, Nepal, Micronesia, the Cook Islands, the New Hebrides, Brazil and Mexico. Reprints of articles about the Center and its activities are available by mail.

Referral Service

175 U.S. (Smithsonian) National Collection of Fine Arts

Library
9th and G Streets, NW

Mailing Address:
Washington, D.C. 20560
(202) 381-5118

10:00 A.M.-5:00 P.M.   Monday-Friday

William Walker, Librarian

Eligibility

Open to graduate students and serious adult researchers.

Referral Aids

The library collection focuses on American art and has some materials on video art and artists.

Other Materials

The National Collection has a large catalogued collection of slides and photographs of American art and artists.

Collection

176 U.S. (Smithsonian) National Gallery of Art

Extension Programs
6th Street and Constitution Avenue, NW
Washington, D.C. 20565
(202) 737-4215

9:00 A.M.-5:30 P.M.   Monday-Friday

Laura Schneider, Curator, Extension Program

Eligibility

The film collection and slide programs are available to the public.

Collection

26 titles. The films explore the history of art, focusing on the collection held by the National Gallery and those loaned to the Gallery for exhibitions. Individual titles and topics include Leonardo, American painting, *On Loan from Russia: Forty-One French Masterpieces*, and *The Eye of Thomas Jefferson.*

Catalogue

A descriptive catalogue is available by mail.

Access

> Borrowing is by mail and in person.
> To borrow films by mail it is recommended that the request be sent three months in advance. Borrowing of films in person for a one-day period, can be arranged by calling the day before to check on whether the film is available.
> There are no viewing facilities.
> For information on TV rights and purchase of copies, contact the Office of the General Counsel, National Gallery of Art.

Other Materials

> The library, which is open 10:00 A.M.-4:30 P.M., Tuesday-Friday, may be used by graduate students and adult researchers. Its holdings include a slide library, a photographic archive, and the Index of American Design.

Collection

177 U.S. (Smithsonian) National Zoological Park

Education Office
3000 block Connecticut Avenue, NW
Washington, D.C. 20008
(202) 381-7235

8:45 A.M.-5:15 P.M.   Monday-Friday

Judith King, Program.Assistant

Eligibility

> The current collection is available to other zoos and to scholars. The archival collection is not currently available.

Collection

> 5 current titles; 40 archival titles. General audience films on events at the zoo and a research film on the Uganda Kob make up the current collection. Archival films include records of trips to capture animals by Dr. William Mann (zoo director, 1925-1955), panda films, and TV programs from NBC and WTTG.

Catalogue

> There is no printed catalogue but Ms. King will provide information about the collections by phone or by mail.

Access

> Zoos may borrow the current collection by mail.
> Scholars should contact the Education Office to request to view the current collection at the zoo.
> A projector is available.

For information on TV rights and purchase of copies, contact the Education Office.

Collection

178 U.S. (Smithsonian) Office of Museum Programs

2235 Arts & Industries Building
900 Jefferson Drive, SW
Washington, D.C. 20560
(202) 381-6551

8:45 A.M.-5:15 P.M.   Monday-Friday

Mary Nugent, Conservation Program

Eligibility

The collection is loaned to museums and shown periodically at the Smithsonian. There is a small fee.

Collection

86 titles: conservation. Eighty of the videotapes are illustrated lectures by Robert Organ, Chief of the Conservation-Analytical Lab at the Smithsonian. The other titles also deal with the handling of museum objects.

Catalogue

A descriptive catalogue is available by mail.

Access

Borrowing is by mail and in person.
    Advanced reservations are required.
    Viewing facilities might be arranged for scholars.
    For information on TV rights and purchase of copies, contact the Conservation Program.

Collection

179 U.S. (Smithsonian) Office of Telecommunications

2410 Arts & Industries Building
900 Jefferson Drive, SW
Washington, D.C. 20560
(202) 381-6414

8:45 A.M.-5:15 P.M.   Monday-Friday

Nazaret Cherkezian, Director

Eligibility

The collection is for in-house use.

Collection

40 titles. Many of the films are about the Smithsonian, including one Eames film, and several CBS and NBC documentaries. Others feature the museums' collections and activities. More specialized subjects include an enthnographic film about the Himba, films on meteorites, and one on the multiple mirror telescope.

Catalogue

Descriptive lists of the films are available for in-house use.

Referral Service

180 U.S. (Smithsonian) Renwick Gallery

17th Street and Pennsylvania Avenue, NW
Washington, D.C.
  Mailing Address:
Washington, D.C. 20560
(202) 381-5811

9:30 A.M.-5:00 P.M.   Monday-Friday

Kitty Coiner, Film Consultant
Allen Bassing, Education

Eligibility

Scholars may use the reference materials.

Referral Aids

The large collection of catalogues covers both art films and documentaries on art, crafts, and design.

Other Materials

Prints of a few films used in past exhibits at the gallery are in the staff offices.

Note: See Appendix IV for information on the Creative Screen Film Series.

Collections

181 U.S. State Department

Bureau of Public Affairs
21st and C Streets, NW
Washington, D.C. 20520
(202) 632-2353

Elaine McDevitt, Chief, Special Programs Staff

Information about films and video within the Department of State is available from the Bureau of Public Affairs. Three specialized collections are described below.

FOREIGN SERVICE INSTITUTE
Audiovisual Collections, Room 212
1400 Key Boulevard
Arlington, Virginia 22209
(703) 235-8721

The Foreign Service Institute (FSI) offers training for State Department employees and others. Its audiovisual collections include about 60 films and over 150 videotapes. There are a few technical titles about consular affairs but the majority of the collection explores different countries and regions of the world.

The collection is for in-house use but scholars may contact FSI and ask to view materials in the FSI screening facilities.

AGENCY FOR INTERNATIONAL DEVELOPMENT
Office of Public Affairs
21st Street and Virginia Avenue, NW
Washington, D.C. 20523
(202) 632-9309

Kay Chernush

The Agency for International Development (AID) has produced only one film recently. All others have been retired to the National Archives and Record Service (entry #155). A small training collection is for in-house use.

OFFICE OF POPULATION
Information and Education Division
1621 N. Kent Street
Arlington, Virginia
  Mailing Address:
AID, Washington, D.C. 20523
(703) 235-8081

Marshall Roth, Public Information Officer

This office maintains a small collection of films on family planning methods and information on a larger collection of AID films on population and family planning. Most of these films are in Spanish. There is also information on films on population from sources outside of AID.

Colection

182 U.S. (Transportation) Coast Guard

Boating Education Reference Film Library
Room 4302
2nd and V Streets, SW
  Mailing Address:
G-BAE-4
Washington, D.C. 20590
(202) 426-1077

7:30 A.M.-3:30 P.M. Monday-Friday

Eligibility

Open to the public.

Collection

51 titles. Boating and water safety are the focus of this collection. There are six films on the work of the Coast Guard, water safety films by the Red Cross, and a number of sponsored films which combine boating safety messages with spectacular boating scenes.

Catalogue

A descriptive catalogue is available by mail.

Access

Borrowing is by mail and in person.
Reservations are not necessary.
A projector is available. Call ahead to make arrangements to view films at the library.
The catalogue has information on TV rights.

Referral Service

183 U.S. (Transportation) Federal Aviation Administration

Public Affairs
800 Independence Avenue, SW
Washington, D.C. 20591
(202) 426-3895

Sue Silverman, Chief, Plans and Audiovisual Division

The Federal Aviation Administration (FAA) film collection is primarily geared to the aviation community. There are, however, a number of films which have been produced for a more general audience. All films are available for free loan through:

FAA Film Service
5000 Park Street N.
St. Petersburg, Florida 33709

This collection was formerly located in Oklahoma City, Oklahoma.
The FAA collection is available for purchase from the National Audiovisual Center (entry #156).

Collection

184 U.S. (Transportation) Federal Highway Administration

Publications and Visual Aids Branch
Room 6419, 400 7th Street, SW
Washington, D.C. 20590
(202) 426-0835

7:45 A.M.-4:15 P.M.   Monday-Friday

George Hay, Motion Picture Producer and Director

Eligibility

Educational institutions, organizations, and government agencies may borrow the films free. The public should contact the National Highway Institute (entry #185). Scholars may request to view the collection in the Branch.

Collection

185 titles. Twenty-five of the titles are available for loan, although only about ten are of general interest. There are films on how to drive in winter conditions and the history of highways, but the majority of the films are on technical subjects for engineers and road builders. The collection includes both in-house productions and acquired motion pictures.

Catalogue

A descriptive list of the 25 loan films is available by mail. The other 160 films are listed in a file in the Branch.

Access

Borrowing is by mail and in person.
  Reservations to borrow films or to view them in the Branch should be made in advance.
  A projector is available.
  Films may be purchased from the National Audiovisual Center (entry #156).

Collection

185 U.S. (Transportation) Federal Highway Administration National Highway Institute

Film Library
Room 6404
400 7th Street, SW
Washington, D.C. 20590
(202) 426-9143

7:45 A.M.-4:15 P.M.   Monday-Friday

Robert Cox, Training Assistant

Eligibility

The FHWA distributes a free loan collection of films and videotapes to institutions and groups. Many of the titles are available to the public through the National Audiovisual Center (entry #156). Scholars may request to view the collection at the Institute.

Collection

> 180 titles: transportation, engineering. This primarily technical collection does include a few films of general interest. There are films on the history of highways, the Inter-American Highway, safe driving, and car pooling. Many of the films are FHWA productions, but the majority have been acquired from outside sources.

Catalogue

> Monthly bulletins providing the latest film and video titles are available by mail to groups and institutions.

Access

> Borrowing is by mail.
> Reservations should be made in advance.
> There are projectors and video analysis equipment at the Institute. Scholars should make reservations to use these facilities.
> For information on TV rights and purchase contact the National Audiovisual Center (entry #156).

Referral Aids

> Twice each year the film library issues a bulletin which lists films and other audiovisual materials on highways and transportation available from sources other than the Institute.

Collection

186 U.S. Veterans Administration Central Office Film Library

801 Vermont Avenue, NW
Washington, D.C. 20420
(202) 389-2780

8:30 A.M.-4:30 P.M.   Monday-Friday

Dorsey Jackson, Chief Librarian

Eligibility

> Open to the public for viewing in the library screening room. Many films have restrictions on borrowing.

Collection

> 700 titles. The great majority of the films are specialized medical and dental films. There are also about 60 chaplain films produced in the 1950s and early 1960s and acquired by the Veterans Administration (VA). Individual films of interest include a group of drug and alcohol abuse films, a 1947 film on grief in infancy, a 1958 KOED-TV documentary titled *Sick Minds & Crime,* a 1949 American Legion film about the lack of jobs for veterans entitled *No Help Wanted,* a 1970 VA film about Bataan and Corregidor *The Flame and the Sea* and the 1963 CBS documentary *Age of Anxiety.*

Catalogue

A descriptive catalogue is available from the Superintndent of Documents, U.S. Government Printing Office, Washington, D.C. 20420 for about $3.00. The title is *VA Film Catalogue* and the stock number is 051-000-00111-7.

Access

Borrowing is by mail and in person. Regular borrowers should get copies of the VA form for ordering films.

Reservations for borrowing films by mail should be made one month in advance. One-day loans are possible on short notice.

A preview room large enough for six people is available and can be reserved by calling the library.

VA-produced films may be duplicated in some cases. Contact the film library. VA films may be purchased from the National Audiovisual Center (entry #156).

APPENDIXES

Appendix I. Television Stations, Services, Broadcasts

The Washington area television stations have large libraries of entertainment films and their news departments have hours of news film and tape. Although the stations are not in business to serve scholars and researchers, staff members in each of them expressed a willingness to be of assistance. This appendix describes the holdings and policies of the respective stations and provides information on the Radio and TV Monitoring Service and the U.S. House of Representatives' recordings of its floor proceedings. Those interested in television news are also referred to the Television News Study Service at George Washington University (entry #94).

TELEVISION STATIONS, GENERAL INFORMATION

LIBRARIES OF ENTERTAINMENT FILMS

In general scholars and others interested in the non-profit use of films may request to view titles in the film libraries. It should be understood that the exact holdings change day by day since the titles are leased by the stations for a limited period of time, and that many titles remain at the station for only a few days. Most stations do have a core collection of prints which remain at the station for a number of years. There are no printed catalogues although the librarian can determine if an individual title is in the library.

Requests to view films should specify titles and include a description of the research being undertaken. The station may ask the researcher to first contact the owner for permission to view a film. There may be a fee if an equipment operator is required. All films must be viewed at the station. In all cases, the station's work is the first priority of the limited staff.

The film libraries generally include feature films, cartoon packages, and syndicated series. Scholars should specify the titles of the films, episodes, or cartoons they wish to view.

NEWS FILM AND TAPE

Scholars and others interested in the non-profit use of film and videotape may request to view materials in the news archives. Each request should include a description of the relevant research project and specific subjects and dates of the footage. A station may have recordings of its news programs but in most cases only the film and video inserts are kept. The outtakes at all stations are quickly disposed of. Finding aids vary greatly from station to station.

Little is predictable about a news department's schedule or ability to serve scholars. There may be a fee if technical personnel are needed to show the material.

Scholars interested in TV news should first explore the facilities and services of the George Washington University Television News Study Service (entry #94), which can provide information on scholarly resources of TV news broadcasts and helpful advice on approaching the local stations and the networks.

Although it may be too expensive for scholarly research, the Radio and TV Monitoring Service can provide dubs of television and radio news and news specials. Videotapes of all network and local news on six local channels and audiotapes of all radio broadcasts on six local radio stations are available for a number of weeks after broadcast. Written transcripts are also available. This service is for information purposes only, not for commercial use. For fees and more information contact Radio and TV Monitoring Service, Inc., 3408 Wisconsin Avenue, NW, Washington, D.C. 20016. (202) 244-1901.

WASHINGTON AREA TELEVISION STATIONS

Channel 4   WRC   (NBC affiliate)
4001 Nebraska Avenue, NW
Washington, D.C. 20016
Information: (202) 686-4000
Film Library: (202) 686-4493
News Department: (202) 686-4111

Channel 5   WTTG   (Metromedia)
5151 Wisconsin Avenue, NW
Washington, D.C. 20016
Information: (202) 244-5151
Film Library: Ext. 481
Legal Department: Ext. 412
For requests to view materials in the news archives, contact Preston Paddon of the Legal Department.

Channel 7   WJLA   (ABC affiliate)
4461 Connecticut Avenue, NW
Washington, D.C. 20008
Information: (202) 686-3000
Film Library: (202) 686-3239   Sandy Reedy
Film and Tape: (202) 686-3170   Dave Gross

Channel 9   WDVM   (CBS affiliate)
4001 Brandywine Street, NW
Washington, D.C. 20016
Information: (202) 686-6000
Programming (Film): (202) 686-6130
News: (202) 686-6026

Channel 20   WDCA
5202 River Road
Bethesda, Maryland 20016
Information: (301) 654-2600
Ask for the Programming Department for films.
There is no news department.

Channel 26 WETA (public television)
3620 S. 27th Street
Arlington, Virginia
Information: (703) 998-2600
Mail: Box 2626, Washington, D.C. 20013
Film Library: (703) 998-2671
News Department: (703) 998-2830
Inquiries should be first made to the PBS Archive (entry #131) since most materials from WETA are transferred to the Archive.

PROCEEDINGS OF THE U.S. HOUSE OF REPRESENTATIVES

The House of Representatives records its procedings on videotape and audiotape and transmits the signal live via satellite to television stations and cable systems throughout the U.S. The recordings are limited to the images and voices of speakers at the podiums on the floor of the House. The transmissions can be viewed in the press gallery.

Copies of the videotapes are kept for 60 days and then erased. Duplicate color copies can be purchased. Copies of the audiotapes are kept for 30 days and then sent to the Library of Congress (entry #165) for its permanent collection. Duplicates of the audiotapes may be purchased. For more information contact the Clerk of the House of Representatives, Washington, D.C. 20515. (202) 225-7000. Ask for Bill Hartnett.

Appendix II. Public School System Media Collections

School systems have collections of 16mm films and videotapes for use in their classrooms. Many are instructional, produced to teach a specific part of a curriculum, but many others are within the broader category of "educational" and include filmed plays, animations, and documentaries originally produced for television. Often these educational materials are also found in the large public library film collections but many are located only in the school system collections.

None of the following collections was intended to serve those outside of the school systems, but each administrator offered some assistance to scholars. Please note the restrictions on each collection.

ALEXANDRIA PUBLIC SCHOOLS

> Educational Media Center
> 1207 Madison Street
> Alexandria, Virginia 22314
> (703) 548-2294 (Film Library)
> (703) 548-3971 (Dale Brown)
>
> Dale Brown, Library and Media Services
>
> Scholars may view materials at the Center by appointment. Under special circumstances materials will be loaned to scholars.
>
> 1,800 titles. Films and a few videotapes. A descriptive catalogue is available and may be used at the Center and at city schools.

ARLINGTON COUNTY PUBLIC SCHOOLS

> Teaching Materials Center
> 1426 North Quincy Street
> Arlington, Virginia 22207
> (703) 558-2306
>
> Richard Kubalak, Supervisor
>
> Residents of Arlington County may view films at the Center by appointment.

4,000 titles. Films and a few videotapes which include both in-house productions and instructional broadcasts. A card catalogue is available at the Center.

DISTRICT OF COLUMBIA PUBLIC SCHOOLS

Educational Media Center
1709 3rd Street, NE
Washington, D.C. 20002
(202) 576-6315 (Film Library)
(202) 576-6317 (Harry Burke)

Harry S. Burke, Supervising Director

Scholars may preview films at the Center by appointment. Short-term loans are possible for institutions and graduate students with memos from the directors of their programs.

2,500 titles. A descriptive catalogue is available.

FAIRFAX COUNTY PUBLIC SCHOOLS

James Lee Media Center
2855 Annandale Road
Falls Church, Virginia 22042
(703) 536-2600

Bob Summers, Supervisor of Media Services

Residents of Fairfax County may view materials at the Center by appointment.

3,000 titles. Film and videotape, purchased and in-house produced titles. A descriptive catalogue is available and may be used at the Center and at county schools.

MONTGOMERY COUNTY PUBLIC SCHOOLS

Film Library
850 Stone Street
Rockville, Maryland 20850
(301) 279-3101

Sara Poling, Film Supervisor

Scholars may view the collection at the Library by appointment.

7,000 titles. Purchased film and videotape, a few in-house video productions. A descriptive catalogue is available and may be used at the Center and at county schools.

PRINCE GEORGE'S COUNTY PUBLIC SCHOOLS

Palmer Park Services Center
Audiovisual Services
8437 Landover Road
Landover, Maryland 20785
(301) 777-9790

Doris Turman, Preview Librarian

Scholars may view materials at the Center by appointment.

4,900 titles. Films and a few videotapes which include both in-house productions and instructional broadcasts. A descriptive catalogue is available and may be used at the Center and at county schools.

Appendix III.   Other Film and Video Collections in the U.S.

Many scholars expect all embassy and government collections to be housed in Washington, but in fact several large libraries are at other locations. This appendix lists and briefly describes large embassy collections, government libraries, and major archives of films and video located outside the Washington area. Very small collections or those duplicated in Washington are not included. The list of film and television archives is limited to ten major collections.

EMBASSY COLLECTIONS

AUSTRALIA

> Australia Information Service
> Australia Consulate General
> 636 Fifth Avenue
> New York, N.Y. 10020
> (212) 245-4000
> Over 200 titles. Rental fee.

AUSTRIA

> Austrian Institute
> Attention: Film Librarian
> 11 East 52nd Street
> New York, N.Y. 10022
> (212) 759-5165
> 19 feature films; 70 documentary shorts.

BULGARIA

> Bulgarian Tourist Office
> 50 East 42nd Street, Suite 1508
> New York, N.Y. 10017

DENMARK

> Royal Danish Consulate General
> Danish Information Service
> 280 Park Avenue
> New York, N.Y. 10017
> (212) 697-5107
> 59 titles.

FINLAND

> Films from Finland
> Films of the Nations
> 7820 20th Avenue
> Brooklyn, N.Y. 11214
> (212) 331-1045
> 33 documentaries. Emphasis on arts and architecture.

FRANCE

> F.A.S.C.E.A.
> Ambassade de France
> 972 Fifth Avenue
> New York, N.Y. 10021
> Large film library.

GREAT BRITAIN

> Fourteen different American distributors handle British classic documentaries, travel films, documentaries and theatrical films. For a list write:
> Embassy of Great Britain
> 3100 Massachusetts Avenue, NW
> Washington, D.C. 20008
> (202) 462-1340

GREECE

> A.C. & R. Public Relations, Inc.
> 437 Madison Avenue
> New York, N.Y. 10022
> (212) 758-5780
> 18 titles.

ITALY

> Instituto Italiano Di Cultura
> 686 Park Avenue
> New York, N.Y. 10021
> 360 documentaries and short films; 17 features on videotape, 12 interviews with filmmakers.

SRI LANKA

> Tribune Films, Inc.
> 38 West 32nd Street
> New York, N.Y. 10001
> 11 titles.

SWEDEN

> Audience Planners, Inc.
> One Rockefeller Plaza
> New York, N.Y. 10020
> (212) 489-7789
> 17 titles.

Yugoslav Press and Cultural Center
488 Madison Avenue
New York, N.Y. 10022
(212) 838-2306
Large collection.

U.S. GOVERNMENT LIBRARIES

DEFENSE DEPARTMFNT

Air Force Film Depository
C. M. Schlofner, Chief of Depository
Norton Air Force Base
Norton, California 92409
(714) 382-2513
Stock footage; completed Air Force productions.

Army Audiovisual Depository and Records Center
Thomas M. Sheridan, Chief
U.S. Army Training Support Center
Training Materiel Support Detachment, ATTN: ATTSC-TP-TM
Tobyhanna, Pennsylvania 18466
(717) 894-8301, Ext. 7945
35,000 cans of documentary footage; 12,000 training film titles on
film and videotape.

Navy Film Lending Library
Commanding Officer, Naval Education and Training Support Center
(Atlantic)
Building W313, Fleet Branch
Norfolk, Virginia 23511
(804) 444-3013
Completed Navy productions.

Navy Film Lending Library
Commanding Officer, Naval Education and Training Support Center
(Pacific)
San Diego, California 92132
(714) 235-3877
Completed Navy productions.

ENERGY DEPARTMENT

Department of Energy
Oak Ridge Operations Office, Willie Clark, Film Librarian
P.O. Box 62
Oak Ridge, Tennessee 37830
(615) 483-8611, Ext. 3-4161
Films formerly in the film library of the Atomic Energy Commission.

HEALTH, EDUCATION AND WELFARE DEPARTMENT

This collection of both educational and entertainment films is located

at the University of Indiana but all reservations and applications are handled by:
Captioned Films for the Deaf Distribution Center
5034 Wisconsin Avenue, NW
Washington, D.C. 20016
(202) 363-1308
The captioning and distribution of hundreds of films is a program of the Bureau of Education for the Handicapped, Office of Education, Washington, D.C. 20202.

National Medical Audiovisual Center
1600 Clifton Road, NE
Atlanta, Georgia 31333
(404) 633-3351 (switchboard)
This distribution center for audiovisual products is part of the National Institutes of Health. Many of the titles are also in the Library of Medicine (entry #159).

INTERIOR DEPARTMENT

Bureau of Indian Affairs
Don Morrow, Chief
Division of Educational Audiovisual Services
Box 450
Brigham City, Utah 84302
(801) 723-4321
7,000 titles, a majority of which are for classroom use by schools run by the Bureau. There are a number of anthropological films and others produced or acquired by BIA. A few titles are available to Washington area scholars and schools from the BIA Office of Information, Room 4071, 18th and C Streets, NW, Washington, D.C. 20245. (202) 343-7445. Ask for Tanna Chappin.

LABOR DEPARTMENT

Mining Enforcement and Health Administration
Audiovisual Services
4800 Forbes Avenue
Pittsburgh, Pennsylvania 15213
(412) 621-4500
A large collection on mine safety. Many made in cooperation with the mining industry.

MAJOR FILM AND TELEVISION ARCHIVES IN THE U.S.

The ten archives described below have major collections of motion pictures, television productions, television news, and video art. All collections are for scholarly research. The list includes neither the large and important Canadian collections nor other archives outside of the U.S.

Academy of Television Arts and Sciences—UCLA Television Library
Department of Theater Arts
University of California at Los Angeles
Los Angeles, California 90024
(213) 825-4480

Robert Rosen, Director

11,000 television programs of all kinds. Open to scholars. Catalogue available.

Anthology Film Archives
80 Wooster Street
New York, New York 10012
(212) 226-0010

Jonas Mekas, Director

300 titles in repertory program; 750 titles in study collection; 200 video-tapes. Emphasis on American avant-garde and independent filmmakers. Scholarly use of collections by appointment. Card catalogue of holdings.

George Foster Peabody Collection
School of Journalism and Mass Communication
University of Georgia
Athens, Georgia 30602
(404) 542-3785

Worth McDougald, Director

5,000 television programs. An accumulation of entries to the annual competition for the Peabody Awards for Distinguished Broadcasting since 1940. Equivalent radio collection. Scholars may apply to use the collection.

International Museum of Photography at George Eastman House
Department of Film
900 East Avenue
Rochester, New York 14607
(716) 271-3361

John B. Kuiper, Director

7,000 items including feature films and shorts. Television from the mid-1950s: *Kraft Theater, Hallmark Hall of Fame,* Edward R. Murrow's programs. Descriptive catalogue available. Facilities open to scholars.

Museum of Broadcasting
1 East 53rd Street
New York, New York 10022
(212) 752-4690

Robert Saudek, President

1,500 television programs back to the 1940s. 2,000 hours added each year from both network and public television. Printed catalogue available. Open to the public for a fee. Radio back to the 1920s.

Museum of Modern Art
Department of Film

11 West 53rd Street
New York, New York 10019
(212) 956-4212

Charles Silver, Supervisor of the Film Study Center
Bob Summers, Circulation

8,000 titles including features, documentaries, personal and independent films; some television, newsreels, and video art. Collection is international and spans the history of film. Scholars may view the collection. There is a small service fee.
   The Museum also has a circulating collection. A catalogue is available.

Pacific Film Archive
University Art Museaum
Berkeley, California 94720
(415) 642-1412

Linda Provinzano

4,000 titles including Japanese and Soviet silent features; avant-garde films; contemporary animated films. Open and free to anyone with a need to study film.

UCLA Film Archive
Melnitz Hall, Room 1438
Department of Theater Arts, University of California-Los Angeles
Los Angeles, California 90024
(213) 825-4142

Robert Rosen, Director

7,000 titles, mostly American feature films. Open to scholars by appointment. There is a card catalogue.

Vanderbilt Television News Archive (See entry #97.)
Joint University Libraries
Vanderbilt University
Nashville, Tennessee 37203
(615) 322-2927

James F. Pilkington, Administrator

6,000 hours of television broadcasts including 4,500 evening newscasts. Open to the public. There is a fee for viewing the collection. Dubbing services are available by mail. They publish the *Television News Index and Abstracts.*

Wisconsin Center for Theatre Research
Film Archives
816 State Street
Madison, Wisconsin 53706
(608) 242-0585

Susan Dalton, Archivist

1,750 feature films and numerous television series prints, shorts and cartoons. United Artists Collection includes films from Warner Brothers-First National, RKO, Monogram, and others. Title list of features available. Descriptive catalogue of paper materials in UA Collection also available. The Center is open to scholars.

Appendix IV. Theaters/Film Series

This appendix reproduces, with revisions, the American Film Institute's *Fact-sheet: Alternative Showcases in the Washington, D.C. Area,* prepared in 1979 by Abby Nelson. A few foreign film series have been added. Scholars should be especially interested in the offerings of the American Film Institute Theater and the commercial Circle, Biograph, and Key theaters.

THEATERS, LIBRARIES, EDUCATIONAL INSTITUTIONS

The following is a list of the major repertory theaters and independent showcases in the Washington, D.C. area. For information on the films being shown, consult *The Washington Post* "Weekend" section, published every Friday, which carries an extensive calendar of events, including synopses of films currently playing in the area. *The Washington Star* also publishes a listing of film showings. A comprehensive source of information on alternative film and cultural events of all kinds—especially music—is *The Unicorn Times,* a free monthly newspaper available at such local bookstores and restaurants as Kramers, Discount Books, and Food for Thought.

> Alexandria Public Library
> Burke Branch
> 4701 Seminary Road
> Alexandria, VA 22304
> (703) 370-6050

> Repertory Films on Wednesday evenings. Free.

> The American Film Institute
> J. F. Kennedy Center for the Performing Arts
> Washington, D.C. 20566
> (202) 785-4600

> Repertory, theme programs, and occasional premieres. Reduced ticket prices for AFI members.

> The American University
> The Media Center
> 310A Ward Circle Building
> Washington, D.C. 20016
> (202) 686-2103

Free programs of independent, documentary, and feature films.

Arlington Central Library
1015 North Quincy Street
Arlington, VA 22201
(703) 527-4777

Repertory films on Tuesdays at 7:30. Free.

Biograph Theater
2819 M Street, NW
Washington, D.C. 20007
(202) 333-2696

Repertory films in series. Ticket books available.

Black Film Institute
University of the District of Columbia
Library and Media Services Division
425 Second Street, NW
Washington, D.C. 20001
(202) 727-2396

Black and Third World films with lectures. Free.

Catholic University
Loft Coffeehouse
620 Michigan Avenue, NE
Washington, D.C. 20064
(202) 635-5291

Recent releases at popular prices.

Center for Adult Education
University of Maryland
College Park, MD 20742
(301) 779-5100

Repertory. Usually $1.50.

Circle Theater
2105 Pennsylvania Avenue, NW
Washington, D.C. 20037
(202) 331-7480

Repertory, year-old releases, series.
10 tickets for $10.00.

Community Cafe
4949 Bethesda Avenue
Bethesda, MD 20014
(301) 986-0848

Free films in the cafe. Features, repertory, documentaries.

Institute for Policy Studies
1901 Q Street, NW
Washington, D.C. 20009
(202) 234-9382

Films shown in conjunction with seminars.

Key Theatre
1222 Wisconsin Avenue, NW
Washington, D.C. 20007
(202) 333-5100

Repertory, series.

Key Theatre
7242 Baltimore Boulevard
College Park, MD 20742
(301) 927-4848

Repertory, series. 10 tickets for $15.00.

Magic Lantern Theater
c/o District Creative Space (d.c. space)
443 Seventh Avenue, NW
Washington, D.C. 20004
(202) 347-1445

Independent and political films; occasional video programs.

Martin Luther King Library
901 G Street, NW
Washington, D.C. 20001
(202) 727-1111

Films on Tuesdays at noon and films for children Saturdays at 1:00. Free.

Ontario Theater
1700 Columbia Road, NW
Washington, D.C. 20009
(202) 462-7118

Eclectic programing includes Spanish-language features, documentaries, repertory, and feature films.

Prince George's County Library
6532 Adelphi Road
Hyattsville, MD 20782
(301) 779-9330

Features and shorts from the library's collection. Free.

Takoma Theater
4th and Butternut Streets, NW
Washington, D.C. 20012
(202) 829-0001

Eclectic weekend programming of repertory and recent releases.

University of Maryland
Student Union Theatre
College Park, MD 20742
(301) 454-2596

Recent releases at $1.50 for general admission.

Washington Project for the Arts
1227 G Street, NW
Washington, D.C. 20005
(202) 347-8304

Video performances and independent films.

MUSEUMS

The following is a list of museums with film programs, compiled from the *Official Museum Directory* (Washington, D.C.: American Association of Museums, 1975). Check the "Weekend" section on Friday in *The Washington Post* at the beginning of each month for a listing of events at the Smithsonian Institution. Many of the museums which make up the Smithsonian Institution show films, and a monthly calendar of events at each museum is compiled and published by the Office of Public Affairs, The Smithsonian Institution, Washington, D.C. 20560.

Air and Space Museum
The Smithsonian Institution
4th and Independence Avenue, SW
Washington, D.C. 20560
(202) 381-6264

Films on flying. Free.

Anacostia Neighborhood Museum
2405 Martin Luther King, Jr. Avenue, SE
Washington, D.C. 20020
(202) 381-6731

Films pertaining to Afro-American history and Africa. Free.

Hirshhorn Museum and Sculpture Gardens
8th and Independence Avenue, SW
Washington, D.C. 20560
(202) 381-6264

Independent, animated, and avant-garde films as well as films about art. Free.

Museum of African Art
Education Department
318 A Street, NE
Washington, D.C. 20002
(202) 547-6222

Films about Africa and African art are shown as part of exhibits and special programs. Free. (The Museum's Eliot Elisofon Archives of photographs and motion pictures is being catalogued and will be available to scholars.)

National Archives and Records Service
8th and Pennsylvania, SW
Washington, D.C. 20408
(202) 523-3006

Documentaries, newsreels, television programs, commercial and government-made films. Free.

National Collection of Fine Arts
8th and G Streets, NW
Washington, D.C. 20560
(202) 381-4215

Films pertaining to current exhibits.

National Gallery of Art
6th and Constitution Avenue, NW
Washington, D.C. 20565
(202) 737-6264

Feature-length and short films pertaining to exhibits.

National Geographic Society—Explorers Hall
17th and M Streets, NW
Washington, D.C. 20036
(202) 857-7588

Daily film showings. Mostly scientific films and film versions of the N.G. television specials. Free.

National Museum of History and Technology
14th and Constitution Avenue, NW
Washington, DC 20560
(202) 381-6264

Lunchtime screenings Tuesday through Friday. Free. Films in conjunction with Smithsonian special events.

Renwick Gallery
17th and Pennsylvania Avenue, NW
Washington, D.C. 20560
(202) 381-6264

Films pertaining to the exhibits twice a month on Tuesday. Free.

FOREIGN FILMS

Many foreign films are part of the offerings listed above. The wide range of foreign film series offered by the AFI Theater has included German, French, Czechoslovak, Third World, and Swedish series. The Black Film Institute shows films from Third World countries. The Circle, Biograph, Key, and other repertory theaters have presented French and German series as well as individual titles from many other countries.

For those interested in films from Asia or the Middle East, the following series are offered.

Asia Society Film Festival
Washington Center of the Asia Society, Sponsor
1785 Massachusetts Avenue, NW
Washington, D.C. 20036
(202) 387-6500

Documentaries about Asia are showcased once each year in a five-day festival. Screenings are at the Austrialian Embassy, 1601 Massachusetts Avenue, NW

Georgetown University Film Lecture Series
Center for Contemporary Arab Studies, Sponsor
Georgetown University
Washington, D.C. 20057
(202) 625-3128

Documentaries produced in or about the Middle East and Africa are combined with lectures and the series is offered twice each year. Free.

Pakistan Film Club, Sponsor
(703) 751-9210

Feature films from Pakistan are shown on one weekend evening every two weeks. Screenings are at Thomas Jefferson High School in Arlington, Virginia, or at the Takoma Theater in Washington. Admission is charged.

Young India Forum
P.O. Box 5993
Bethesda, Maryland 20014
(703) 528-7538 (Film information)
(301) 279-0879·(General information)

Indian feature films are shown on Saturday night and Sunday afternoon at the Wilson Theater in Arlington, Virginia. Admission is charged.

Appendix V. Media Organizations and Publications

The Washington, D.C. area is the home of many organizations, agencies, and publications which maintain no collections of film or videotape but may nonetheless be of interest to media scholars. There surely are many more than those listed below but this Appendix attempts to reveal the richness and variety of Washington's resources for scholars. Telephone numbers have been omitted since the latest information is available from the telephone directory or long distance information. See also the most recent edition of *Aspen Handbook on the Media* prepared by the Aspen Institute listed below.

RESEARCH CENTERS

Aspen Institute Program on Communications and Society
1785 Massachusetts Avenue, NW
Washington, D.C. 20036

Brookings Institution
1775 Massachusetts Avenue, NW
Washington, D.C. 20036

Bureau of Social Science Research
1990 M Street, NW
Washington, D.C. 20036

National Research Council
2101 Constitution Avenue, NW
Washington, D.C. 20418

BROADCASTING ORGANIZATIONS

American Women in Radio and Television, Inc.
1321 Connecticut Avenue, NW
Washington, D.C. 20036

Association of Maximum Service Telecasters, Inc.
1735 De Sales Street, NW
Washington, D.C. 20036

Broadcast Education Association
National Association of Broadcasters Building
1771 N Street, NW
Washington, D.C. 20036

Joint Council on Educational Telecommunications
1126 16th Street, NW
Washington, D.C. 20036

National Association of Broadcasters
1771 N Street, NW
Washington, D.C. 20036

National Association of Educational Broadcasters
1346 Connecticut Avenue, NW
Washington, D.C. 20036

National Public Radio
2025 M Street, NW
Washington, D.C. 20036

Public Broadcasting Service (PBS)
475 L'Enfant Plaza West, SW
Washington, D.C. 20024

Radio-Television News Directors Association
1735 De Sales Street, NW
Washington, D.C. 20036

EDUCATIONAL AND INSTRUCTIONAL MEDIA ORGANIZATIONS

Association for Educational Communications and Technology
1126 16th Street, NW
Washington, D.C. 20036

Association of Media Producers
1707 L Street, NW
Washington, D.C. 20036

Educational Communication Association
822 National Press Building
14th and F Streets, NW
Washington, DC. 20045

National Audio-Visual Association
3150 Spring Street
Fairfax, Virginia 22030

FILM ORGANIZATIONS

Council on International Nontheatrical Events (CINE)
1201 16th Street, NW
Washington, D.C. 20036

Motion Picture Association of America, Inc.
1600 I Street, NW
Washington, D.C. 20006

Washington Area Film/Video League, Inc. (WAFL)
P.O. Box 6475
Washington, D.C. 20009

Washington Film Council
2755 Macomb Street, NW
Washington, D.C. 20008

INDUSTRIAL, IN-HOUSE, AND CABLE TELEVISION

American Society for Information Science
1155 16th Street, NW
Washington, D.C. 20036

Cable Television Information Center
2100 M Street, NW
Washington, D.C. 20037

Cablecommunications Resource Center
2000 K Street, NW
Washington, D.C. 20036

International Television Association (ITVA)
c/o George Manno
American Red Cross
5816 Seminary Road
Falls Church, Virginia 22041

National Cable Television Association
918 16th Street, NW
Washington, D.C. 20006

Speech Communication Association
5205 Leesburg Pike
Falls Church, Virginia 22041

MEDIA ACTION GROUPS

Accuracy in Media
77 14th Street, NW
Washington, D.C. 20005

Citizens Communications Center (a public interest law firm)
1424 16th Street, NW, Suite 404
Washington, D.C. 20036

Council for Public Interest Law
1250 Connecticut Avenue, NW
Washington, D.C. 20036

Council on Children, Media and Merchandising
1346 Connecticut Avenue, NW
Washington, D.C. 20036

Media Access Project (a public interest law firm)
1910 N Street, NW
Washington, D.C. 20036

National Citizens Committee on Broadcasting
1530 P Street, NW
Mail: P.O. Box 12038
Washington, D.C. 20005

National Organization for Women (NOW)
Task Force on Broadcast Media and the FCC
425 13th Street, NW
Washington, D.C. 20004

INDEPENDENT GOVERNMENT CORPORATIONS

Communications Satellite Corporation (COMSAT)
950 L'Enfant Plaza, SW
Washington, D.C. 20024

Corporation for Public Broadcasting (CPB)
1111 16th Street, NW
Washington, D.C. 20036

Radio Free Europe, Radio Liberty, Inc.
1201 Connecticut Avenue, NW
Washington, D.C. 20036
Direct questions to (202) 457-6923.

U.S. GOVERNMENT AGENCIES AND COMMISSIONS

Federal Communications Commission
1919 M Street, NW
Washington, D.C. 20554
Direct questions to the Consumer Assistance Office, (202) 632-7000.

Federal Trade Commission
6th and Pennsylvania Avenue, NW
Washington, D.C. 20580
The Library contains studies of TV and radio advertising. Call (202) 523-3768. Also contact the Division of Advertising Practices, (202) 724-1499.

U.S. Commission on Civil Rights
1121 Vermont Avenue, NW
Washington, D.C. 20425
In 1977 the Commission published a report on women and minorities in television. That report and additional information is available from the Press and Communications Division, (202) 254-6697.

Scholars interested in congressional committee hearings concerning the media should consult Brightbill, George D., *Communications and the U.S. Congress: A Selectively Annotated Bibliography of Congressional Hearings, 1870-1976* (Washington, D.C.: Broadcast Education Association, 1978).

House of Representatives
Clerk of the House
Washington, D.C. 20515
The proceedings on the floor of the U.S. House of Representatives are recorded on audio and videotape. For detailed information see Appendix I.

Library of Congress
(see entry #165 for the LC film, video, and related collections)
General Reading Rooms
10 First Street, SE
Washington, D.C. 20540
The collections of books, periodicals and newspapers are available free to the public in the General Reading Rooms. The stacks are closed but titles may be requested. Several specialized Reading Rooms have their own reference collections. For more information call (202) 287-5000.

Library of Congress Copyright Office
Crystal Mall Annex
Arlington, Virginia 20559

INTERNATIONAL ORGANIZATIONS

Clearinghouse on Development Communication
1414 22nd Street, NW
Washington, D.C. 20037

International Association of Independent Producers
P.O. Box 2801
Washington, D.C. 20013

International Telecommunications Satellite Organization (INTELSAT)
490 L'Enfant Plaza, SW
Washington, D.C. 20024

PUBLICATIONS (PERIODICALS, GUIDES, CATALOGUES)

The following publications have been listed because their editorial offices, sponsoring organizations or editors are in the Washington area. In each case the address listed may be the location of information on film and television. Not included are the many publications which are described in the individual entries and those listed in the Bibliography. The frequency of appearance for regularly published serials is noted.

American Film: Journal of the Film and Television Arts (monthly)
The American Film Institute (publisher)
John F. Kennedy Center for the Performing Arts
Washington, D.C. 20566

Broadcasting (weekly)
1735 DeSales Street, NW (editorial offices)
Washington, D.C. 20036

Broadcasting Yearbook and *Cable Sourcebook* (annuals)
1735 DeSales Street, NW (editorial offices)
Washington, D.C. 20036

Federal Communications Bar Journal
Federal Communications Bar Association (publisher)
1730 M Street, NW
Washington, D.C. 20036

Films for a Changing World
Society for International Development (publisher)
1346 Connecticut Avenue, NW
Washington, D.C. 20036

Films for Anthropological Teaching
American Anthropological Association (sponsor)
1703 New Hampshire Avenue, NW
Washington, D.C. 20009

Funny World (an animation quarterly)
Michael Barrier (editor)
226 N. St. Asaph Street
Alexandria, Virginia
  Subscription information:
Box 1633
New York, New York 10001

Media Report to Women (monthly)
Media Report to Women Index/Directory (annual)
Women's Institute for Freedom of the Press (publisher)
3306 Ross Place, NW
Washington, D.C. 20008

Public Telecommunications Review (bi-monthly)
National Association of Educational Broadcasters (sponsor)
1346 Connecticut Avenue, NW
Washington, D.C. 20036

Scholar's Guide to Washington, D.C.
Woodrow Wilson International Center for Scholars (sponsor)
Smithsonian Institution Building
1000 Jefferson Drive, SW
Washington, D.C. 20560

Television Digest, Public Broadcasting Report, Satellite Week (weeklies)
1836 Jefferson Place, SW (editorial offices)
Washington, D.C. 20036

Televisions (quarterly)
Washington Community Video Center, Inc. (publisher)
P.O. Box 21068
Washington, D.C. 20009

Editorial offices:
1509 19th Street, NW
Washington, D.C. 20009

Video News (bi-weekly)
8401 Connecticut Avenue (editorial offices)
Chevy Chase, Maryland 20015

*The WAFL Book: A Guide to Film and Video in the
Washington, D.C. Area*
Washington Area Film/Video League, Inc. (publisher)
P.O. Box 6475
Washington, D.C. 20009

Appendix VI.   Films in a Washington Setting

By Raoul Kulberg

Huge and varied collections of motion pictures and television are found in the Washington area but there is another side to Washington's relationship with the world of movies and TV. The following list, compiled by Raoul Kulberg with help from other Washington film folk, includes those productions in which Washington, D.C., plays some significant part. Those who wish to add to the list or argue with an item or two can reach Mr. Kulberg at the University of the District of Columbia.

1898:
Secretary Long and Captain Sigsbee

1901:
*President McKinley and Escort Going
   to the Capitol*
President McKinley Taking Oath
*President McKinley's Funeral Cortege
   at Washington, D.C.*

1902:
*Prince Henry Arriving in Washington
   and Visiting the German Embassy*

1903:
*Theodore Roosevelt Leaving the White
   House*

1904:
The Late Senator Mark Hanna
Military Maneuvers, Manassas, Virginia

1905:
The Inauguration of President Roosevelt
President Roosevelt's Inauguration

1915:
Birth of a Nation

1918:
Washington Sky Patrol

1921:
The Great Moment

1924:
Abraham Lincoln
Flames of Desire
The Iron Horse
Laughing at Danger
Marriage in Transit
Oh, You Tony;

1925:
His Secretary
The Mad Dancer
Sackcloth and Scarlet

1926:
The Border Sheriff

1927:
A Texas Steer

1928:
Wallflowers

1929:
Behind Closed Doors
The Lost Zeppelin

1930:
Abraham Lincoln

1931:
Alexander Hamilton

1932:
Washington Masquerade
Washington Merry-Go-Round

232

1933:
Gabriel over the White House

1934:
The President Vanishes

1936:
The President's Mystery

1937:
First Lady

1939:
Mr. Smith Goes to Washington
Washington Cowboy

1941:
Adventure in Washington
Washington Melodrama

1942:
Tennessee Johnson
The World at War
Yankee Doodle Dandy

1943:
Government Girl
Mission to Moscow
The More the Merrier
Sherlock Holmes in Washington
This Is the Army

1944:
Heavenly Days
Wilson

1945:
Without Love

1946:
The Magnificent Doll

1947:
13 Rue Madelaine

1950:
Born Yesterday
The Magnificent Yankee

1951:
The Day the Earth Stood Still

1952:
Washington Story

1955:
The Court Martial of Billy Mitchell
Davy Crockett, King of the Wild Frontier

1956:
Earth vs. Flying Saucers

1958:
Damn Yankees
Houseboat

1959:
The FBI Story

1961:
The Absent-Minded Professor
Bridge to the Sun
Dead to the World
The Flight that Disappeared

1962:
Advise and Consent

1963:
Son of Flubber

1964:
Babo
The Candidate
A Distant Trumpet
Dr. Strangelove: Or How I Learned to
*   Stop Worrying and Love the Bomb*
Fail Safe
Four Days in November
Kisses for the President
Point of Order
Seven Days in May

1965:
The Bus
The Eleanor Roosevelt Story
The Great Sioux Massacre

1966:
Murderer's Row

1967:
The President's Analyst
Way Out Topless
Who's Minding the Mint
Young Americans

1968:
The Ballad of Josie
The Edge
The Horse in the Grey Flannel Suit
Wild in the Streets

1969:
King: Montgomery to Memphis
Medium Cool
Pendulum

1970:
Baby, Light My Fire
Colossus: The Forbin Project
Story of a Woman

1971:
The President's Plane Is Missing
Vanished

1973:
The Exorcist
Scorpio

1974:
The Last Detail

1975:
Hearts and Minds
Three Days of the Condor

1976:
The Adams Chronicles (TV)
All the President's Men
Eleanor and Franklin (TV)
Give 'Em Hell Harry (TV)
Logan's Run

1977:
The Other Side of Midnight

1978:
Washington: Behind Closed Doors (TV)

1979:
Blind Ambition (TV)
Hair

Appendix VII. Note on Government Paper Records/Bibliographic Guide for Film and Video Studies

By David Culbert

A. Note on Government Paper Records

How does a scholar do research on a particular film? What about films which were never distributed? The release print cannot tell us what we need to know about conception, changes demanded, ideas found wanting; only print records can provide answers to these matters of interest to students of aesthetics and those concerned with locating film within the context of the society which produced it. How can one find materials relating to film in the voluminous, poorly catalogued government records in the Washington, D.C., area?

The answers to these questions are obviously a function of each scholar's particular research subject; they cannot exist as a single universally applicable "how to" guide. It is nevertheless useful to witness a specific step-by-step example of one scholar's odyssey through the rich but sometimes labyrinthine resources available to film scholars in Washington. Accordingly, this appendix will describe the sources which I uncovered in conducting research for *The American Military's Use of Film in World War II*, during 1976 and 1977. Although there is some additional information about other records relating to film, I make no claim to being exhaustive.

The value of a "paper chain" of documents in recovering a "lost" film by a major Hollywood director is evident in the specific experience of Barry Sabath, a young scholar who with Robert L. Carringer wrote *Ernst Lubitsch: A Guide to References and Resources* (1978). Sabath had worked carefully in sources familiar to the film scholar but when he arrived in Washington to locate archival material about Lubitsch's one film for the U.S. Army, *Know Your Enemy Germany,* he was stymied. Sabath reported in detail what he found in the trade press and other film books. He wondered if Lubitsch made more than one film, and whether a 1945 Army film, *Your Job in Germany*, contained Lubitsch footage. Above all he wondered how one found information since government records are not arranged by film title or director. He had a legitimate problem, for Lubitsch's film was completed but never shown and no prints survive.

Exhibit 1 is a page from a standard 20th Century Fox picture estimate for October, 1942, Record Group (RG) 159, Box 1160, 333.9, Records of the Inspector General, Washington National Records Center, Suitland, Maryland. It indicates that Lubitsch decided to shoot much of his film on Hollywood sets.

Though his original script has not survived, the names of the sets tell us a good bit about what he planned to do:

TWENTIETH CENTURY-FOX FILM CORPORATION								
PRODUCTION BUDGET					Production No. U.S. #18			
SET COSTS					Production Days 7			
SET DRESSINGS								

	SETS			SET DRESSINGS			
NAME OF SET	New-Revamp Pickup or Rented	Location	Acct. Nos. 115-01 115-04 Construction	Acct. No. 123-11 Prop Purchases	Acct. No. 123-12 Prop Rentals	Acct. No. 123-14 Mfd. Labor	Acct. No. 123-15 Mfd. Material
German Barracks 1913		Uplifter's					
" " 1862	P.U.	Golf Course	75.00				
" Inn	Rev.	Stage A	100.00				
Reichstag & Parliament	Rev.		300.00				
Bismarck Chancellory	P.U.	Stage 16	150.00				
2nd Floor Window	Units		150.00				
Boundary Line-Denmark			100.00				
" " Austria			100.00				
" " France			100.00				
" " Belgium			100.00				
German Civilians Singing		Fr. Sq.	50.00				
" Family Dining Room	P.U.	Stage B	25.00				
" University	Rev.	Stage B	250.00				
Sampler on Wall			100.00				
Court Room	Rev.	Stage B	450.00				
Kaiser on Horse		Uplifters					
Street (Vendor) (Karl at Curb)		Chicago St.	180.00				
Woman Reading Bible (Nursery)	P.U.		150.00				
" " N.Y.	P.U.		-				
Protestant Church	P.U.	Stage 9	50.00				
Large Room (youths Saluting)	P.U.		150.00				
Karl & Companions (C.U. SC.107)	P.U.		-				
Windows (Stones)			50.00				
Bunnery	P.U.	Chicago St.	60.00				
Cell A Boor			200.00				
Class Room - Boys	New		800.00				
Girls School	P.U.	Colonial Hm	50.00				
Schmidt's Apt. House	P.U.	Wash. Sq.	60.00				
" Room			700.00				
Cheap Hotel	P.U.	Stage 11	25.00				
Berlin Apt. House	Rev.	Fr. Sq.	200.00				
Dr.Ziemer Lecturing(Gas Chamber)	P.U.		-				
Karl's Grandfather & Father	P.U.	Uplifter's	-				

Exhibit 1: Production Cost Estimates for Ernest Lubitsch's *Know Your Enemy Germany*

Actual scripts were located for several later versions of Lubitsch's film. Exhibit 2, pages from a working script dated June 27, 1944, from RG 319, 062.2, Box 370, Troop Information and Education Division, Chief of Staff, Modern Military Records, National Archives, show exact sections of Lubitsch's film which were used in later revisions:

```
        DISSOLVE TO:

    LUBITCH FILM                      Here is a German soldier...
                                      Let's call him Karl Schmidt...
                                      he is a representative of his nation.


    INSERT OF Swastika on             What made him choose the crooked cross
    Helmet.   (PRODUCTION)            as the symbol of what he is fighting
                                      for.


    INSERTS OF older types of         The first clue lies in Germany's past...
    helmets.   (PRODUCTION)           for it has taken generations of people...


        DISSOLVE TO:

    Young Germans learning to         ...with the same thoughts...the same
    goosestep...LUBITCH FILM          emotions...to produce this soldier...
                                      and his goosestepping comrades in arms.

                                      The father of our Karl Schmidt did
                                      the same goosestep...and felt the
                                      same urge for conquest.

    OLD PRUSSIAN SEQUENCE             And the grandfather of our Karl, though
                                      he wore a different uniform, did the
                                      same goosestep and had the same lust
                                      for mastery.
```

Exhibit 2: Excerpt from the Working Script of *Know Your Enemy Germany* (1st page)

OLD PRUSSIANS MARCHING	Always the same goose-stepping...
BOOTS MARCHING	...always the same desire for power.
CLOSE UP HITLER	Today the leader is Hitler.
CLOSE UP KAISER	Your father knew the leader as Kaiser Wilhelm.
CLOSE UP OF BISMARCK	Your grandfather remembers Bismarck.
NEWSPAPER HEADLINES AS IN LUBITCH FILM	Today there is a Nazi menace.
	Your father's generation was threatened by the Huns.
	In your grandfather's day...the threat was the Prussians.
	The Nazis...the Huns...the Prussians.
	Three different names for the same people. Three generations attempting to inflict their will upon others by force.
FILM AS CUT	Here is Germany in peace time...
	...very much the same as it was 80 years ago.
	Quaint medieval towns and villages.

Exhibit 2: Excerpt from the Working Script of *Know Your Enemy Germany* (2nd page)

Shown in Exhibit 3 is the final script (a moviola transcription of the release print) for *Here Is Germany,* dated October 8, 1945, RG 111, Box 9, Miscellaneous Production Files OF-11, Room 20E, Motion Picture Section, National Archives. Lubitsch's 1942 character Karl Schmidt appears, as does the director's idea of having this typical German march off to war three times; the narration is the same as for the 1944 script. The "paper chain" (along with a great deal of correspondence from other government records) proves what cannot be learned any other way: Sections of the 1942 film were used in 1945 for a film which—while depicting the aggressive tendencies of Germany—also showed what an American soldier might expect in an occupied country. Specific sections of *Your Job in Germany* are in fact a "lost" Lubitsch film.

HERE IS GERMANY

And the grandfather of Karl
Schmidt did the same goose-step
and trod the same path of
agression.

The same goose-step...

The same will of aggression.

The same lust for conquest.

Close-up of Hitler   You knew their leader as Hitler.

Close-up of Kaiser   Your father knew the leader
                            as the Kaiser...

Close shot of Bismarck   Your grandfather remembers
                            Bismarck.

Newspaper montage   You faced the Nazi menace.

                            Your father's generation was
                            threatened by the Huns.

Matching shots of Germans   In your grandfather's day there
                            were the Prussians.

                            The Nazis...The Huns...The
                            Prussians.

                            Three different names for three
                            generations of Gormans attempting
                            to inflict their will upon others
                            by force...three generations
                            following a tradition so
                            different from ours.

Exhibit 3: Excerpt from the Final Script of *Your Job in Germany*

A number of primary print records are available to the student of film. The most voluminous textual records for World War II film material are found at the Washington National Records Center (WNRC), Suitland, Maryland, and at the main branch of the National Archives (NA) on Pennsylvania Avenue in downtown Washington. A free shuttle bus runs from NA to WNRC and back several times a day, starting at 9:00 A.M. from the Pennsylvania Avenue NA entrance. Xerox copies of all materials found in either collection may be purchased for $.15 per page.

WNRC-NA, RG 208, Office of War Information. Those interested in feature films, wartime distribution of government films to schools and colleges, or wartime propaganda, should begin here. Although RG 208 is physically located at Suitland, it is in the section of the WNRC controlled by NA. This means that there are finding aids for this immense record group and a staff which can be of great assistance. The branch is headed by Daniel Goggin, (202) 763-1710. An inventory in the Suitland Search Room roughly describes contents of the hundreds of boxes in this collection. There is no list of films by title but alphabetical groupings will point to appropriate boxes. The personal files of OWI Director Elmer Davis and records relating to the Hollywood Branch of the OWI's Bureau of Motion Pictures are particularly helpful. The footnotes to Clayton Koppes and Gregory Black's article relating to OWI film activities, published in the June 1977 *Journal of American History,* are also useful. The scholar who has prepared beforehand could be actually looking at boxes of material after only two hours with the RG 208 inventory.

WNRC-NA, RG 229, Office of Inter-American Affairs. Those interested in Latin America or Walt Disney's wartime work will want to look at these well-catalogued records of the agency headed by Nelson Rockefeller. A published inventory of this record group may be had without cost by writing the Publications Office, National Archives and Records Service, Washington, D.C. 20408. Ask for *Records of the Office of Inter-American Affairs,* Inventory Series No. 7 (1973). The references to film are found on pages 24, 25, 44, and 47. Copies of the inventory may be available in the government documents sections of local or university libraries.

WNRC-NA, RG 333.9, Boxes 1159-68, The Inspector General. IG records normally deal with individual crimes and are therefore closed to scholars for a very long time, but I requested that these records be declassified. They cover a massive 1942 investigation of training film production in Hollywood and include 2,500 pages of verbatim testimony from Hollywood directors, over 10,000 pages of supporting documents, detailed financial records for some of the studios, and picture estimates such as the one for the Lubitsch film shown in Exhibit 1. The material is self-indexed, although some of the documents are out of order. The records range much more widely than the aim of the investigation, which was to determine whether Hollywood had cheated the federal government by charging too much for training films, indicates.

WNRC-FRC. The largest number of print records relating to film are physically located in the Federal Records Center at Suitland. FRC records are not catalogued by record group (RG) and are harder to use since they are still physically in the custody of the Army but serviced by the FRC. To use these records a scholar must first contact Mr. Paul Taborn, Security Specialist, HQDA (DAAG-AMR), Room GAO76, Forrestal Building, 1000 Independence Avenue, SW, Washington, D.C. 20314. (202) 693-0970. Taborn is an employee of the Army's Adjutant General's office, and his written permission is required for access to any FRC records at Suitland. He will explain over the telephone precisely what information is required in the letter requesting access to the records. Under the current system, the next step is to visit Taborn's office in the Forrestal Building (across from the old Smithsonian Castle on the Mall and a five-minute walk from downtown NA) to use inventories which describe FRC holdings. The inventories are likely to be confusing, for they often describe material long since destroyed or combined in other FRC classifications. Nothing is arranged by film title. Other inventories, stored in file cabinets in the FRC Reference Branch at Suitland, may help those stymied by the inventories, for these are the finding aids used at the time the records were generated in World War II. The FRC has abundant material on post-1945 film production and some material for World War I.

It may be difficult to go from Taborn's inventories to the print-out which the FRC uses as part of its computerized retrieval system, but specific records cannot be located in the stacks without having first been discovered on that print-out. Paul Taborn will provide scholars with access to the current print-out; in general, the applicable records are identified by military decimal numbers 062.2, 413.56, 319.1, and 004.52. Such numbers appear on most of the documents eventually needed. The following actual example from the print-out points the way to twenty-two enormous cartons of film records: A52-248, 062.2 ocsigo, Boxes 1-22, 11-39-11-2-0. The first number is in effect the record group and is used in all citations; then follows the 062.2 decimal number; ocsigo is the abbreviation for Office of the Chief Signal Officer—the Army division charged with film production; the number of boxes is self-evident, and the final digits tell the archivist where the material is located in the warehouse. The records I have found most useful are:

A43-B28, 062.2 Boxes 748-9, 752-3, 759, 3-10-29-1-0
A45-196, 062.2 Boxes 43-50, 11-39-17-1-0
A52-248, 062.2 Boxes 1-22, 11-39-11-2-0

Receipt of these boxes does not mark the end of the scholar's difficulties. The files are arranged by film production number—which bears no relation to the film's release number. The Frank Capra *Why We Fight* series, for example, is a 6000 series, so a good deal of looking is necessary even after locating the materials I have described.

When clearance is approved by Taborn (a formality) a scholar should call Mr. Roland Wilson, head of the FRC Reference Branch (202-763-7430) a week in advance and again the day before visiting the FRC to make sure the appropriate records have been moved to the Search Room. The procedure upon arriving at FRC is to sign in at Wilson's office, to the left as you enter the building, where a separate FRC identification card can also be picked up. Remember that the FRC is not like NA—it is only supposed to provide boxes for the scholar; it does not offer research assistance.

National Archives. Another major source of material is downtown at NA. Film material can be found in Modern Military Records (Mr. Edward Reese, Room 13W, 523-3340), State Department Records (Mr. Gerald Haines, Room 6W, 523-3174), and the Motion Picture Branch (Mr. William Murphy, Room 20E, 523-3294).

NA, Production Files, RG 111, Office of the Chief Signal Officer. The Motion Picture Branch, where government films and newsreels (see description in entry #155) may be reviewed, provides several shelves of print records relating to production. Although there are no complete records for any single film, scripts, source sheets, memoranda relating to required script changes, or general correspondence exist for many titles. The films are arranged by title and the records are thus quickly accessible.

NA, RG 59, State Department. These files are surprisingly rich. A decimal system designates each film according to country. The Soviet Union, for example, is 811.4061. Topics include the export of American films abroad, the situation for film production abroad, and foreign responses to American films. Particularly rich are files for the Soviet Union, Great Britain, and much of Latin America. The staff for this division can be of great assistance, although the chronological arrangement of the records generally precludes instant location of a particular title. Other reference materials include an immense central card file indexing directors' names and film titles and the large bound purport books arranged by decimal number (such as 811.4061). The purport books give cross references to other decimal files.

NA, RG 165, RG 330, RG 331, RG 319, RG 407, Modern Military Records (MMR). Only in the past few years have scholars begun to use these record groups for topics relating to film. There is abundant material, and RG 165 and RG 319 contain particularly valuable memoranda relating to high-level decision-making. Look for records with the following decimal numbers: 062.2, 319.1, 413.56, and 004.5. The boxes I have found most helpful are:

RG 165, Records of the Chief of Staff, Boxes 14, 19, 20-22, 27-30, 133.
RG 319, Records of the Chief, Troop I & E, Chief of Staff, Boxes 302-4, 353-5, 370-1.
RG 330, Records of the Secretary of Defense, Assistant Secretary of Defense Manpower, Research, *What the Soldier Thinks* (psychological testing), Boxes 972-3, 990-1001, 1011-12.
RG 407, Records of the Adjutant General, Boxes 18, 193. Especially note: 413.56, Boxes 3255-64.

MMR also has separate record groups for the various theaters of war. For Europe (ETOUSA) I found important material in RG 331 (Allied Operational and Occupation HDQ, WWII, SHAEF), Box 3 (062.2); Box 8 (062.2) which concerns the Psychological Warfare Division's use of film, and Box 11, where decimal 334 concerns the Joint Anglo-American Film Planning Commission, responsible for *The True Glory.*

One other unusual source of material is not filed by decimal number but is part of RG 165. Boxes 5-10, Public Relations Division, News Branch, Motion Picture Scripts, 1942-46, contain—arranged by film title—complete scripts for thousands of feature films and serials with military themes. Often there is correspondence relating to censorship or questions about borrowing equipment.

Library of Congress (LC), Motion Pictures, Broadcasting and Recorded Sound Division (entry #165). A third significant source of paper records on World War II films is the LC, a fifteen-minute walk from the downtown NA. The Division has OWI evaluations of Hollywood feature and short films produced during the 1940s. Materials are arranged by title; for each there may be a script or continuity, some correspondence, an OWI evaluation, and often a number of stills.

LC, Manuscript Division. A number of collections, arranged by the individual's name, relate to film and television. The George Creel Papers contain some correspondence relating to World War I film production but have more to say about propaganda. The Woodrow Wilson Papers have a good deal of correspondence to and from Creel. The Joseph Davies Papers contain extensive material about *Mission to Moscow.* The Henry Arnold Papers deal with Air Force film production. Other collections are described in entry #165.

For each catalogued collection there is a shelf list describing the contents of each box, which speeds access to the material. Still, it is wise to write in advance to give the staff time to think about other collections appropriate to specific research topics. Discussion of a research project with a staff librarian invariably results in some excellent ideas.

Naval Research Laboratory Library. Located at Bolling Air Force Base, this library is generally closed to researchers. It contains numerous unpublished naval studies about the value of instructional film. It is possible to use this material by calling Doris Baster, director (767-2357) and making prior arrangements.

Naval Historical Center Library, Washington Navy Yard, Washington, D.C. 20374. This collection includes a number of in-house administrative studies relating to naval film in World War II. The helpful though limited amount of unpublished material available in this library is available without prior arrangements.

Center for Military History Library, Forrestal Building, Room 6AO49, 1000 Independence Avenue, SW, Washington, D.C. 20314. This library contains a substantial number of unpublished Army administrative histories. Call the librarian, Hannah Zeidlik (693-5045), to set up an appointment.

Office of Air Force History Library. Building 5681, Bolling Air Force Base, (202) 767-5088. Scholars interested in Air Force film production should not ignore the MMR at NA, since RG 165 has much about Air Corps policy-making. Film production files, and post-1945 material is on microfilm in the Library. The original documents are stored at Maxwell Air Force Base in Alabama. Finding aids, also on microfilm, facilitate location of some material by director or film title, but these records much less significant than those at Suitland or NA.

Access to Classified Documents. Scholars wishing to use records in the custody of the FBI, or which are restricted, should request a copy of a handy pamphlet published by NA, "Know Your Rights to Mandatory Review of Classified Documents," which explains the procedure. In your research at Suitland or NA you may encounter a slip which tells you a document has been removed. If so, the staff both places will be happy to explain how to file a request asking to see the document in question. Another practical source of information on this subject is Alonzo L. Hamby and Edward Weldon, eds., *Access to the Papers of Recent Public Figures: The New Harmony Conference* (1977). The specific experiences of scholars, none of them students of film or television, are of obvious relevance. A copy may be ordered for $3.00 by writing the Executive Secretary, Organization of American Historians, 112 North Bryan Street, Bloomington, Indiana 47401.

Finally, I should mention *Film and Propaganda in America: A Documentary History,* a five-volume collection to be published by Greenwood Press sometime in 1981. Dr. Richard Wood of NA will edit the volume on World War I; I will edit two volumes on World War II; and Lawrence Suid will edit the post-1945 volume. Each 500-page volume will include a table of documents, detailed introduction, and index. A fifth volume, in microfiche, will make available an additional 4,000 pages of material. The emphasis will be on government propaganda, censorship, and the evolution of scripts. Most of this material will be published here for the first time.

B. Bibliographic Guide for Film and Video Studies

This guide to published English-language sources for the study of film and television is designed for the scholar unfamiliar with the ever-expanding literature of these fields. Materials are arranged in the following subject categories: General Guides and Finding Aids, Film History, Aesthetics, Documentary, Social and Cultural History, Photography, Propaganda and Public Opinion, Television, Sociology of Film and Television, and Journals. In each category the first work discussed is the one most useful to those interested in that particular subject; the remaining organization in each category is dictated by a logical progression of ideas. There is an alphabetical listing with complete citations at the end of this appendix.

1. GENERAL GUIDES AND FINDING AIDS

For a fine example, see Peter C. Rollins, "Film and American Studies: Questions, Activities, Guides" (1974). Rollins emphasizes classroom use and literature and film, two subjects purposely excluded from this bibliography. An updated version of his essay has been published in the Spring, 1980, *American Quarterly,* a special issue on film which Rollins edited. Also essential are William Rivers *et al., Aspen Handbook on the Media: 1977-79* (1977) and Paul Smith, ed., *The Historian and Film* (1976).

All who work in film should be acquainted with standard finding aids, such as Leonard Maltin, *TV Movies: 1979-80 Edition* (1978), which provides credits and plot summaries for over 12,000 films. Of the many general guides the best are Leslie Halliwell, *The Filmgoer's Companion* (1978), and Liz-Anne Bawden, ed., *The Oxford Companion to Film* (1976); the former is inexpensive and regularly revised, the latter very strong in technical descriptions of film production. The American Film Institute. located at the Kennedy Center in Washington, is engaged in a longterm project to publish credits and summaries for every American feature film. See their *American Film Institute Catalog: Feature Films 1921-1930* (1971) and *Feature Films 1961-1970* (1976), both two-volume works and both elaborately indexed. Two other helpful guides in paperback are Georges Sadoul, *Dictionary of Film Makers* (1972) and his *Dictionary of Films* (1972).

For published material relating to films, see Peter J. Bukalski, *Film Research: A Critical Bibliography with Annotations and Essay* (1972); for Nazi film see the outstanding three-part survey by Richard Alan Nelson, "Germany and the German Film, 1930-1945: An Annotated Research Bibliography," which appeared in the *Journal of the University Film Association* (1977-78). For other sources see John C. and Lana Gerlach, *The Critical Index: A Bibliography of Articles on Film in English, 1946-1973* (1974); Harold Leonard, ed., *The Film Index* (1941); and Richard Dyer MacCann and Edward S. Perry, *The New Film Index: A Bibliography of Magazine Articles in English, 1930-1970* (1975). To discover what reviewers thought of a particular film consult Stephen E. Bowles, ed.. *Index to Critical Film Reviews* (1974); and *The New York Times Film Reviews, 1913-1968* (1970). fully indexed in six volumes plus supplements.

Before visiting the National Archives or the Library of Congress in search of textual records relating to film and television it is a good idea to check another volume in the series of guides sponsored by the Woodrow Wilson International Center for Scholars. Steven A. Grant, *Scholars' Guide to Washington, D.C. for Russian/Soviet Studies* (1977). which contains concise guidelines for locating specific materials. Also important is *The National Union Catalog of Manuscript Collections: 1959-61* (1962) and *1962-present* (1963-), which lists individuals whose papers may be in Washington; for the West consult Linda Mehr, compiler, *Motion Pictures, Television and Radio: A Union Catalogue of Manuscript and Special Collections in the Western United States* (1977). Also important is the *Guide to the National Archives of the United States* (1974), nearly 900 pages long. To ascertain whether records have already been microfilmed, check the *National Archives Microfilm Publications* (1974).

Those interested in the records of World War II should write the National Archives and Records Service, Washington, D.C., 20408, for a free copy of Mayfield S. Bray and William T. Murphy, *Audiovisual Records in the National Archives of the United States Relating to World War II* (1974). Although it relates primarily to photography, Shirley I. Green and Diane Hamilton, comps., *Pictorial Resources in the Washington, D.C. Area* (1976) also covers other visual materials; see also Ann Gourley Caffrey, comp., *Using Your Nation's Capital: An Indexed Guide to Multimedia Resources in Washington, D.C.* (1972).

If current military audiovisual resources are needed, consult the U.S. Army, *Index of Army Motion Pictures for Public Non-Profit Use* (1975), describing films available free from selected military bases throughout the country; see also the fuller *Index of Army Motion Pictures and Related Audio-Visual Aids* (1977). For purchase of government films, see the Washington National Audiovisual Center, *A Reference List of Audiovisual Materials Produced by the United States Government* (1978).

Three harder-to-locate government reports discuss current audiovisual production by the government: Assistant Secretary of Defense (Manpower and Reserve Affairs), *Audio-Visual Management Task Force Report* (1974); Office of Federal Management Policy, *Review of Audiovisual Facilities in Washington, D.C., and San Bernardino, California Areas* (1975) and Government Accounting Office, "Valuable Government-Owned Motion Picture Films are Rapidly Deteriorating," the latter particularly important in light of the devastating fire which destroyed nitrite footage at Suitland, Maryland, in late 1978.

To rent a film, check Kathleen Weaver, compiler, *Film Programmer's Guide to 16mm Rentals* (1975); see also James L. Limbacher, *Feature Films on 8mm and 16mm: A Directory of Feature Films Available for Rental, Sale, and Lease in the United States* (1977). Both works are likely to be updated regularly. For information about video resources in communities throughout the United States, see Olga Weber, *North American Film and Video Directory* (1976) which, however, only lists places which responded to a questionnaire; or Abigail Nelson, comp., *Guide to Film and Video Resources in New England* (1977). For folklore, see Bill Ferris and Judy Peiser, eds., *American Films and Videotapes: An Index* (1976); for anthropological film the best source is Karl G. Heider, *Films for Anthropological Teaching* (1977) and his *Ethnographic Film* (1976); more generally, consult Ernest D. Rose, *World Film and TV Study Resources: A Reference Guide to Major Teaching Centres and Archives* (1974); for stock footage, see the *World Directory of Stockshot and Film Production Libraries* (1969) but also see the experience of those who have already used such resources as described in Smith (1976).

2. FILM HISTORY

Begin with Gerald Mast, *A Short History of the Movies* (1976); for comedy see his *The Comic Mind: Comedy and the Movies* (1973). A good illustrated history is Richard Griffith and Arthur Mayer, *The Movies* (1970). For the early history of film, begin with C. W. Ceram, *Archaeology of the Cinema* (1965); George C. Pratt, *Spellbound in Darkness: A History of the Silent Film* (1973), which includes many primary documents; Gordon Hendricks, *The Edison Motion Picture Myth* (1961), a bitter assault on Edison; and Kevin Brownlow, *The Parade's Gone By* (1968), one of the finest examples of oral history in print.

The financial side of the industry is clearly introduced in Tino Balio, ed., *The American Film Industry* (1976); for censorship and blacklisting two major sources are Richard S. Randall, *Censorship of the Movies: The Social and Political Control of a Mass Medium* (1970) and John Cogley, *Report on Blacklisting I: Movies* (1956); for educational film, see the excellent articles in Film Council of America, *Sixty Years of 16mm Film 1923-1983* (1954).

War and film is a subject covered by a large number of books. Lawrence H. Suid, *Guts and Glory; Great American War Movies* (1978) uses extensive oral history interviews; Kevin Brownlow, *The War, the West, and the Wilderness* (1979) has some good material on World War I; Clyde Jeavons, *A Pictorial History of War Films* (1974) is a serious piece of work; Tom Perlmutter, *War Movies* (1974) is useful only for its numerous illustrations. Robert Hughes, ed., *Film: Book 2, Films of Peace and War* (1962) contains complete scripts for John Huston's *Let There Be Light* (1946) and Alain Renais's *Night and Fog* (1958). For World War II, none of the following are really satisfactory: Roger Manvell, *Films and the Second World War* (1974); Thomas William Bohn, *An Historical and Descriptive Analysis of the 'Why We Fight' Series* (1977); and *Look* (editors of), *Movie Lot to Beachhead* (1945).

Two of the best studies of national cinema concern Germany: Lotte H. Eisner, *The Haunted Screen: Expressionism in the German Cinema and the Influence of Max Reinhardt* (1973) and Siegfried Kracauer, *From Caligari to Hitler: A Psychological History of the German Film* (1947); on Nazi film the documentary appendices in Erwin Leiser, *Nazi Cinema* (1975) are valuable. For Soviet film. the standard work is Jay Leyda, *Kino: A History of the Russian and Soviet Film* (1973); the best study of Sergei Eisenstein is Yon Barna, *Eisenstein: The Growth of a Cinematic Genius* (1975). Other standard works in this field are Rachael Low and Roger Manvell, *The History of the British Film*, 3 vols. (1948-51); Georges Sadoul, *French Film* (1953); Pierre Leprohon, *The Italian Cinema* (1972); Peter Cowie, *Swedish Cinema* (1966); Joseph L. Anderson and Donald Richie, *The Japanese Film: Art and Industry* (1960), and Joan Mellen, *The Waves at Genji's Door; Japan through its Cinema* (1976); and Erik Barnouw and S. Krishnaswamy, *Indian Film* (1963). The Barnouw book will be updated and published by Oxford University Press in 1981.

For many films (though rarely documentaries) there are published film scripts. Sometimes such editions are very good indeed. for example, Pauline Kael, *The Citizen Kane Book* (1974) or Marcel Ophuls, *The Sorrow and the Pity* (1972). An important new series of Warner feature film scripts to be published by the University of Wisconsin Press under the general editorship of Tino Balio began in the spring of 1979. Some twenty titles are already in production.

The bane of film scholarship is the Hollywood memoir, unreliable and based on the assumption that what really happened cannot possibly be lively enough for the film buff. A representative example is Frank Capra, *The Name Above the Title: An Autobiography* (1971), full of fabricated dialogue and factual errors. Unusual because of its extreme hostility is Richard Schickel, *The Disney Version: The Life, Times, Art and Commerce of Walt Disney* (1968); for one kind of corrective see my " 'A Quick Delightful Gink'; Eric Knight at the Walt Disney Studio" (1978); on the subject of animation Michael Barrier is writing a full treatment for Oxford University Press.

Most film scholarship presumes a knowledge of many technical terms. If these are unfamiliar a regular dictionary may not be of much help. Instead choose Harry M. Geduld and Ronald Gottesman, *An Illustrated Glossory of Film Terms* (1973) or John Mercer, comp., *Glossary of Film Terms* (1978), though the latter contains some sloppy definitions.

3. AESTHETICS

Begin with J. Dudley Andrew, *The Major Film Theories: An Introduction* (1976), clearly-written and helpful for semiotics; see also John Harrington, *The Rhetoric of Film* (1973), with a slightly different focus. The problem of aesthetics is also dealt with as part of a larger problem in Richard P. Alder, "What is Visual Literacy?" (1978).

For the classic film theories, begin with Richard Dyer MacCann, *Film: A Montage of Theories* (1966); Bill Nichols, ed., *Movies and Methods* (1976), which emphasizes structuralism; and two classics: Erwin Panofsky, "Style and Medium in the Motion Pictures," reprinted in Gerald Mast and Marshall Cohen, eds., *Film and Theory and Criticism: Introductory Readings* (2d ed., 1979) and Siegfried Kracauer, *Theory of Film: The Redemption of Physical Reality* (1965) which includes an important chapter on photography.

Linguistic theory offers a potential source for film criticism. Will Wright, *Sixguns & Society: A Structural Study of the Western* (1977) is excellent; for the original materials of semiotics, see Christian Metz, *Film Language: A Semiotics of the Cinema* (1974); for the beginner Andrew (1976) is most helpful: also excellent, and brief, is Terence Hawkes, *Structuralism and Semiotics* (1977).

4. DOCUMENTARY

Begin with Erik Barnouw, *Documentary* (1974), clearly-written and well-organized; another good introduction is Richard Meran Barsam, *Nonfiction Film: A Critical History* (1973). Brief and original is Jay Leyda, *Films Beget Films: A Study of the Compilation Film* (1971). The best analysis of the documentary movement of the 1930s remains Paul Rotha, *Documentary Film* (1952), whose third edition contains Richard Griffith's excellent appendix on American military film. Rotha's *Documentary Diary* (1973) adds important information about the British experience up to 1939. For the war years in Britian, The Arts Enquiry, *The Factual Film* (1947) is essential reading.

Documentary film has never been shy of theorists. Begin with Richard Maran Barsam, ed., *Nonfiction Film Theory and Criticism* (1976); and A. William Bluem, *Documentary in American Television: Form, Function, Method* (1965), which in spite of its title has much to say about film and photography. The classic theorist of documentary film is covered in Forsyth Hardy, ed., *Grierson on Documentary* (1966). The role of documentary film in official propaganda is discussed in Leif Furhammar and Folke Isaksson, *Politics and Film* (1971); William Stott, *Documentary Expression and Thirties America* (1973) generally ignores film but has much to say about photography which relates to film.

William T. Murphy, *Robert Flaherty: A Guide to References and Resources* (1978) is a good guide to one of the very best documentary filmmakers. For the history of official documentary film in America, see Richard Dyer MacCann, *The People's Films: A Political History of U.S. Government Motion Pictures* (1973). Raymond Fielding, *The American Newsreel 1911-1967* (1972) provides a general overview of its subject. Fielding's *The March of Time 1935-1951* (1978) covers a special sort of newsreel. Robert Snyder, *Pare Lorentz and the Documentary Film* (1968) is unsatisfactory but contains useful material; the best autobiography by any documentary filmmaker is Joris Ivens, *The Camera and I* (1969).

5. SOCIAL AND CULTURAL HISTORY

Begin with Garth Jowett, *Film: The Democratic Art* (1976) and John O'Connor and Martin Jackson, eds., *American History/American Film* (1979), with essays by leading scholars on selected feature films; see also Paul Smith, ed., *The Historian and Film* (1976), mostly on British film, and Robert Sklar's beautifully written *Movie-Made America: A Cultural History of American Movies* (1976). All of these books include extensive bibliographies.

The idea of studying film to understand the ideas of a given society, or the placing of film within a proper historical context, is very much a recent historiographical trend. On the subject of women, see Molly Haskell, *From Reverence to Rape: The Treatment of Women in the Movies* (1974); on thirties America there are a few interesting ideas in Andrew Bergman, *We're in the Money: Depression America and Its Films* (1971); blacks have been covered fully in several recent studies, in particular Daniel J. Leab, *From 'Sambo' to 'Superspade': The Black Experience in Motion Pictures* (1975) and the exhaustive analysis in Thomas Cripps, *Slow Fade to Black: The Negro in American Film, 1900-1942* (1977); Cripps serves as a model for film research based on primary sources. A fine essay analyzing the societal significance of a single film is Thomas J. Knock, " 'History with Lightning': The Forgotten Film *Wilson*" (1976).

6. PHOTOGRAPHY

Begin with Marsha Peters and Bernard Mergen, " 'Doing the Rest': The Use of Photographs in American Studies" (1977). See also my bibliographic essay, "Historians and the Visual Analysis of Television News" in William Adams and Fay Schreibman, eds., *Television Network News: Issues in Content Research* (1978). Stott (1973) has much to say about Walker Evans which relates to documentary film; see also the discussions of photography in Bluem (1965) and Kracauer (1965). Susan Sontag's *On Photography* (1977) contains essays about the photographic image and historical context. Two classic essays relating photography to symbol and historical context are E. H. Gombrich, "The Visual Image" (1972), and Walter Benjamin's "A Short History of Photography" (1977). Finally John Berger, *Ways of Seeing* (1977) has some overstated ideas about the societal significance of images.

7. PROPAGANDA AND PUBLIC OPINION

Begin with Jacques Ellul, *Propaganda* (1973), a brilliant book, and Bernard C. Cohen, *The Public's Impact on Foreign Policy* (1973). Students of the visual image can hardly afford to ignore these topics. For Ellul, compare his changing ideas with his discussion of the same topic in his earlier *The Technological Society* (1964). A fine, though dated, bibliography can be found in Harold Lasswell, *et al.*, *Propaganda and Promotional Activities—An Annotated Bibliography* (1969), originally published in 1935.

Propaganda has its own vast bibliography. Representative titles include Terence H. Qualter, *Propaganda and Psychological Warfare* (1962); Jay W. Baird, *The Mythical World of Nazi War Propaganda, 1939-1945* (1974); and Allan M. Winkler, *The Politics of Propaganda: The Office of War Information 1942-1945* (1978), which says little about the OWI's visual productions. For a visual survey of propaganda, see Anthony Rhodes and Victor Margolin, *Propaganda, The Art of Persuasion in World War II* (1976) with a valuable filmography by William Murphy.

For public opinion the classic, still informative work is Walter Lippmann, *Public Opinion* (1965) which appeared in 1922. V. O. Key, Jr., *Public Opinion and American Democracy* (1961) says something valuable about mass persuasion, though the matter is dealt with more rigorously in Robert O. Carlson, ed., *Communications and Public Opinion: A Public Opinion Quarterly Reader* (1975). Some material about the visual media is found in the later chapters of James E. Pollard, *The Presidents and the Press* (1947) and a sequel, *The Presidents and the Press, Truman to Johnson* (1964). The best analysis of the reporter as mythmaker is Evelyn Waugh's cynical *Scoop* (1966); Phillip Knightley, *The First Casualty: From the Crimea to Vietnam—The War Correspondent as Hero, Propagandist, and Myth Maker* (1975) is not always accurate.

8. TELEVISION

Begin with George Comstock *et al., Television and Human Behavior* (1978), which summarizes over 2,500 studies of television's effect on human beings. See also the bibliographical essays on television research in Adams and Schreibman (1978). It is a convention to separate the literature of television from that of film. Every student must realize that the principles of visual analysis of the two media are often similar, and that any informed understanding of television as a medium must be grounded in a thorough study of what has been written about film and photography.

The best one-volume history of television is Erik Barnouw, *Tube of Plenty: The Evolution of American Television* (1975), a condensation and updating of his earlier *A Tower in Babel* (1966), *The Golden Web* (1968), and *The Image Empire* (1970); for the topic of sponsor relations, see his closely argued *The Sponsor: Notes on a Modern Potentate* (1978). There is some interesting material on CBS in David Halberstam's gossipy *The Powers That Be* (1979). Two fine textbooks which place television within the context of mass broadcasting are Christopher Sterling and John M. Kittross, *Stay Tuned: A Concise History of American Broadcasting* (1978) and Sydney W. Head, *Broadcasting in America: A Survey of Television and Radio* (1976). A helpful collection of articles, with some important statistical data, can be found in Lawrence W. Lichty and Malachi C. Topping, eds., *American Broadcasting: A Source Book on the History of Radio and Television* (1975).

Horace Newcomb, ed., *Television: The Critical View* (2d ed., 1979) has some material which places television programming within societal context; for economic matters the best survey is Les Brown, *Televi$ion: The Business Behind the Box* (1971); Martin Mayer, *About Television* (1972) is an informed overview, though now a bit outdated.

Russel B. Nye, *The Unembarrassed Muse: The Popular Arts in America* (1970) places television alongside other popular media. Audience attitudes are covered in Gary A. Steiner, *The People Look at Television: A Study of Audience Attitudes* (1963) and an updated version, Robert T. Bower, *Television and the*

Public (1973), both of which are in turn related to a series of books about radio audiences written by Paul Lazarsfeld in the 1940s. Short essays of widely varying quality on an important topic can be found in Randall M. Miller, ed., *Ethnic Images in American Film and Television* (1978). For actual examples of television programming, see Museum of Broadcasting, *A Subject Guide to the Radio & Television Collection of the Museum of Broadcasting* (1978), with regular supplements planned.

Government policy looms large in any consideration of television. Begin with John M. Kittross, ed., *Documents in American Telecommunications Policy* (1976); to survey what the new copyright law says about television, see U.S. Congress, House of Representatives, 94th Congress, 2d Session, *Copyright Law Revision* (1976). For public television, a recent overview can be found in Douglass Cater and Michael J. Nynan, *The Future of Public Broadcasting* (1976); for cable television, see Steven R. Rivkin, *Cable Television: A Guide to Federal Regulations* (1973); Walter B. Emery, *Broadcasting and Government: Responsibilities and Regulations* (1971) is the standard, now somewhat dated, source for its subject.

Television has proved to be an industry easily intimidated. See Barnouw (1978); John Cogley, *Report on Blacklisting II: Radio-Television* (1956); and the fascinating account of one who eventually triumphed over his persecutors, John Henry Faulk, *Fear on Trial* (1976). The Twentieth Century Fund Task Force on the Government and the Press, *Press Freedoms Under Pressure* (1972) provides a more recent variant of the problem.

The social effects of television-viewing have exercised many parents who tend to forget that the same fears were raised about movies, for example in Henry James Forman, *Our Movie Made Children* (1935). Comstock (1978) summarizes over 2,500 such studies and is very reluctant to attribute much to television. For the possibility that television increases juvenile delinquency, see the Surgeon General's Scientific Advisory Committee on Television and Social Behavior, *Television and Growing Up: The Impact of Televised Violence* (1972), and Douglass Cater and Stephen Strickland, *TV Violence and the Child: The Evolution and Fate of the Surgeon General's Report* (1975); also valuable is M. S. Heller and S. Polsky, *Studies in Violence and Television* (1976).

The impact of television on voting has also led to considerable discussion. One of the best books on the subject is Kurt and Gladys Lang, *Politics and Television* (1968); for the 1960 presidential campaign, see Sidney Kraus. ed., *The Great Debates: Background—Perspective—Effects* (1968); for 1972, see Thomas E. Patterson and Robert D. McClure, *The Unseeing Eye: The Myth of Television Power in National Politics* (1976). The British experience offers some important contrasts. See Jay G. Blumler and Denis McQuail, *Television in Politics: Its Uses and Influence* (1968); Blumler's *The Challenge of Election Broadcasting: Report of an Enquiry by the Centre for Television Research, University of Leeds* (1978) is remarkably lively.

The serious analysis of television news is an emerging field. Begin with Adams and Schreibman (1978) and the fine bibliography in Robert Schmuhl, ed., *The Classroom and The Newsroom* (1979). The history of television news is covered in Fred W. Friendly, *Due to Circumstances Beyond Our Control* (1967) and William Small, *To Kill a Messenger: Television News and the Real World* (1970). Ben H. Bagdikian, *The Information Machines: Their Impact on Men and Media* (1971) contains some good ideas.

Critics of television news abound. Daniel J. Boorstin, *The Image: A Guide to*

Pseudo-Events in America (1964) makes an important point about the practical relationship between public relations and news. Edith Efron, *The News Twisters* (1971) is a diatribe; so too is Ernest W. Lefever, *TV and National Defense: An Analysis of CBS News, 1972-1973* (1974). Edward Jay Epstein, *News from Nowhere: Television and the News* (1973) argues that institutional constraints shape news coverage.

The war in Vietnam has resulted in one superb body of data about television's coverage of that conflict. Peter Braestrup, *Big Story: How the American Press and Television Reported and Interpreted the Crisis of Tet 1968 in Vietnam and Washington* (1977), for which Lawrence Lichty compiled the data relating to CBS. Lichty and George Bailey are currently finishing up ten years of research for their important book on this subject. Finally, for a variety of topics, particularly the Vietnam war, the best television criticism is found in Michael Arlen, *Living-Room War* (1969) and *The View from Highway 1: Essays on Television* (1976).

9. SOCIOLOGY OF FILM AND TELEVISION

Begin with Jeremy Tunstall, *The Media Are American* (1977) and Denis Mc-Quail, *Towards a Sociology of Mass Communications* (1969). This heading combines two kinds of literature—studies which deal with the impact of media on society from a theoretical point of view and those which attempt to measure precisely certain effects, such as are listed in Comstock (1978). Marshall Mc-Luhan, *Understanding Media* (1964) still merits careful attention. Raymond Williams, *Television: Technology and Cultural Form* (1975) is well-argued; much less helpful than Tunstall is Herbert I. Schiller, *Mass Communications and American Empire* (1971).

Statistical analyses are few and far between. One of the best is Fredric Stuart, *The Effects of Television on the Motion Picture and Radio Industries* (1976); for movies, see Leo A. Handel, *Hollywood Looks at Its Audience* (1950); for the more recent period, I. C. Jarvie, *Movies and Society* (1970) is important. A very handy source of data, now outdated, is Richard E. Chapin, *Mass Communications: A Statistical Analysis* (1957). Christopher H. Sterling and Timothy R. Haight, eds., *The Mass Media: Aspen Guide to Communication Industry Trends* (1978) covers the more recent period admirably.

Attempts by social psychologists to gauge media effects can be found in Wilbur Schramm and Donald F. Roberts, eds., *The Process and Effects of Mass Communication* (1974); World War II work is described in C. I. Hovland, *et al.*, *Experiments on Mass Communications* (1965). A large group of scattered studies is summarized in Charles F. Hoban, Jr., and Edward B. Van Ormer, *Instructional Film Research 1918-1950* (1976). Finally a model study relating to radio is relevant: Robert K. Merton, *Mass Persuasion: The Social Psychology of a War Bond Drive* (1946).

10. JOURNALS

Begin with *Mass Media Booknotes* (Christopher H. Sterling, Dept. Radio-TV-Film, Temple University, Philadelphia, PA 19122). In a field such as mass media, current journals are a must. Many are obscure and found only in larger libraries. The best journals to subscribe to for film are the *Journal of the University Film Association* (School of Communication, Agnes Arnold Hall, University of Houston, Houston, TX 77004); and a fine magazine, *American Film* (American Film Institute, John F. Kennedy Center, Washington, DC 20560).

For animation see *Funnyworld* (P.O. Box 1633, New York, NY 10001). To see what historians are doing with film and television, subscribe to *Film & History* (The Historians Film Committee, c/o The History Faculty, New Jersey Institute of Technology, Newark, NJ 07102).

Other journals might be consulted in a larger library. For film, see in particular *Cinema Journal, Journal of Popular Film and Television, Film Comment, Cineaste, Film Quarterly, Jump Cut, Sight and Sound,* and the *Quarterly Review of Film Studies.* For television, by all means look at the weekly issues of *Variety,* which always include a vast amount of material about film as well; see also *Broadcasting,* the trade journal of the broadcasting industry; and the scholarly articles in the *Journal of Broadcasting* and *Journalism Quarterly.*

WORKS CITED

Adams, William and Fay Schreibman, eds. *Television Network News: Issues in Content Research.* Washington, D.C.: George Washington University Press, 1978.

Adler, Richard P. "What is Visual Literacy?" *American Film,* III (June, 1978), pp. 22-25 *et seq.*

American Film Institute Catalog: Feature Films 1921-1930. Edited by Kenneth Munden. New York: Bowker, 1971. 2 vols.

American Film Institute Catalog: Feature Films 1961-1970. Edited by Richard Krafsur. New York: Bowker, 1976. 2 vols.

Anderson, Joseph L. and Donald Richie. *The Japanese Film: Art and Industry.* New York: Grove Press, 1960.

Andrew, J. Dudley. *The Major Film Theories: An Introduction.* New York: Oxford, 1976.

Arlen, Michael. *Living-Room War.* New York: Viking Press, 1969.

―――. *The View from Highway 1: Essays on Television.* New York: Farrar, Straus & Giroux, 1976.

Arts Enquiry, The. *The Factual Film.* London: Oxford, 1947.

Assistant Secretary of Defense (Manpower and Reserve Affairs). *Audio-Visual Management Task Force Report.* Washington, D.C.: Department of Defense, August 1, 1974.

Bagdikian, Ben H. *The Information Machines: Their Impact on Men and the Media.* New York: Harper & Row, 1971.

Baird, Jay W. *The Mythical World of Nazi War Propaganda, 1939-1945.* Minneapolis: University of Minnesota, 1974.

Balio, Tino, ed. *The American Film Industry.* Madison: University of Wisconsin, 1976.

Barna, Yon. *Eisenstein: The Growth of a Cinematic Genius.* Boston: Little, Brown, 1975.

Barnouw, Erik. *Documentary: A History of the Non-Fiction Film.* New York: Oxford, 1974.

————. *The Golden Web: A History of Broadcasting in the United States 1933-1953.* New York: Oxford, 1968.

————, and S. Krishnaswamy. *Indian Film.* New York: Columbia University Press, 1963.

————. *The Sponsor: Notes on a Modern Potentate.* New York: Oxford, 1978.

————. *A Tower in Babel: A History of Broadcasting in the United States to 1933.* New York: Oxford, 1966.

————. *Tube of Plenty: The Evolution of American Television.* New York: Oxford, 1975.

Barsam, Richard Meran. *Nonfiction Film: A Critical History.* New York: Dutton, 1973.

Bawden, Liz-Anne, ed., *The Oxford Companion to Film.* New York: Oxford, 1976.

————, ed. *Nonfiction Film Theory and Criticism.* New York: Dutton, 1976.

Benjamin, Walter. "A Short History of Photography." *Art Forum,* XV (February, 1977), pp. 46-51.

Berger, John. *Ways of Seeing.* Baltimore: Penguin Books, 1977.

Bergman, Andrew. *We're in the Money: Depression America and Its Films.* New York: New York University Press, 1971.

Bluem, A. William. *Documentary in American Television: Form, Function, Method.* New York: Hastings House, 1965.

Blumler, Jay G. and Denis McQuail. *Television in Politics: Its Uses and Influence.* London: Faber & Faber, 1968.

————et al. *The Challenge of Election Broadcasting: Report of an Enquiry by the Centre for Television Research, University of Leeds.* Leeds, England: Leeds University, 1978.

Bohn, Thomas William. *An Historical and Descriptive Analysis of the "Why We Fight" Series.* New York: Arno, 1977.

Boorstin, Daniel J. *The Image: A Guide to Pseudo-Events in America.* New York: Harper Colophon, 1964.

Bower, Robert T. *Television and the Public.* New York: Holt, Rinehart and Winston, 1973.

Bowles, Stephen E., ed. *Index to Critical Film Reviews.* New York: Burt Franklin, 1974.

Braestrup, Peter. *Big Story: How the American Press and Television Reported and Interpreted the Crisis of Tet 1968 in Vietnam and Washington.* 2 v. Boulder, Col.: Westview, 1977.

Bray, Mayfield S. and William T. Murphy. *Audiovisual Records in the National Archives of the United States Relating to World War II.* Washington, D.C.: National Archives and Records Service, 1974. (Reference Information Paper No. 79.)

Brown, Les. *Television: The Business Behind the Box.* New York: Harcourt Brace Jovanovich, 1971.

Brownlow, Kevin. *The Parade's Gone By . . .* New York: Knopf, 1968.

————. *The War, the West, and the Wilderness.* New York: Knopf, 1979.

Bukalski, Peter J., *Film Research: A Critical Bibliography with Annotations and Essay.* Boston: G. K. Hall, 1972.

Caffrey, Ann Gourley, comp. *Using Your Nation's Capital: An Indexed Guide to Multimedia Resources in Washington, D.C.* Washington, D.C.: Office of Education, 1972.

Capra, Frank. *The Name Above the Title: An Autobiography.* New York: New York: Macmillan, 1971.

Carlson, Robert O., ed. *Communications and Public Opinion: A Public Opinion Quarterly Reader.* New York: Praeger, 1975.

Cater, Douglass and Stephen Strickland. *TV Violence and the Child: The Evolution and Fate of the Surgeon General's Report.* New York: Russell Sage Foundation, 1975.

———— and Michael J. Nyman. *The Future of Public Broadcasting.* New York: Praeger, 1976.

Ceram, C. W. *Archaeology of the Cinema.* New York: Harcourt Brace and World, 1965.

Chapin, Richard E. *Mass Communications: A Statistical Analysis.* East Lansing: Michigan State University, 1957.

Cogley, John. *Report on Blacklisting I: Movies.* New York: Fund for the Republic, 1956.

———— *Report on Blacklisting II: Radio-Television.* New York: Fund for the Republic. 1956.

Cohen, Bernard C. *The Public's Impact on Foreign Policy.* Boston: Little, Brown, 1973.

Comstock, George *et al. Television and Human Behavior.* New York: Columbia University, 1978.

Cowie, Peter. *Swedish Cinema.* London: Zwemmer; New York: Barnes, 1966.

Cripps, Thomas. *Slow Fade to Black: The Negro in American Film, 1900-1942.* New York: Oxford, 1977.

Culbert, David. " 'A Quick, Delightful Gink': Eric Knight at the Walt Disney Studio." *Funnyworld* No. 19 (Fall, 1978), pp. 13-17.

Efron, Edith. *The News Twisters.* Los Angeles: Nash, 1971.

Eisner, Lotte H. *The Haunted Screen: Expressionism in the German Cinema and the Influence of Max Reinhardt.* Berkeley: University of California, 1973.

Ellul, Jacques. *The Technological Society.* New York: Knopf, 1964.

———— *Propaganda: The Formation of Men's Attitudes.* New York: Vintage Books, 1973.

Emery, Walter B. *Broadcasting and Government: Responsibilities and Regulations.* 2d ed. East Lansing: Michigan State University, 1971.

Epstein, Edward Jay. *News from Nowhere: Television and the News.* New York: Random House, 1973.

Faulk, John Henry. *Fear on Trial.* New York: Tempo Books, 1976.

Ferris, Bill and Judy Peiser, eds. *American Folklore Films and Videotapes: An Index.* Memphis: Center for Southern Folklore, 1976.

Fielding, Raymond. *The American Newsreel 1911-1967.* Norman: University of Oklahoma, 1972.

——— *The March of Time 1935-1951.* New York: Oxford, 1978.

Film Council of America. *Sixty Years of 16mm Film 1923-1983. A Symposium.* Evanston: Film Council of America, 1954.

Forman, Henry James. *Our Movie Made Children.* New York: Macmillan, 1935.

Friendly, Fred W. *Due to Circumstances Beyond Our Control.* New York: Random House, 1967.

Furhammar, Leif and Folke Isaksson. *Politics and Film.* New York: Praeger, 1971.

Geduld, Harry M. and Ronald Gottesman. *An Illustrated Glossary of Film Terms.* New York: Holt, Rinehart and Winston, 1973.

Gerlach, John C. and Lana Gerlach. *The Critical Index: A Bibliography of Articles on Film in English, 1946-1973.* New York: Teachers College, 1974.

Gombrich, E. H. "The Visual Image." *Scientific American,* CCXXVII (September, 1972), pp. 82-96.

Government Accounting Office, "Valuable Government-Owned Motion Picture Films are Rapidly Deteriorating." LCD-78-113. Washington, D.C.: Government Accounting Office, June 19, 1978.

Grant, Steven A. *Scholars' Guide to Washington, D.C. for Russian/Soviet Studies.* Washington, D.C.: Smithsonian Institution Press, 1977.

Green, Shirley L. and Diane Hamilton, comps. *Pictorial Resources in the Washington, D.C. Area.* Washington, D.C.: Library of Congress, 1976.

Griffith, Richard and Arthur Mayer. *The Movies.* Rev. ed. New York: Simon and Schuster, 1970.

Guide to the National Archives of the United States. Washington, D.C.: National Archives and Records Service, 1974.

Halberstam, David. *The Powers That Be.* New York: Random House, 1979.

Halliwell, Leslie, *The Filmgoer's Companion.* 6th ed. New York: Avon, 1978.

Handel, Leo A. *Hollywood Looks at Its Audience.* Urbana: University of Illinois Press, 1950.

Hardy, Forsyth, ed. *Grierson on Documentary.* Rev. ed. Berkeley: University of California, 1966.

Harrington, John. *The Rhetoric of Film*. New York: Holt, Rinehart and Winston, 1973.

Haskell, Molly. *From Reverence to Rape: The Treatment of Women in the Movies*. New York: Holt, Rinehart and Winston, 1974.

Hawkes, Terence. *Structuralism and Semiotics*. Berkeley: University of California, 1977.

Head, Sydney W. *Broadcasting in America: A Survey of Television and Radio*. 3rd ed. Boston: Houghton Mifflin, 1976.

Heider, Karl G. *Ethnographic Film*. Austin: University of Texas, 1976.

——— *Films for Anthropological Teaching*. 6th ed. Washington, D.C.: American Anthropological Assoc., 1977.

Heller, M. S. and S. Polsky. *Studies in Violence and Television*. New York: American Broadcasting Company, 1976.

Hendricks, Gordon. *The Edison Motion Picture Myth*. Berkeley: University of California, 1961.

Hoban, Charles F., Jr. and Edward B. Van Ormer. *Instructional Film Research 1918-1950*. New York: Arno, 1976.

Hovland, C. I. *et al. Experiments on Mass Communications*. New York: Wiley, 1965.

Hughes, Robert, ed. *Film: Book 2, Films of Peace and War*. New York: Grove, 1962.

Ivens, Joris. *The Camera and I*. New York: International Publishers, 1969.

Jarvie, I. C. *Movies and Society*. New York: Basic Books, 1970.

Jeavons, Clyde. *A Pictorial History of War Films*. Secaucus, N.J.: Citadel Press, 1974.

Jowett, Garth. *Film: The Democratic Art*. Boston: Little, Brown, 1976.

Kael, Pauline. *The Citizen Kane Book*. New York: Bantam, 1974.

Key, V. O. Jr. *Public Opinion and American Democracy*. New York: Knopf, 1961.

Kittross, John, ed. *Documents in American Telecommunications Policy*. New York: Arno, 1976.

Knightley, Phillip. *The First Casualty: From the Crimea to Vietnam—The War Correspondent as Hero, Propagandist, and Myth Maker*. New York: Harcourt Brace Jovanovich, 1975.

Knock, Thomas J. " 'History with Lightning': The Forgotten Film *Wilson*." *American Quarterly*, XXVIII (Winter, 1976), pp. 523-43.

Kracauer, Siegfried. *From Caligari to Hitler: A Psychological History of the German Film*. Princeton: Princeton University, 1947.

——— *Theory of Film: The Redemption of Physical Reality*. New York: Oxford, 1965.

Kraus, Sidney. *The Great Debates: Background-Perspective-Effects.* Gloucester, Mass.: Peter Smith, 1968.

Lang, Kurt and Gladys Lang. *Politics and Television.* Chicago: Quadrangle Books, 1968.

Lasswell, Harold *et al. Propaganda and Promotional Activities—An Annotated Bibliography.* Chicago: University of Chicago, 1969.

Leab, Daniel J. *From 'Sambo' to 'Superspade': The Black Experience in Motion Pictures.* Boston: Houghton Mifflin, 1975.

Lefever, Ernest W. *TV and National Defense: An Analysis of CBS News, 1972-1973.* Boston, Va.: Institute for American Strategy, 1974.

Leiser, Erwin. *Nazi Cinema.* NewYork: Collier, 1975.

Leonard, Harold, ed. *The Film Index.* New York: Wilson, 1941

Leprohon, Pierre. *The Italian Cinema.* New York: Praeger, 1972.

Leyda, Jay. *Films Beget Films: A Study of the Compilation Film.* New York: Hill & Wang, 1971.

———— *Kino: A History of the Russian and Soviet Film.* New York: Collier, 1973.

Lichty, Lawrence W. and Malachi C. Topping, eds. *American Broadcasting: A Source Book on the History of Radio and Television.* New York: Hastings House, 1975.

Limbacher, James L. *Feature Films on 8mm and 16mm: A Directory of Feature Films Available for Rental, Sale, and Lease in the United States.* 5th ed. New York: Bowker, 1977.

Lippmann, Walter. *Public Opinion.* New York: Free Press, 1965.

Look, editors of. *Movie Lot to Beachhead: The Motion Picture Goes to War and Prepares for the Future.* Garden City, N.Y.: Doubleday, Doran, 1945.

Low, Rachel, and Roger Manvell. *The History of the British Film.* 3 v. London: Allen & Unwin, 1948-1951.

MacCann, Richard Dyer. *Film: A Montage of Theories.* New York: Dutton, 1966.

———— *The People's Films: A Political History of U.S. Government Motion Pictures.* New York: Hastings House, 1973.

———— and Edward S. Perry. *The New Film Index: A Bibliography of Magazine Articles in English, 1930-1970.* New York: Dutton, 1975.

McLuhan, Marshall. *Understanding Media.* New York: McGraw-Hill, 1964.

McQuail, Denis. *Towards a Sociology of Mass Communications.* London: Collier-Macmillan, 1969.

Maltin, Leonard, ed. *TV Movies: 1979-80 Edition.* New York: NAL, 1978.

Manvell, Roger, ed. *International Encyclopedia of Film.* London: Joseph, 1972.

Mast, Gerald. *The Comic Mind: Comedy and the Movies.* Indianapolis: Bobbs-Merrill, 1973.

―――― *A Short History of the Movies.* 2nd ed. Indianapolis: Bobbs-Merrill, 1976.

Mayer, Martin. *About Television.* New York: Harper & Row, 1972.

Mehr, Linda, compiler. *Motion Pictures, Television and Radio: A Union Catalogue of Manuscript and Special Collections in the Western United States.* Boston: G. K. Hall, 1977.

Mellen, Joan. *The Waves at Genji's Door: Japan Through Its Cinema.* New York: Pantheon Books, 1976.

Mercer, John, comp. *Glossary of Film Terms.* Houston: University Film Association, 1978. (UFA Monograph No. 2.)

Merton, Robert K. *Mass Persuasion: The Social Psychology of a War Bond Drive.* New York: Harper, 1946.

Metz, Christian. *Film Language: A Semiotics of the Cinema.* New York: Oxford, 1974.

Miller, Randall M., ed. *Ethnic Images in American Film and Television.* Philadelphia: The Balch Institute, 1978.

Murphy, William T. *Robert Flaherty: A Guide to References and Resources.* Boston: G. K. Hall, 1978.

Museum of Broadcasting. *A Subject Guide to the Radio & Television Collection of the Museum of Broadcasting (as of September 1, 1977).* I (No. 1). New York: Museum of Broadcasting, 1978.

National Archives Microfilm Publications. Washington, D.C.: National Archives and Records Service, 1974.

The National Union Catalog of Manuscript Collections, Ann Arbor: J. W. Edwards, 1962, and Washington, D.C.: Library of Congress, 1963-.

Nelson, Abigail, compiler. *Guide to Film and Video Resources in New England.* Cambridge: University Film Study Center, 1977.

Nelson, Richard Alan. "Germany and the German Film, 1930-1945: An Annotated Research Bibliography." *Journal of the University Film Association,* XXIX (Winter, 1977), pp. 45-66; (Spring, 1977), pp. 67-80; and XXX (Winter, 1978), pp. 53-72.

Newcomb, Horace, ed. *Television: The Critical View.* 2d ed. New York: Oxford, 1979.

The New York Times Film Reviews, 1913-1968. 6 v. New York: New York Times, 1970.

Nichols, Bill, ed. *Movies and Methods.* Berkeley: University of California, 1976.

Nye, Russel B. *The Unembarrassed Muse: The Popular Arts in America.* New York: Dial, 1970.

O'Connor, John E., ed. *Film and the Humanities.* New York: The Rockefeller Foundation, August, 1977.

———— and Martin A. Jackson, eds. *American History/American Film.* New York: Ungar, 1979.

Office of Federal Management Policy. *Review of Audiovisual Facilities in Washington, DC and San Bernardino, California Areas.* Washington, D.C.: Office of Federal Management Policy, December, 1975.

Ophuls, Marcel. *The Sorrow and the Pity.* New York: Dutton, 1972.

Panofsky, Erwin. "Style and Medium in the Motion Pictures," reprinted in Gerald Mast and Marshall Cohen, eds. *Film Theory and Criticism: Introductory Readings.* 2d ed. New York: Oxford, 1979, pp. 151-69.

Patterson, Thomas E. and Robert D. McClure. *The Unseeing Eye: The Myth of Television Power in National Politics.* New York: Putnam's Sons, 1976.

Perlmutter, Tom. *War Movies.* Secaucus, N.J.: Castle Books, 1974.

Peters, Marsha, and Bernard Mergen. " 'Doing the Rest': The Use of Photographs in American Studies." *American Quarterly,* XXIX (No. 3, 1977), pp. 280-303.

Pollard, James E. *The Presidents and the Press.* New York: Macmillan, 1947.

———— *The Presidents and the Press, Truman to Johnson.* Washington, D.C.: Public Affairs, 1964.

Pratt, George C. *Spellbound in Darkness: A History of the Silent Film.* Greenwich, Conn.: New York Graphic Society, 1973.

Qualter, Terence H. *Propaganda and Psychological Warfare.* New York: Random House, 1962.

Randall, Richard S. *Censorship of the Movies: The Social and Political Control of a Mass Medium.* Madison: University of Wisconsin, 1970.

A Reference List of Audiovisual Materials Produced by the United States Government 1978. Washington, D.C.: National Audiovisual Center, 1978.

Rhodes, Anthony and Victor Margolin. *Propaganda, The Art of Persuasion: World War II.* New York: Chelsea, 1976.

Rivers, William L. *et al. Aspen Handbook on the Media: 1977-79 Edition—A Selective Guide to Research, Organizations and Publications in Communications.* New York: Praeger, 1977.

Rivkin, Steven R. *Cable Television: A Guide to Federal Regulations.* Santa Monica, Calif.: Rand Corporation, 1973.

Rollins, Peter C. "Film and American Studies: Questions, Activities, Guides." *American Quarterly,* XXVI (No. 3), 1974, pp. 245-65.

Rose, Ernest D. *World Film and TV Study Resources: A Reference Guide to Major Training Centers and Archives.* Bonn: Friedrich-Ebert Stiftung, 1974.

Rotha, Paul. *Documentary Film.* 3d ed. London: Faber & Faber, 1952.

————. *Documentary Diary: An Informal History of the British Documentary Film, 1928-1939.* London: Secker & Warburg, 1973.

Sadoul, Georges. *Dictionary of Film Makers.* Rev. ed. Berkeley: University of California, 1972.

———— *Dictionary of Films.* Rev. ed. Berkeley: University of California, 1972.

———— *French Film.* London: Falcon Press, 1953.

Schickel, Richard. *The Disney Version: The Life, Times, Art and Commerce of Walt Disney.* New York: Simon and Schuster, 1967.

Schiller, Herbert I. *Mass Communications and American Empire.* Boston: Beacon, 1971.

Schmuhl, Robert, ed. *The Classroom and The Newsroom: The Citizen and the News Project.* Bloomington: The Poynter Center, January 1979.

Schramm, Wilbur and Donald F. Roberts, eds. *The Process and Effects of Mass Communication.* Rev. ed. Urbana: University of Illinois, 1974.

Sklar, Robert. *Movie-made America: A Cultural History of American Movies.* New York: Vintage Books, 1976.

Small, William. *To Kill a Messenger: Television News and the Real World.* New York: Hastings House, 1970.

Smith, Paul, ed. *The Historian and Film.* Cambridge, Eng.: Cambridge University, 1976.

Snyder, Robert. *Pare Lorentz and the Documentary Film.* Norman: University of Oklahoma, 1968.

Sontag, Susan. *On Photography.* New York: Farrar, Straus & Giroux, 1977.

Steiner, Gary A. *The People Look at Television: A Study of Audience Attitudes.* New York: Knopf, 1963.

Sterling, Christopher and John M. Kittross. *Stay Tuned: A Concise History of American Broadcasting.* Belmont, Cal.: Wadsworth, 1978.

———— and Timothy R. Haight, eds. *The Mass Media: Aspen Guide to Communication Industry Trends.* New York: Praeger, 1978.

Stott, William. *Documentary Expression and Thirties America.* New York: Oxford, 1973.

Stuart, Fredric. *The Effects of Television on the Motion Picture and Radio Industries.* New York: Arno, 1976.

Suid, Lawrence H. *Guts and Glory: Great American War Movies.* Reading, Mass.: Addison-Wesley, 1978.

Surgeon General's Scientific Advisory Committee on Television and Social Behavior. *Television and Growing Up: The Impact of Televised Violence.* Washington, D.C.: Government Printing Office, 1972.

Twentieth Century Fund Task Force on the Government and the Press. *Press Freedoms Under Pressure.* New York: Twentieth Century Fund, 1972.

Tunstall, Jeremy. *The Media Are American.* New York: Columbia University, 1977.

U.S. Army. *Index of Army Motion Pictures for Public Non-Profit Use.* Washington, D.C.: U.S. Army, May, 1975. (Pamphlett 108-4.)

———— *Index of Army Motion Pictures and Related Audio-Visual Aids.* No. 108-1. Washington, D.C.: U.S. Army, January 1977.

U.S. Congress. House of Representatives. 94th Congress, 2d session. Report 94-1476. *Copyright Law Revision.* Washington, D.C.: Government Printing Office, 1976.

Waugh, Evelyn. *Scoop.* Boston: Little, Brown, 1966.

Weaver, Kathleen, compiler. *Film Programmer's Guide to 16mm Rentals.* Berkeley: Reel Research, 1975. 2d ed. [Available from Reel Research, Box 6037, Albany, Cal. 94706.]

Weber, Olga, comp. *North American Film and Video Directory.* New York: Bowker, 1975.

Williams, Raymond. *Television: Technology and Cultural Form.* New York: Schocken, 1975.

Winkler, Allan M. *The Politics of Propaganda: The Office of War Information 1942-1945.* New Haven: Yale University, 1978.

World Directory of Stockshot and Film Production Libraries. London: Pergamon Press, 1969.

Wright, Will. *Sixguns & Society: A Structural Study of the Western.* Berkeley: University of California, 1977.

Appendix VIII.   Technical Services/Commercial Distributors

TECHNICAL SERVICES

Screening facilities available for rent range from 16mm projectors and video cassette units which can be picked up for use at any location to plush screening rooms at the commercial labs to full-sized commercial theaters which can be rented for an afternoon or evening. Check the Yellow Pages under "Audio-visual Equpiment and Supplies," "Motion Picture Equipment—Rental," and "Television Rental," or contact the Washington commercial labs or area movie theaters.

Dubbing services are available from the commercial labs. Also see entry #109 for services available at the University of Maryland.

The handiest source of information on technical services available in Washington is *The WAFL Book,* a publication of the Washington Area Filmmakers League, Inc. (See Appendix V.) It has an excellent section called "Using the Capital City." The focus of the book is film production rather than scholarly use of film and video.

COMMERCIAL DISTRIBUTORS

The following are distributors of 16mm entertainment motion pictures located in the Washington area:

> FILM CENTER
> 908 12th Street, NW
> Washington, D.C. 20005
> (202) 393-1205

Collection

> 400 feature length films and hundreds of shorts. The bulk of the collection is contemporary American entertainment films. There are some classic documentaries and the shorts include cartoons, serials, and live action films of interest to children. Early shorts include Chaplin, Mack Sennett, Laurel & Hardy, Our Gang, and W. C. Fields.

Rentals

> The rentals are moderate and there is a special rate for many of the films if shown in one's own home.

262

Catalogue

A descriptive catalogue is available by mail.

RE-RUNS UNLIMITED, INC.
4907 Cordell Avenue
Bethesda, Maryland 20014
(301) 986-9440

Collection

70 feature length films and 32 shorts. The emphasis of this collection is older and classic American and British films. There are a number of literary classics and single films of note such as *Yellow Submarine* and *Night of the Living Dead.* A special group of films for children includes animated features, *Our Gang,* and television episodes from *Hot Dog* and *The Lone Ranger.*

Rentals

The rental rates are low to moderate. (*Cat Ballou* is $40 from Re-Runs, $65 from Film Center, and $97.50 from Swank.) A special 50 percent discount is available to individuals.

Catalogue

A descriptive catalogue is available by mail.

SWANK MOTION PICTURES, INC.
7926 Jones Branch Road
McLean, Virginia 22102
(703) 821-1040

Collection

500 feature length films, hundreds of shorts. The emphasis is on recent American films, with smaller collections of film classics, foreign films and horror films. All films seem to have been chosen for their entertainment value. The shorts include silent comedies, animations, and early sound comedies.

Rentals

The rental rates are high with no special advantages for local groups. Swank does not rent to individuals.

Catalogue

A descriptive catalogue is available through the mail to groups and institutions.

The distribution of entertainment films and TV programs on videocassettes is just beginning to provide another valuable resource for those interested in viewing older TV and films. Numerous companies are gaining the rights to hundreds of older and many recent titles from American commercial film and television production companies. Little specific information was available at press time. One publication that should be helpful is the National Video Clearinghouse's *The Video Sourcebook* (Syosset, N.Y.: National Video Clearinghouse, 1979), a subject-indexed guide to over 15,000 titles in distribution.

Appendix IX.   Transportation/Housing/Services

This section has been prepared to assist visiting scholars with information about transportation and short-term housing, and to describe the special services available to international visitors.

TRANSPORTATION

The great majority of the collections described in the *Guide* are located in downtown Washington, D.C. Parking is expensive but this area is well-served by our new subway system, the Metro. Metrobuses serve the outer areas of the city and the Maryland and Virginia suburbs. Maps of the Metro subway, which does link some suburban locations to the city, and information booths at each stop can provide guidance to visitors. Information on metrobus routes is available at (202) 637-2437.

Taxi fares in Washington are reasonable compared to those in other large cities. The rates increase substantially for trips which cross the D.C. line into Maryland or Virginia. Rates within D.C. are based on zones, which can be confusing to a newcomer.

ARRIVING AND LEAVING

Those arriving by bus or train will find themselves right in downtown Washington. The Greyhound and Trailways bus stations are near several Metro subway stops. All trains come into Union Station, which has its own Metro subway stop and is within easy walking distance of the Library of Congress. The National Visitors Center at Union Station is a fine source of maps and advice on getting around Washington.

Three airports serve the Washington area. National Airport is close to the city and linked to it by subway, Metrobus, and taxi. Those who can carry their own luggage may prefer to take the subway, which is both quicker and less expensive than a taxi. There is a walk of several blocks from the terminals to the Metro subway stop, but a free shuttle bus runs frequently.

Both Dulles International Airport and Baltimore-Washington International Airport are linked to the city by taxi and airport limousine service. The limousine drops off passengers at several downtown locations including some major hotels. For further information, call Greyhound Airport Service (202) 471-9801.

HOUSING

Perhaps the best first stop is one of the university housing offices. Their services are available to the public and they have information on dormitories, apartments for rent and sublease, copies of *The Apartment Shoppers Guide and Housing Directory,* and maps of Washington.

George Washington University Off-Campus Housing Resources Center
2121 I Street, NW, 4th Floor
Washington, D.C. 20052
(202) 676-6688

Georgetown University Off-Campus Housing Office
Healy Building Basement
37th and O Streets, NW
Washington, D.C. 20057
(202) 625-3026

Catholic University Off-Campus Housing Office
St. Bonaventure Hall, Room 106
4th Street and Michigan Avenue, NE
Washington, D.C. 20064
(202) 635-5618

Northern Virginia Community College
Annandale Campus Housing Office
Science Building, Room 225-A
8333 Little River Turnpike
Annandale, Virginia 22003
(703) 323-3143

Near the Library of Congress are two apartment buildings which have furnished apartments available for short term (3 months) lease:

The Capitol Park
800 4th Street, SW
Washington, D.C. 20024
(202) 484-5400

The Coronet Apartment
200 C Street, SE
Washington, D.C. 20003
(202) 547-6300

Those interested in very short term housing might check the following low cost alternative to a hotel open to everyone:

International Guest House
1441 Kennedy Street, NW
Washington, D.C. 20011
(202) 726-5808

The Guest House is located on good bus routes into the downtown area. Accommodations are available at a daily rate and children are permitted. There is a curfew.

SERVICES FOR INTERNATIONAL VISITORS

The International Visitors Information Service (IVIS) is a private nonprofit community organization which offers services to international visitors to the Washington area. Over 1,200 volunteers support the program. The multilingual staff and volunteers are available to help visitors with sightseeing arrangements, hotel accommodations, bilingual medical assistance and opportunities to visit American families. Persons in need of language assistance may call (202) 872-8747. There are two locations:

Main Information and Reception Center
801 19th Street, NW
Washington, D.C. 20006
Monday-Friday 9:00 A.M.-5:00 P.M.

Information Booth
Dulles International Airport
12 noon-7:00 P.M. daily

International college and university students may be interested in the Foreign Student Service Council (FSSC) which provides home hospitality, sightseeing, and other services:

1623 Belmont Street, NW
Washington, D.C. 20009
(202) 232-4979

Appendix X.   Federal Government Holidays

Federal government offices are closed on the following holidays:

New Year's Day	January 1
Washington's Birthday	3rd Monday in February
Memorial Day	last Monday in May
Independence Day	July 4*
Labor Day	1st Monday in September
Columbus Day	2nd Monday in October
Veterans' Day	November 11*
Thanksgiving	4th Thursday in November
Christmas	December 25*

* If this date is on a Saturday, the holiday is on Friday. If this date is on a Sunday, the holiday is on Monday.

The public areas of the Smithsonian Institution and the General Reading Rooms of the Library of Congress are open on most holidays.

Bibliography

Information on catalogues and publications about individual collections is found in each entry. The general reference works listed below are those used by the author to locate collections in Washington and elsewhere in the United States. Factfile, Number 11, listed below, is a good basic media research bibliography.

Adams, William, and Schreibman, Fay. *Television Network News: Issues in Content Research.* Washington, D.C.: School of Public and International Affairs, George Washington University, 1978.

Aspen Handbook on the Media 1977-1979: A Selective Guide to Research Organizations and Publications in Communications. New York: Praeger, 1977.

CINE (Council on International Non-Theatrical Events). *Golden Eagle Film Awards.* Unpublished. Washington, D.C.: CINE, 1978.

American Film Institute. "Film and Television: A Research Guide," *Factfiles,* Number 11, 1977.

Educational Film Library Association. *Film Resource Centers in New York City.* New York: Educational Film Library Association, 1976.

Green, Shirley L. *Pictorial Resources in the Washington, D.C. Area.* Washington, D.C.: Library of Congress. 1976.

Jennings, Margaret S., ed. *Library and Reference Facilities in the Area of the District of Columbia.* 10th ed. Washington, D.C.: American Society for Information Science, 1979.

Mehr, Linda Harris, ed. *Motion Pictures, Television, and Radio: A Union Catalogue of Manuscript and Special Collections in the Western United States.* Boston: G. K. Hall, 1977.

Perry, Ted, ed. *Performing Arts Resources.* 2 v. New York: Drama Book Specialists, 1974-5.

Rose, Ernest D. *World Film & TV Study Resources: A Reference Guide to Major Training Centers and Archives.* Bonn: Friedrich-Ebert-Stiftung, 1974.

U.S. Department of State. *Diplomatic List.* Washington, D.C.: Government Printing Office, January 1979.

U.S. National Audiovisual Center. *Directory of U.S. Government Audiovisual Personnel.* Washington, D.C.: Government Printing Office, 1977.

U.S. White House, Office of Telecommunications Policy. *Summary of Findings and Recommendations on Federal Audiovisual Activities.* Prepared by Robert Lissitt. Photocopied. Washington, D.C.: Department of Commerce, National Telecommunications and Information Administration, April 1978.

WAFL Book: A Guide to Film and Video in the Washington, D.C. Area. Washington, D.C.: Washington Area Filmmakers League, Inc., 1978.

Washington V. Washington, D.C.: Potomac Books, 1979.

Weber, Olga, comp. *North American Film and Video Directory: A Guide to Media Collections and Services.* New York: R. R. Bowker, 1976.

Yakes, Nancy, and Akey, Dean, eds. *Encyclopedia of Associations.* 13th ed. 2 v. Detroit: Gale, 1979.

Organization Index

Arranged by type of organization or institution. Unless otherwise specified, references are to entry numbers.

ASSOCIATIONS, ORGANIZATIONS, RESEARCH CENTERS

Alexander Graham Bell Association, 1
American Association of Community and Junior Colleges, 2
American Federation of Labor and Congress of Industrial Organizations, 3
American Federation of State, County, and Municipal Employees, 4
American Federation of Teachers, 5
American Film Institute, 6
American Institute of Architects, 7
American Mining Congress, 8
American Petroleum Institute, 9
American Red Cross, 10
American Trucking Association, 11
Anti-Defamation League of B'nai B'rith, 16
Association for Childhood Education International, 18
Association of American Railroads, 19

Catholic Archdiocese of Washington, 23
Catholic Diocese of Arlington, 24
Coordination Council for North American Affairs, 26

Farm Film Foundation, 82
Fondo Del Sol, 84

International Visual Literacy Association, 103

Japan Foundation, 104
Jewish Teacher Center, 105

Middle East Institute, 111

National Association for Foreign Student Affairs, 118
National Geographic Society, 120
National Trust for Historic Preservation, 121
Organization of American States, 125

Project HOPE, 129
Public Broadcasting Service—Public Television Library, 130
Public Broadcasting Service—Public TV Program Archive and Study Center, 131
Public Citizen Visitors' Center, 132

Resources for the Future, 133

Special Olympics, 134

UNICEF Information Center, 137
United Nations Information Center, 138
United States Catholic Conference, 139
United Way of America, 140
U.S.-China Peoples Friendship Association of Washington, D.C. 141

BUSINESSES

Association Films, 17

BNA Communications, Inc., 20

Independent Curators, Inc., 102

Modern Talking Pictures Service, Inc., 112

Narcotics Education, Inc., 119

Named Collections Index

This index directs the user to the entries which hold special collections not readily identified by the title of the entry. Collections within the federal government are not prefaced with U.S. and common names and abbreviations are used.

Unless otherwise specified, references are to entry numbers. The alphabetical designations of sections within entries 165 and 172 and the Record Group numbers within entry 155 have been provided to allow rapid location of the desired collection descriptions in these complex entries.

Foreign Productions Index

This index includes collections of motion pictures produced outside of the United States. Many other films *about* foreign countries are located in collections and can be found through the Geography and History listings in the Content Index. Also see Appendixes III and IV.

The Library of Congress (entry #165) has many foreign productions in its copyright collection because many foreign films are released in this country and registered for copyright with the Library. The copyright collection is not included in this index.

Scholars interested in foreign-produced films should note that the American Film Institute Theater regularly shows series of films produced in individual foreign countries. The AFI Library has files with information on these films and the film industry of countries which have been spotlighted by the Theater (entry #6).

References in this index are to entry numbers. The alphabetical designations of sections within entry #165 have been provided to allow rapid location of the desired collection descriptions in this complex entry.

NATIONS

Australia, 33, 91
Austria, 34, 83

Barbados, 35
Belgium, 36
Bolivia, 81, 84
Brazil, 37

Canada, 3, 16, 27, 38, 81, 91, 100, 116, 127
China, 26, 39, 141
Cyprus, 40
Czechoslovakia, 14, 41

Denmark, 128

Egypt, 42
France, 14, 81, 83, 88, 96, 100, 127, 128, 135, 155, 173

Germany, 14, 43, 44, 81, 83, 112, 124, 127, 128, 135, 155, 165G, 173
Ghana, 46
Great Britain, 2, 14, 16, 20, 27, 32, 40, 81, 83, 96, 110, 114, 119, 127, 128, 135, 155, 173
Guyana, 46

Hungary, 47

Iceland, 48
India, 49, 128
Indonesia, 33, 50
Iran, 51
Ireland, 52
Israel, 16, 53, 105
Italy, 83, 128, 135, 155, 165H, 173

Jamaica, 54
Japan, 55, 104, 128, 155, 165I

Production Date Index

This index covers collections which contain groups of films produced before 1960. In the case of the silent film years, the categories overlap (the category "pre-1930" includes also the category "pre-1910"). The separate additional listing of the "pre-1910" category will be of interest to scholars concerned with the earliest film-making efforts or events. References in this index are to entry numbers. The alphabetical designations of sections within entries #165 and #172 have been provided to allow rapid location of the desired collection descriptions in these complex entries.

Type Index

This index identifies groups of films and videotapes within collections according to their format, purpose, length, and technique. References are to entry numbers. The alphabetical designations of sections within entries #165 and #172 have been provided to allow rapid location of the desired collection descriptions in the complex entries.

FICTION

Fiction Features, 6, 14, 26, 27, 36, 43, 44, 47, 81, 83, 88, 96, 99, 110, 114, 124, 127, 128, 135, 141, 155, 162, 165

Fiction Serials (Theatrical), 6, 81, 128, 165

Fiction Series (TV), 6, 135, 165A

Fiction Shorts, 6, 14, 15, 16, 27, 32, 33, 36, 38, 75, 81, 83, 88, 114, 124, 127, 128, 135, 155, 162, 165, 166, 172G

DOCUMENTARY, NEWS

Documentary Features, 16, 27, 36, 44, 45, 60, 81, 99, 104, 110, 114, 128, 135, 155, 162, 165

Documentary Shorts. All but the following collections have short documentaries: 23, 44

Newsreels (Theatrical), 74, 110, 155, 165

TV News, 94, 155

TV News Specials, 10, 16, 30, 32, 38, 94, 96, 110, 114, 155, 162

TV Documentary Series, 2, 27, 32, 38, 81, 93, 96, 99, 100, 110, 114, 127, 128, 130, 133, 149, 155, 156, 165A, 165J, 165K, 166, 172F

Unedited News Footage, 155

Unedited Documentary Footage, 92, 97, 120, 129, 140, 142, 148, 149, 151, 153, 155, 157, 161, 173, 174

Video Documents, 13, 15, 27, 32, 84, 89, 101, 116, 133, 142, 159, 165, 167, 169, 176

OTHER

Advertising, 10, 97, 112, 134, 139, 140, 155, 172C, 172E

Animation, 14, 16, 27, 32, 36, 38, 47, 62, 67, 81, 83, 88, 105, 108, 119, 124, 127, 128, 135, 148, 155, 162, 165A, 165B, 165C, 165L, 166

Experimental, 14, 15, 27, 33, 36, 38, 81, 84, 128, 135, 162, 165A, 166

Filmed Theater, 83, 110, 114, 127, 165, 166

Instruction, 1, 2, 3, 10, 21, 26, 30, 32, 81, 83, 86, 93, 96, 100, 108, 109, 114, 116, 123, 124, 127, 130, 140, 148, 149, 155, 156, 165A, 178, 186

Student Films, 81, 121, 135

Content Index

This index identifies groups of films and videotapes by their content or subject. References are to entry numbers.

Collections of newsreels and TV news contain material on all subjects and are not included in this index. For a special content index to the National Archives motion picture collection, see entry #155. The alphabetical designations of sections within entries #165 and #172 have been provided to allow rapid location of the desired collection descriptions in these complex entries.

The author, Bonnie Gail Rowan, attended the University of Wisconsin, Madison (B.A. 1964; M.A. Film, Asian Theatre 1968) and New York University (Cinema Studies). She worked for the Defense Department in Korea and the U.S. Information Agency. From 1970 to 1977 she taught film history and production as an Assistant Professor at Towson State College in Baltimore. She is currently a free-lance writer and researcher in Washington, D.C.

Contributor David Culbert is Associate Professor of History at Louisiana State University, Baton Rouge.

Consultant Thomas Cripps is Professor in the Department of History at Morgan State University, Baltimore.

Consultant Lawrence Lichty is Professor in the Department of Communication Arts at the University of Wisconsin, Madison.

Series Editor Zdeněk V. David, has been librarian of the Wilson Center since 1974. Previously he served as the Slavic Bibliographer of the Princeton University Library, and as Lecturer in the Department of History at Princeton University.